THE
NORFOLK BROADS
AND FENS

THE
NORFOLK BROADS
AND FENS

A Cruising Guide to the Waterways of the East of England

by

Derek Bowskill

OPUS Book Publishing Limited

First published 1999
by
OPUS Book Publishing Limited
Millhouse, Riseden Road, Wadhurst, East Sussex TN5 6NY

ISBN 1-898574-06-5

Cover design: Dave Steele
Photographs:©Derek Bowskill
Cartography: © Estate Publications Limited

Printed in Hong Kong through
World Print Ltd

Contents

The Broads   **9**

North Broads   **15**

Great Yarmouth   16

River Bure   25

River Thurne   42

River Ant   50

Fishing on the North Broads   55

South Broads   **58**

Breydon Water   58

River Waveney   61

Oulton Dyke to Lowestoft   71

River Yare   78

River Chet   81

Fishing on the South Broads   97

The Fens   **99**

River Great Ouse   105

River Cam   148

River Nene   152

Middle Levels   169

Rivers Welland and Glen   182

Witham and Fossdyke Navigation   193

Witham Navigable Drains   202

Useful Addresses   **220**

Index   **221**

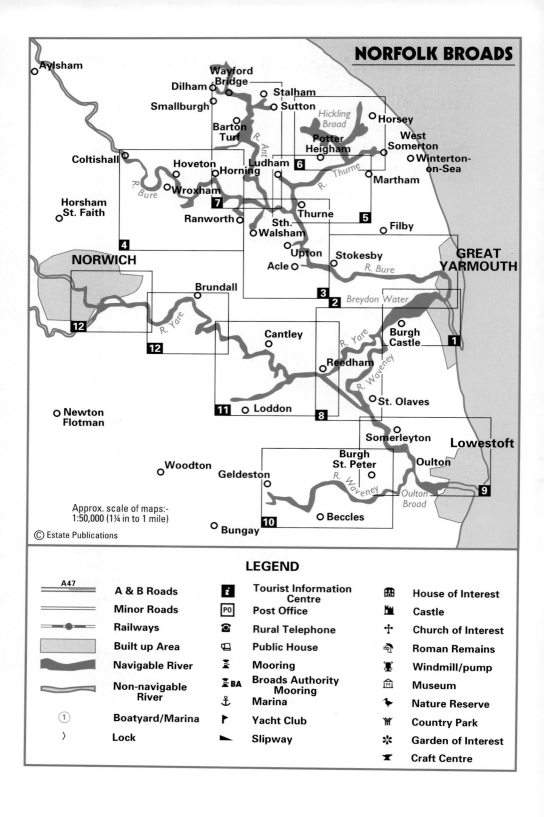

NORFOLK BROADS

Aylsham
Wayford Bridge
Dilham
Smallburgh
Stalham
Sutton
Hickling Broad
Horsey
Barton Turf
Potter Heigham
West Somerton
Coltishall
Hoveton
Horning
Ludham
6
Winterton-on-Sea
Horsham St. Faith
R. Bure
Wroxham
R. Ant
R. Thurne
Martham
7
Ranworth
Thurne
5
Sth.-Walsham
Filby
4
Upton
Stokesby
NORWICH
Acle
R. Bure
GREAT YARMOUTH
Brundall
3
2
Breydon Water
12
R. Yare
Cantley
R. Yare
Burgh Castle
1
12
Reedham
R. Waveney
Newton Flotman
11
Loddon
8
St. Olaves
Somerleyton
Lowestoft
Woodton
Geldeston
Burgh St. Peter
Oulton
R. Waveney
Oulton Broad
9
Approx. scale of maps:-
1:50,000 (1¼ in to 1 mile)
10
Beccles
© Estate Publications
Bungay

LEGEND

A47 — A & B Roads	**i**	Tourist Information Centre	🏛 House of Interest
Minor Roads	PO	Post Office	🏰 Castle
Railways	☎	Rural Telephone	✝ Church of Interest
Built up Area	🍺	Public House	Roman Remains
Navigable River	⚓	Mooring	🏺 Windmill/pump
Non-navigable River	⚓BA	Broads Authority Mooring	🏛 Museum
① Boatyard/Marina	⚓	Marina	Nature Reserve
〉 Lock	►	Yacht Club	Country Park
	►	Slipway	❋ Garden of Interest
			⚒ Craft Centre

List of Maps covering the Norfolk Broads

Area covered		Page
1	Great Yarmouth & Breydon Water	18 & 59
2	River Bure: Yarmouth to Stokesby	24
3	River Bure: Stokesby to Ant Mouth	27
4	River Bure: Ranworth to Coltishall	32
5	River Thurne: Thurne Mouth to Martham	43
6	River Thurne: Martham to Hickling & Horsey	45
7	River Ant: Ant Mouth to Wayford Bridge	49
8	Breydon Water to Reedham & St Olaves	62 & 77
9	River Waveney: St Olaves to Oulton Broad	65 & 72
10	River Waveney: Burgh St Peter to Geldeston	67
11	River Yare: Reedham to Buckenham Ferry	82
12	River Yare: Buckenham Ferry to Norwich	85

Broads Authority

Navigation in this area comes under the jurisdiction of the Broads Authority. Before entering or launching into the waterways, visitors must obtain, either an annual toll, or a short visit toll from the Broads Information Centres, Broads Authority in Norwich, or some boatyards.

For visits of more than 28 days craft must be registered with the Broads Authority.

Broads tolls do not include harbour dues payable by vessels entering from the sea via Great Yarmouth or Lowestoft. Further details are available from the Great Yarmouth Port Authority or Associated British Ports at Lowestoft.

This book is published by:

OPUS Book Publishing Limited

Other titles from OPUS include

Inland Cruising Logbook ISBN 01898574 14

A logbook designed for the river cruiser or narrowboat owner. Inside the colourful cover there are 44 double page spreads for recording daily mileages, engine log, cruising notes and photographs

Where to Launch Around the Coast ISBN 1898574022

a guide to launching sites around the coast of mainland Britain - new edition due March 2000 will include sites on the Canals and Rivers currently covered in -

'Launching on Inland Waterways' ISBN 1898574006.

Trailing Down Channel ISBN 1898574081

a guide to launching sites on the French Channel and Atlantic coasts from Calais to St Nazaire including sites on the Western Rivers.

Sea Angling Charter Boat Directory ISBN 01898574073

Details of boats available for charter covering coast of mainland Britain. Information given includes harbours where boats are based, skipper's name and contact number, operating area, passenger capacity, on-board facilities, sailing season and rates.

The Channel to the Med ISBN 01898574030

detailed coverage of the main inland routes from the Channel ports to the Mediterranean. Derek Bowskill's lively text is accompanied by 80 schematic maps illustrating the routes, stopping places, locks and other points of interest.

Dinghy & Dayboat Directory ISBN 1898574049

an introduction to the world of small sailing boats, illustrated in full colour, giving design specifications, sail insignia, brief history and description of the class, designers name, builder and class secretary

For further details, catalogues etc. contact:
OPUS Book Publishing Limited,
Millhouse, Riseden Road, Wadhurst, East Sussex TN5 6NY
Tel/Fax 01892 782047 E-mail opus@dmac.co.uk

THE BROADS

The word 'Broad' has far more meanings than its antonym 'narrow'; although when used in the plural, both are concerned with waterways. An East Anglian Broad is a large piece of water or lake-like expansion formed by the widening of a river and that is what we are dealing with here; except and notwithstanding that many of the dykes and little broads are shallow in the extreme and so unbroad that they deserve to be designated narrows.

These strange shallow lagoons, lakes, meres, pools, ponds or puddles that are connected to many of Broadland's rivers were, for years an enigma. Finally, after years of competing, if inadequate, explanations had been offered by experts in the fields of geology, hydraulics, hydrographics - even religion and mysticism, the simple suggestion was made that they had been ... just dug! Dug for the peat, as in Holland. Evidence then flooded in to establish that these forty or so shallow lakes dated back to late Saxon and early Norman times. Definitive depth-soundings finally verified that the watery holes were factitious: nothing else could explain the regular depths and straight connecting channels into the nearby rivers. Clearly, commerce had been at work in shipping peat out through the five navigable rivers that make up the area: the Yare, Bure, Ant, Thurne and Waveney. Together, they comprise just under 130 miles of navigable waterways, and are completely free of locks, other than the famous Mutford Lock which controls entry from Lowestoft and the North Sea via Lake Lothing.

Indeed, so substantial was the growth of the needs of commerce, that a number of Acts of Parliament through the 17th, 18th and 19th centuries brought about much betterment and development of the rivers for trading craft. Earlier this century however, many of the upper reaches of the rivers and their locks were abandoned and there is still a great need for much repair, replacement and refurbishment. One move that would totally enhance the navigation and its state of health would be to furnish a link between the mini subordinate rivulets of the Broads and the mini tributaries of the Great Ouse and the Fens. Only a few miles separate the two systems; what a prospect!

However, our main concern is with their present 'unconnected' use as domains devoted almost entirely to leisure and pleasure. The Victorians were the first to exploit the hazy, lazy Broads waterways for holidays; and ever since, they have been popular with conservationists, tourists, fishing folk, boating enthusiasts, caravan devotees and holiday-makers at large. The Broadwaters with their surrounding Flatlands, offer a

Introduction

rural landscape that is now well-preserved by its controlling authority and well-protected by parliamentary law; its legal status being almost that of a national park.

The Broads Authority is supreme. It is responsible for the safety and upkeep of the navigation and is financed partly by the fees exacted upon boat owners plying the waters. In return, it provides and maintains moorings along the banks of the rivers and broads - and also engages river inspectors to advise and help law-abiding boaters ... and sort out those who contravene their quite strict by-laws.

Inspectors

Broads Authority's Inspectors come in various forms: alert, oblivious, friendly, not-quite-affable, happy-go-lucky and bend-over-backwards-to-help-you. Some are land-based while others work from their easily distinguishable launches. They are all issued with regulation uniforms, but some of them wear them with a difference; none at all ruefully and all with a singular style. If you don't notice them and don't follow the by-laws they enforce - you will no doubt rue the day. Don't hesitate to make use of their knowledge or their services.

Wildlife

The vast Broads' landscapes, like a patient etherised upon a table, lie open to the sky with nary a hill or even hillock to disturb or catch your line of sight. Nevertheless, it is a place where wildlife can thrive; and many uncommon species (for example, the swallowtail butterfly and the norfolk hawker dragonfly, found uniquely here) can live a peaceful life - in the main unthreatened by humans. Indeed, the Broads are notable for their treasures of nature, and Norfolk has the claim to be the first county properly to promote nature conservation. Their naturalist's trust, founded in 1926, set out to obtain many of the areas that needed care and/or protection because of their nature-reserve potentialities. The trust has grown considerably over the years, taking on the name of Norfolk Wildlife Trust in the meantime and is now the keeper for nearly forty 'reserves'.

The Broads host species (fish, flesh, fowl - as well as the real thing, the good red herring) many of which have disappeared elsewhere in the UK; a perfect exemplar being the swallowtail butterfly, with its distinctive yellow wings patterned over with red, black and blue. Among the flowers that abound are the yellow flag, a few rare orchids and the intriguingly named hemp agrimony, the roots of which the Greeks used as a specific against indigestion and to cure constipation. And when it comes to birds, there are great crested grebes, mallard, coots and swans in abundance. Grebes live in floating nests which they build in February/ March time among the reeds; which reeds are also host to the rare and small bearded tits and the bigger booming bitterns. Long ago, the waters (NB: in those times crystal-clear) were edged by weed and covered with lilies and other varieties of water plants. Now, the waters are cloudy, under and overcast with few plants and thus none of the wildlife that would have lived on and off them.

The depressingly murky waters have been caused through 'civilisation's' over-abundant generosity in the form of artificially produced nutrients - which in the event are anything but nutritious; and society's leisure craft merely add to the problem by stirring up the trouble - mud on the bottom of the Broads and rivers which has exacerbated the problem. And the consequence is: no sun through water; no plant sustenance and ergo many furry and scaly creatures driven round the bend and down the drains. Things are improving today as excess sewage nutrients are removed at source or through treatment.

An excellent example of 'reclamation' can be seen at Cockshoot Broad, where the Broads Authority has pumped out the bottom mud and built a dam to keep out polluted water. Of course, boats are not permitted to enter. The waters are now much clearer and many plants are returning. The dam is undeniably a watershed, where can be seen, before and after as it were, the dramatic variance between river and Broad waters.

There are, of course, certain places and certain times when quietude is not the order of the day; but there are always plenty of choices: the cathedral city of Norwich (in the west) with its museums and churches makes a fine foil for the foibles of the last resort of Great Yarmouth (in the east) with its Brummagem glitz, its clouds of candy floss, its sassy entertainment and its sand. Nor should one miss the variety of craft to be seen on the water: from the old Norfolk Wherries, through a vast range of wooden and plastic boats to the quite startling powerboats that race on Oulton Broad. And for a different kind of power, there are, scattered throughout the Broads, many classic windpumps, some of which have been kept in good repair; some restored; some unhappily refurbished; and some just dead on their footings. There are many homes and gardens (some stately, some not); many mediaeval churches; an array of castles and abbeys - mostly in ruins; and, above all, lots of waterside watering holes, many of them in riverside villages, with pubs, restaurants and shops.

To visit them by water, there are plenty of sites for launching small (usually trailed) boats as shown on the maps.

Introduction

Windmills and windpumps

Generally speaking, the idea of windmills is associated with Romance: with a capital 'R' as in the world of Don Quixote; but in pedestrian terms they are known more exactly as devices for tapping the energy of the wind by means of a rotating shaft, with sails that are twisted or mounted at an angle so the wind is emplyed to rotate them. These mills are based on the design of the Roman water mill; but the earliest known windmills themselves were used in 7th century Persia and Genghis Khan took Persian prisoners to China to build them for irrigation - for which they are still in use.

Windmills were widespread in Europe from the 12th century until the early 19th century and on the Broads about 150 years ago there were nearly 130 active drainage mills each serving an area called a 'Level' and known by the name of its owner. However, the onset of engine-driven pumps made them redundant - although some did survive for decades. Over the past 20 years, the preservation of nearly 40 mills has been the target of the Broads Authority and the Norfolk Windmills Trust - and nearly 20 have been restored. The Berney Arms Mill is the biggest in full working order while the Stracey Arms Mill is an example of a marsh-drainage pump; together with Thurne and Horsey Mills, these are open during the summer months.

Hire Boats

Broads Hire Boats come in various forms, from the smallest two-seater to the largest of the Bermudan/Caribbean style which will house in floating comfort, an amazingly legal twelve. Generally, boats are hired from Friday/Saturday for seven days; so the time not to be near a hire-boatyard is the week-end! Hirers arrive (all being well at planned intervals) during the day and are shown their chosen craft. They are then taken out for a trial trip, and once the boatyard operator is satisfied that they are compos mentis boat-wise and have an optimum modus operandi, they are allowed to take possession. The rest of the day is usually spent moving on board, coming to terms with being afloat (if not indeed, all at sea); and then setting down to starting the holiday. Although the Hire Boat industry has declined in recent years (and consequently, many of the older Hire Boats have been snapped up for private use), the business is still viable and there continues to be a real sense of community and camaraderie among boatyards and their clientele .

Moorings

Broads moorings come in various forms: first, and predictably the most popular, are those that are closely attached to a hotel, pub, club or restaurant. Some offer free moorings; some charge and then give a refund in the way of food and drink taken in the establishment and some charge a few pounds outright. Second, are the mini-marinas, usually attached to a boatyard - usually attached to a Hire Boat Base. Third are the 'overnight' moorings provided by the Broads Authority, listed at the end of each section: these are free, officially for no more than 24 hours (and some boaters with an eye for a specially selected patch do quite abruptly ask folk to 'Move On' the moment they are a minute over time without any 'Please' or 'Thank you'). Fourth are virtually all the Banks and Braes of the Broads, unless marked 'Private' - as indeed many are. Some simply with the 'NIMBY' intention of guarding their territorial/riparian rights, if not to the last ditch, at least to their front garden; others have it in mind to charge - anything up to £2.00 or £3.00 for the privilege of allowing you to put a couple of your stakes into their muddy field. Some folk believe that there is an old Broads tradition that permits dropping the mud-weight or the anchor anywhere. Such does apply in some Broads, but not in any of the rivers.

Tides

Tides are useful in helping to save time and fuel: going with the flow is the name of the game. Broads tides flood (come in from the sea) for about five hours and ebb (go out to sea again) for about seven hours. There are approximately two high and two low tides a day at any given place, but they occur at times that change from day to day; the average interval betwen consecutive high tides is 12 hours 25mins. Nothing is mathematically easy, but by rule of thumb, tides run about an hour later every day. At their furthest from the sea they rise no more than a few inches and travel at no more than ½ mph; while at their nearest they can rise well over 6'0"/1.8m and attain a speed of as much as 5mph through the bridge arches at Great Yarmouth.

All tides on the Broads are controlled by the tidal stream at Great Yarmouth Bar, and it is these times that are needed to work out the time of slack water for a passage through the bridges of Great Yarmouth, where the tides are about ¾ to 1 hour after the Bar. Skippers need to know that the actual water currents are still running out (namely downstream) for between 1¼ to 1½ hours after the water level has started to rise: this is because the salt water from the sea at the Bar floods in below the top fresh water that is still flowing out to sea. The ebb is usually slightly stronger than the flood.

Introduction

Historic Craft

There are many sailing craft around - including some of the classic Broads Wherries; and 'around' and 'about' is often their favourite occupation. Some of the sailing yachts follow the rules exactly, while others are eccentric. Give them all best courtesy and the benefit of any doubt there may be.

Norfolk Wherries, usually clinker-built in oak, are very special. Originally built as trading craft, they were designed for the special conditions on the Broads. In particular, the fore and aft rig of masts allowed the wherries to sail much closer to the wind than other vessels. The for'ard mast had a tall sail on a long gaff. It was counter-balanced to pivot on the tabernacle so that it could be lowered and raised quickly when negotiating a bridge. These cunning craft were equally cunningly crewed by a skipper and mate (a man and a lad or a lass) who were extremely skilled in their pilotage - and, just like London taxi drivers were possessed of 'the knowledge' ... perhaps to the extent of 'knowing' all the Broads.

The first wherry proper is believed to have been the 'Spread Eagle', a craft dating back to the 17th century. But roads and rails spelt doom for their commercial future. Many went to the rack or the fire, and only a few were saved. The Norfolk Wherry Trust saved the (now famous) 'Albion'. She is in fact carvel-built, (with abutting not overlapping planking), but that apart she is a splendidly typical example of the genre, and can be seen at Ludham.

To sum up: the Broads offer virtually every experience you can think of that might be associated with holiday waterways. The Broads Authority is to be congratulated on the environment and facilities it provides for no more than very modest charges; and conditions are getting better all the time. It is one of the safest places to start boating, whether under sail or engine. Indeed, there are few places where it is quite so pleasing and appealing just to Mess About In Boats!

NORTH BROADS

Pakefield for Poverty
Lowestoft for Poor,
Gorleston for Pretty Girls
Yarmouth for Whores,
Caister for Water Dogs
California for Pluck:
Beggar old Winterton - How Black she do look!

The Broads fall naturally into two geographical areas: North and South, each being possessed of an unique genius loci. While it may appear from a cursory glance at the charts that each can be approached from the sea as easily as the other, this is not the case. Entering the Broads from the North Sea used to be problematic on two counts. First, the eccentricities of the mechanical operations and the working hours of the lock at Mutford, if entering from Lowestoft; and second the lack of welcoming facilities at Great Yarmouth ensuring that it was in no way an agreeable alternative. About ten years ago, I wrote the following about the anomalies at Mutford: 'for years, schemes and stratagems ... have been mooted so that lock and bridge could be brought more into use.' The French are prone to say, 'Plus ça change, plus c'est le même chose'; but, happily, this is not the case at Mutford. Things really have changed and the approach to the Broads through Lowestoft and Mutford has been transformed.

However, little, if anything, has been transformed at Great Yarmouth and passing through the harbour is still a feat made tedious by the failure of the authorities to make life agreeable for yachtsmen. There is no proper facility for mooring for more than a few hours, and the bridge opens for leisure craft only twice a day - and then only as a result of time-consuming booking negotiations if your needs are in any way eccentric ... such as wanting to pass through at a week-end!

Stressing the good news, however, both North and South Broads can now be enjoyed through the recently repaired, refurbished and opened lock at Mutford. Passage through Great Yarmouth is free; while you have to pay to go through Mutford lock and bridge: this is a major difference, of course, and under other circumstances would tempt one to the free passage. But since the 'free passage' refers only to one's personal wealth and not at all to the ease with which one can pass through the Haven Bridge and into Breydon Water or the River Bure, I would recommend Mutford. However, cruising the Broads means sooner or later an encounter with Great Yarmouth,

Great Yarmouth

since it is central to the waterways - separating, as it does, the North Broads from the South. If you are to experience the whole of the Broads, there is no escaping Great Yarmouth; so here we go.

Great Yarmouth

Great Yarmouth grew up as a result of the washing-up and dropping - down of sand, brought perhaps from as far away as Yorkshire, until the Great Spit was formed to bar the estuary. Exits to the sea were difficult to manage, since the moment one door opened, another one closed. This shifting of bars is, of course, quite common on this coast, but historically it was dramatic in its effects here. Finally, the English gave up, and in the 16th century, put the matter in the hands of a Dutchman. With the generous, if not indeed profligate, use of piers, piles, great stakes and a jetty he solved the problem. Great Yarmouth then started the long haul to become 'Great'.

The town has some famous old buildings and streets. For example, Dickens referred to the 100 or more narrow tenfoots and alleyways that riddled the place as the 'Norfolk Gridiron'; another name was 'Yarmouth Rows'. Many of these have disappeared, but there is little doubt that they lived up to their reputation as 'Human's Rabbit Hutches'. The old Fishermen's Hospital was erected for the benefit of some 20 decrepit fishermen - somewhat in the style of The Ancient Mariner. More appealingly, Anna Sewell, of Black Beauty ('my little book') fame was born nearby in 1820, and developed her passion for horses on a farm in the county. Great Yarmouth also gave Dickens Peggotty from David Copperfield: one of her famous sayings was that she was proud to call herself a 'Yarmouth Bloater'.

Great Yarmouth is famous for its summer tourist trade, when folk flock from far and wide (from Scotland to Wales; from Edinburgh to Birmingham to London). The sands are about the only places where it is possible to wander freely when the summer season is at its height. Even then, when the sun shines, there is no space on the beach for the holiday-making Cockneys to put their plates of meat. Entertainment is king and all the court dance their mad whirligig of summer. As one local author, A. D. Bayne, wrote of the tourists: 'a variety of characters, all in pursuit of pleasure, and all more or less amusing. Some few really come for health, some for meditation, some for flirtation, but more for idleness.'

Once ashore in Great Yarmouth you will find that is has all the entertainments and facilities most cruising families are likely to want or need. It may not be a peaceful mooring, but it does permit access to many that are. In order to reach these, you need to travel a few miles up the River Bure.

However, that is to jump the gun a bit: before we make that trip, it is important to consider the ways in which the exits and entrance of Great Yarmouth must be tackled in order to secure an anxiety and trouble-free passage.

Bridges form the nub of the problem. There is much more to the procedure than just observing the restrictions created by how high and wide (or otherwise) any bridge may be, but since they are central to the issues, we will look at them first.

There are four bridges in the area; one of which is only of concern for those with craft wishing to pass in or out from the sea. Let us get this fourth bridge out of our hair to start with. It is the Haven Bridge; the gateway to the strong currents of the tidal section as it moves down to the sea. It may be fourth, but without the stature of the Forth Bridge up north; yet its opening is circumscribed by so much circumstance (in re: the aforementioned tedious booking negotiations) that one would think it were of the significance of Tower Bridge. Passing through the Haven Bridge is forbidden to all hire craft. In fact they are not permitted beyond the confluence of the Rivers Bure and Yare, where there is enough to keep skippers sufficiently busy with just getting from one to the other. One has only to see the stream and the rip on the ebb tide to know why.

Two of the remaining three bridges are on the River Bure: Acle Road Bridge and Vauxhall Bridge, each with only 7'0"/2.13m headroom. The last bridge in the trio is the comparatively new Breydon Bridge across the entrance to Breydon Water. It was opened in March 1986, on an extremely windy, gusty day; so bad in fact that the police warned off the official party from crossing in celebration, after the Transport Minister had cut the tape. However, the passengers in the specially commandeered double-decker buses sardine-packed themselves in downstairs to help ballast the 'craft' and keep them steady. In the event, the navigation was successfully accomplished - albeit in bright and breezy circs. No-one was decker-sick!

Breydon Bridge lies to the west of the town, and is part of the town's traffic-relief system. Unless your craft has a fixed mast, or your air draught exceeds 13'.0"/3.96m at High Water, you just follow the large red arrows, navigating in the normal manner to starboard when passing through. If your air-draught exceeds this figure, special arrangements are needed for the raising of the bridge. This will mean co-operation from the bridge-master at the Haven Bridge, since you will be moving on or out of the stretch to the sea: this can be tedious. The Breydon Bridge master listens on VHF Ch 16 and Ch 12. The three navigation

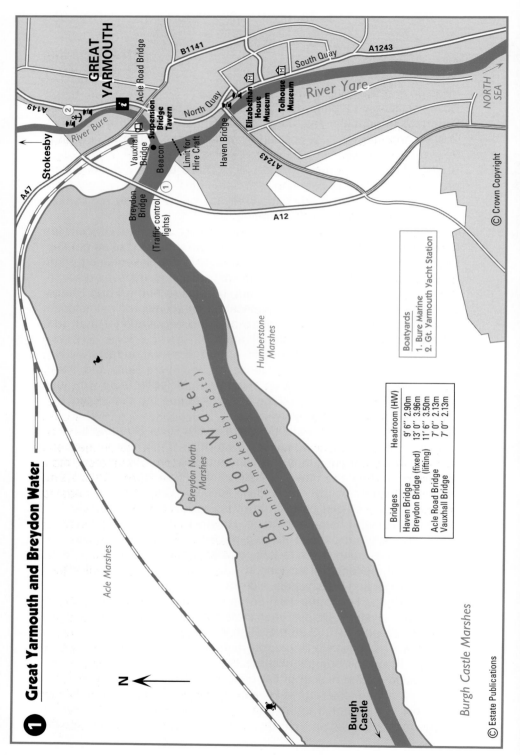

Great Yarmouth and Breydon Water

GREAT YARMOUTH

River Bure

Stokesby ←

A149

A47

A12

River Yare

NORTH SEA

Acle Road Bridge

B1141

A1243

South Quay

Suspension Bridge Tavern

North Quay

Elizabethan House Museum

Tolhouse Museum

Haven Bridge

Vauxhall Bridge

Beacon

Limit for Hire Craft

Breydon Bridge
(Traffic control lights)

Breydon North Marshes

Breydon Water
(channel marked by posts)

Humberstone Marshes

Acle Marshes

Burgh Castle

Burgh Castle Marshes

N ←

Boatyards
1. Bure Marine
2. Gt. Yarmouth Yacht Station

Bridges	Headroom (HW)	
Haven Bridge	9' 6"	2.90m
Breydon Bridge (fixed)	13' 0"	3.96m
(lifting)	11' 6"	3.50m
Acle Road Bridge	7' 0"	2.13m
Vauxhall Bridge	7' 0"	2.13m

© Crown Copyright

© Estate Publications

18

spans are a main lifting span, and the two fixed spans on each side and immediately adjacent. Craft capable of getting under the other two Great Yarmouth bridges can get under these fixed side spans.

Traffic Control Stop Lights (3 vertical reds) operate on the lifting span; but side span traffic is not affected by these signals unless it encroaches into the main channel when it will precipitate the wrath of the bridge master.

Passage from North to South Broads

We now turn to the question of effecting a passage between the North and the South Broads, which means first, crossing the Great Breydon Water; and second, negotiating the Great Yarmouth Bridges. Let me emphasise right at the outset that the passage through Great Yarmouth needs careful navigation and right timing, because of the restrictive bridge heights and the strength of the tides.

The best time for passing through or mooring in Great Yarmouth is at **slack low water**. This is about one and a quarter hours after low water and lasts for about half an hour. The tide turns in the River Yare, and in Breydon Water, about an hour before it does in the River Bure. The tricky aspects in Great Yarmouth are getting the timing right and being able to handle your boat well under tight circumstances. The logistics require that the draught and height of the vessel accord with the strictures laid down by the water depth and bridge heights. When there is too much water, you cannot get under the bridges; and when there is not enough water, you touch bottom. Fortunately, most cruisers using the Broads draw no more than 3'0"/0.9m. Nevertheless, skilled boat-handling can be needed when passing through and mooring-up, since the tide can run fast and furious.

If you are coming from the North Broads (the Bure) and wish to cross Breydon Water, you should time your arrival at the yacht station (just above the two bridges) for slack low water. This will allow you to pass through the bridges without difficulty and give you the best of the flood tide to carry you across Breydon Water.

If you are coming from the South Broads (Breydon Water) you should time your arrival at the entry to the River Bure (below the two bridges) also to coincide with **slack low wate**r. This will bring you across Breydon before the flood starts in earnest and you can then wait at the yacht station for the tide to turn to take you up the Bure. Approaching the entrance to the River Bure from Breydon, you round the large yellow beacon, leaving it to port, and move ahead to the first bridge on the Bure, Vauxhall Bridge. You should keep a central course, watching out for the shoaling to port. This bridge is followed by the Acle Road Bridge, where similar precautions should be observed: red arrows delineate the obligatory channel to be taken under the bridges. However, with sufficiently powerful engines, it is possible to make the passage through Great Yarmouth up to two hours or more after low water. From the south, and only from the south, you can also move through up to an hour before low water. Attempting an entry or departure at any other time will mean one of two things: a delay of hours waiting for sufficient clearance under the two fixed bridges; or an extremely hazardous passage with the force of the tide carrying the boat onward, concluding, in all likelihood, with a damaging and probably terminal encounter with craft at the yacht station, or the pillars of one of the bridges. Either of these could involve the total loss of the craft.

Mooring in Great Yarmouth also requires extra special care and attention. If you are coming from Breydon, you should do so on the last of the ebb in the River Bure. This will enable you to moor easily while facing the current upstream. If you are coming down the Bure, it is best to time your arrival to meet the young flood and use it as your brake. If, however, you are approaching the yacht station and the tide is still running with you, it is essential to go just below the yacht station and turn well before the bridges. This strategy enables you to stem the tide and so moor with some room to manoeuvre. There is a shoal patch almost opposite the yacht station and you can turn there, directing your bows towards the mud. No harm will befall should you touch, since the bottom is very soft. Indeed, such a touch could help turn the boat for you. Best of all, however, is to arrive at the right time and so risk nothing.

Passage from North to South
Arrive at yacht station at slack Low Water and use the flood to cross Breydon Water

Passage from South to North
Arrive below Vauxhall Bridge at slack Low Water: pass under bridges and then wait at yacht station for tide to turn and carry you up the River Bure

---

Final reminder: The restricting factors are, first: the air draught of your boat and the available headroom under the bridges; second, the water draught of your boat, the power of your engines, the height of the tide and the strength of its flow.

Final caution: the dangers of navigating the River Bure at full flood or full ebb either to attempt to moor or to pass through cannot be overstated.

The following is promulgated by the Broads Authority:

How to get through Great Yarmouth:
Great Yarmouth is the gateway between the northern and southern broads. Tides are strong, so follow our guide. Try to time your arrival in Great Yarmouth at around slack water or just afterwards. That's when the outgoing tide has finished but the next incoming tide has not started. This is about an hour after the time of low water at Great Yarmouth Yacht Station.
At slack water it's easier to moor and there is good head-room under the bridges. You'll also save time and fuel because you will have a "fair" tide down the river to Great Yarmouth. It will take about 2¼ hours to Great Yarmouth from Acle and about 1¾ hours through the bridges to turn from Reedham or St Olaves. Remember that there are no safe moorings between Stracey Arms and Great Yarmouth on the River Bure (about 1½ hours) or from Burgh Castle on the Waveney (about 1 hour) and Berney Arms on the Yare (about ¾ hour).
When you approach Great Yarmouth lower your canopy in plenty of time. If you want to stop here, always approach the moorings against the tide. You may have some difficulty turning in the narrow river, so start turning in plenty of time and, if it is busy, be prepared to go down through the bridges to turn where there is more room, but not if three red lights on road bridge are lit.
In Great Yarmouth remember the tide rises and falls by up to 2.2m /7'2"(T) so don't forget to adjust your mooring ropes. The Quay Attendants will advise you. Take extra care when mooring up here and when climbing on and off your boat. If you fall in it's very difficult to climb out and the tide can easily sweep you away.
Keep clear of cargo ships at the wharf at the mouth of the River Bure. Always go round the yellow beacon where the Bure joins the Yare - don't cut the corner as it's very shallow (see map). Remember, hire boats are not allowed in Great Yarmouth commercial harbour.
Breydon Water is very shallow outside the posted navigation channel. Always keep within the posts. It can also get quite rough on Breydon Water. If in doubt make sure your canopy and/or windows etc. are closed and that all loose objects are stowed.
Breydon Bridge has a lifting centre span and two navigable side spans. You should pass through the side span on your right hand side. Look out for larger vessels and keep clear of them - the bridge has to be lifted for them. Keep away from the centre of the main channel and do not try to pass through the lifting span when the 'stop' lights (three red lights in a vertical line) are displayed.

Great Yarmouth

Great Yarmouth Facilities

Bridges	Headroom	
Haven Road Bridge	9'6"	2.90m
Breydon Bridge - fixed	13'0"	3.96m
- lifting	11'6"	3.50m
Acle Road Bridge	7'0"	2.13m
Vauxhall Road Bridge	7'0"	2.13m

Moorings

Broads Authority 24 hour moorings at North Quay
Great Yarmouth Port Authority, 20-21 South Quay Tel. 01493 335500
Moorings on 50m stretch by Town Hall and Haven Bridge

Boatyards

Bure Marine, Breydon Road	Tel. 01493 656996
Great Yarmouth Yacht Station	Tel. 01493 842794
Gorleston Marine Ltd. Beach Road, Gorleston	Tel. 01493 661883

Public Houses and Restaurants

Suspension Bridge Tavern	Tel. 01493 857151
Seafood Restaurant, 85 North Quay	Tel. 01493 856009

Places of interest

Elizabethan House Museum, 4 South Quay, Great Yarmouth
Tel. 01493 855746 (National Trust)
16th century merchant's house with panelled rooms and 19th century
front housing a museum of domestic life

Tolhouse Museum, Tolhouse St, Great Yarmouth
Tel. 01493 858900
former courthouse and gaol and one of the oldest municipal buildings
in the country: tel. for opening times

Marina Leisure Centre, Marine Parade, Great Yarmouth
Tel. 01493 851521
open daily from 1000 all year

Sea Life Centre, Marine Parade, Great Yarmouth
Tel. 01493 330631
display of marine life: open all year daily from 1000

<u>Maritime Museum</u>, Marine Parade, Great Yarmouth
Tel. 01493 842267
maritime history of Norfolk and collection of models: tel. for opening times

<u>Britannia Pier Theatre</u>, Marine Parade, Great Yarmouth
Tel. 01493 842209

<u>Wellington Theatre</u>, Marine Parade, Great Yarmouth
Tel. 01493 842244

<u>Broads Information Centre,</u> North West Tower, North Quay, Great Yarmouth
Tel. 01493 332095
open Easter - October

River Bure: Great Yarmouth to Stokesby

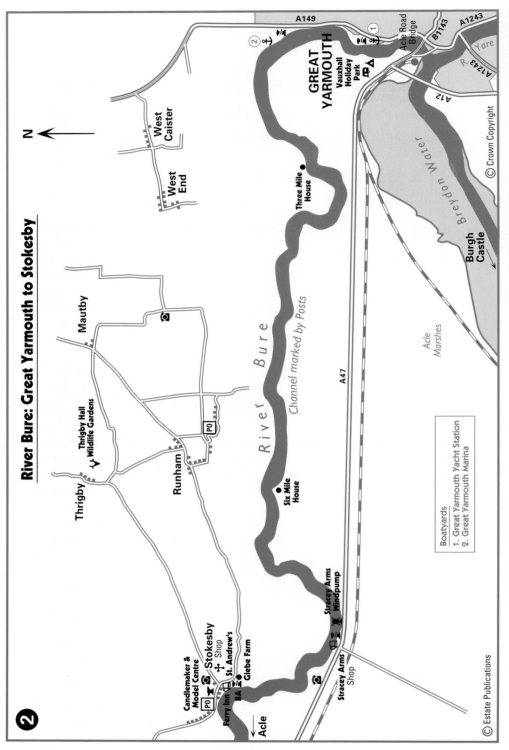

Boatyards
1. Great Yarmouth Yacht Station
2. Great Yarmouth Marina

© Estate Publications

© Crown Copyright

The River Bure from Great Yarmouth to Coltishall
32 miles/51 km

The River Bure, the northernmost of the three main Broads rivers and cruised exclusively by leisure craft, is navigable for 32 miles (51km) to Coltishall Lock. The best known locations on the River Bure in Great Yarmouth itself are the ever-and-over-popular Great Yarmouth Yacht Station, just above Acle Road Bridge (N.B. don't be caught out, this is in Great Yarmouth, not Great Acle), and the Great Yarmouth Marina, just upstream. At one time, the latter was run-down and under-staffed, and, during the summer of 1995 was closed and almost in a state of dereliction. In its lifetime, it has been through many (sea) changes; but since 1998 all the much needed maintenance has been completed and the facility has been so refurbished as to be (almost) unrecognisable. Both mooring places are in the freehold possession of Great Yarmouth Council, but are operated privately. The marina undoubtedly offers easier mooring but is at a distance from the town. However, there is an efficient taxi service available on demand.

You don't get the ethos of the Broads as Broads nor come to terms with them quite so quickly on the North Broads as you do on the South. For a few miles going upstream you will find that the banks are clearly marked with black and white posts to help you keep to the channel, but there are shoals in the insides of the bends. It is important to take note of the markers, since it is only too easy to go into the mud and have a deuce of a time getting off. It is still more important when they are not there to ensure that you keep an eye on the sounder and keep in the middle of the channel even if you draw less than 4'11"/1.5m. Detailed navigational notes are not available for this area so eccentric is it - and so shifting. With a seagoing boat you will be lucky not to find the muddy bottom at least once. The only way to succeed here is to get to know its irregularities for yourself by numerous experiments; or to take advice or even pilotage from the local experts who sail it regularly - frequently cutting corners in their competitive struggles, and consequently getting to know most of the nooks and crannies, hedges, ditches and dykes. Even so, remember that many Broads craft have centre-boards. Continue to beware!

After Great Yarmouth, the river becomes rural, with the occasional windmill and a few willow trees here and there. There are some well-posted houses on some of the maps with names that are supposed to be of linear (distance) guidance: Three Mile House, Five Mile House and Six Mile House. I have never found them to be anything but confusing, but it is fun to try to count them and make sense of the map and your log.

The first attractive stopping place is about five miles upstream at the Stracey Arms, where there are good riverside moorings. (However, before you actually reach here safely, you will have passed what have been known as Duffer's Reach and Slut's Haven. No comment!). The Stracey Arms is the `first and last' pub, and an extremely useful mooring station to sort out all your gear and get everything in order; and this obtains whether you are waiting for the tide to make the return trip to Great Yarmouth or have just left that place and are on the first stage of your adventure: the Great North Road to the Great North Broads. You will be offered a warm welcome by all and sundry, including the donkeys and farmyard inhabitants. Stracey Mill is one of the few old wind-pumps in the area that you can visit. It was built in 1883 on piles sunk about 40'0"/12m and has a boat-shaped cap. It is now fully restored and the engineering innards are open for inspection, daily between April and October. There is also a separate community of other-than-human life: donkeys, geese, strange chickens, rabbits and goats all ramble around almost at their own free will. They are friendly, especially to boat folk whom they know as creatures who have so much food they are more than willing to give it away. Consequently most of the animals are fat and all seem contented. The shop sells a small variety of everyday needs - but has lots of food for broadcasting in the farmyard!

After the Stracey Arms, the North Broads begin to show themselves at their broadest and best. Compared with the South Broads, you will find there is more history and culture to be investigated; there are more ancient and modern buildings to catch the eye and there is more picturesque scenery almost everywhere. All in all, there seems to be more to do, to look at and to think about than on the Southern Waters.

A few miles upriver comes Stokesby, an almost unspoilt red-brick riverside community with a charming village green, shop, post office and the riverside Ferry Inn. The whole area is one of great marshes, with many windmills. Of particular interest is Glebe Farmhouse with its very old and famous mediaeval stone doorway, while the thatched church of St Andrew has benches with pretty open-work backs, and intriguing arm rests decorated with animals and the form of a kneeling woman.

There is no mooring in Muck Fleet, not even in the dyke-mouth, which is the outfall from the vast acres of water that make up the Trinity Broads. However, it is just possible, if really needed, to find a spot just opposite Muck Fleet where there is some depth even at low water.

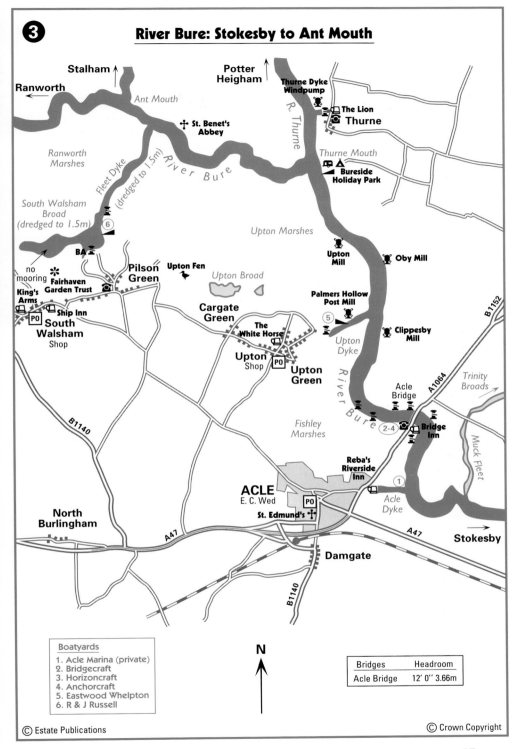

③

River Bure: Stokesby to Ant Mouth

Stalham ↑

Ranworth ←

Potter Heigham

Ant Mouth

Thurne Dyke Windpump

R. Thurne

🏛 The Lion
Thurne

✝ St. Benet's Abbey

Thurne Mouth

🏕 △
Bureside Holiday Park

Ranworth Marshes

Fleet Dyke (dredged to 1.5m)

River Bure

South Walsham Broad (dredged to 1.5m)

⑥

Upton Marshes

Upton Mill

🏭 Oby Mill

BA 🚢

no mooring

✿ Fairhaven Garden Trust

Pilson Green

Upton Fen 🐦

Upton Broad

Palmers Hollow Post Mill

⑤

🏭 Clippesby Mill

B1152

King's Arms 🏛

🏛 Ship Inn

PO

South Walsham Shop

Cargate Green

The White Horse

Upton Shop

PO

Upton Green

Upton Dyke

River Bure

Acle Bridge

A1064

Trinity Broads

B1140

Fishley Marshes

②-④ 🚢 **Bridge Inn**

Muck Fleet

Reba's Riverside Inn

①

North Burlingham

ACLE
E. C. Wed

PO

St. Edmund's ✝

B1140

A47

Acle Dyke

Stokesby →

A47

Damgate

N
↑

Boatyards

1. Acle Marina (private)
2. Bridgecraft
3. Horizoncraft
4. Anchorcraft
5. Eastwood Whelpton
6. R & J Russell

Bridges	Headroom
Acle Bridge	12′ 0″ 3.66m

© Estate Publications

© Crown Copyright

27

River Bure

Once it was possible to pass into the Fleet and get up to the Trinity Broads in a small dinghy but there has been a dam across the mouth for many a year making it completely unnavigable. The three Broads themselves are put to good use by local sailing clubs and are within brisk walking distance. This trio of Broads, (Filby, Rollesby and Ormesby) only three miles from both Heigham Bridge or Acle Bridge, are lonely but picturesque places filled with wildlife. The villages surrounding them - Filby, Rollesby and all the Ormesbys are set in beautiful surroundings and are all well worth a day's outing. Rollesby's 14th century church has a Norman round tower. Nearby Ormesby St Michael is a slightly larger village with splendid houses and battlements and more Norman work in the church: nearby is the Norfolk Rare Breeds Centre.

So, after Stokesby, Muck Fleet and all that exercise, we continue upstream to Acle Dyke, with Reba's Riverside Inn. In the past it was called The Heritage Inn; an appellation promisingly redolent of the essence of the Broads. Further upstream, close to the famous bridge is the community from which it got its name: Acle.

The old bridge here (properly known as Acle Wey Bridge) has been replaced with a new structure with a fractionally increased clearance that is much less arched - more like a motorway flyover. The first bridge was built here in 1101, with a priory; however, that did not prevent the locale becoming a favourite place for executions, those sentenced being hung out to dry over the side. There once was a sign proclaiming the presence of the ghosts of criminals.

Acle Bridge is one of the most popular spots on the river, with plenty of mooring spaces, but some of those immediately next the banks (especially the one on the north side) can be quite shallow. The small town of Acle is more a large village - or the other way round dependant upon your point of view. It is understandably even more popular than its bridge since there is much to attract - including a memorably excellent butcher, and the quaintly intriguing institution of 'Acle Sale', every Thursday. This is an open market about which it is claimed by the locals, "If you can't get it in Acle you don't need it." This flourishing affair has a long-standing reputation for pigs at good prices: all of which makes a clear statement about the appeal and the straight-fowardness of these parts. Thatched St Edmund's church has a Norman tower with 15th century battlements, while inside is a tall screen and an 1410AD font with lions and 'woodwoses', or wild men.

If, on moving downstream to Great Yarmouth, on the way back, you feel at all hesitant about tackling the task of taking your boat into Great Yarmouth yourself, you can phone Great Yarmouth Yacht

Station from here to arrange a tow. Most anxious folk, however, join up with one or two more experienced boats and hope for the best.

The next place of interest is Upton Dyke, just over a mile upstream of Acle Bridge. Palmers Hollow Post Mill, which has been relocated on the dyke bank is the only surviving example of a hollow post mill. Upton village has a post office and shop and much to interest those with a taste for the spiritual as well as the spirituous. There is very good mooring at Upton village staithe, where Eastwood Whelpton's boatyard has basic facilities.The dyke is well sign-posted, but narrow - with a slight bar at its mouth. In general, there is an average depth of just over 3'4"/1.0m, but special care is needed at low water. Indeed, craft drawing more than 4'1"/1.25m need to exercise caution before proceeding into such 'depths' of the Broads. Upton Broad itself is a good distance away and is completely land-locked - and has one of the many 'Private' notices that are a feature of territorial riparians

Now 16 miles/25.6 km from Coltishall, the head of the Bure navigation, we next pass Thurne Mouth, the entrance to the River Thurne on the left bank, to which we return at p.42. It is not far to the ruins of St Benet's (Benedict's) Abbey (on the same bank), spread over its 38 acres of higher land in the surrounding marshes; such upstanding areas being known as 'holms'. The Domesday Book refers to a Benedictine monastery in existence here before the Norman Conquest. It seems that the land was given by King Canute to some eccentric religious squatters led by one Wolfric, around 1020AD. Some believe the sect started as early as the 9th century. Canute's gift consisted of the manors of Horning, Ludham and Neatishead; while local noblemen were 'encouraged' to give more. First there was a timber church which, like Topsy, 'just growed' - but this one also metamorphosed into stone. Thurstan, the second abbot, continued the work. After that, many folk were tempted to gain salvation through gifts, and the money rolled in, until, by the 13th century the Abbey owned a substantial part of Norfolk. St. Benet's register shows payments in cash and kind - indeed almost of kin and kine: for example, some land and a mill were leased for four fat cockerels a year; other lands brought in an annual supply of beer. Other such fees were paid to the Abbey in honey, pepper, cumin and incense. The reverse of the coin was the Abbey's obligation to oblige the king at his summons with three fully equipped knights and retinue.

During the Peasants' Revolt of 1381, on the night of 20th June, a group laid siege to the Abbey, got their papers of serfdom and burned them. On Sunday, 23rd June, a similar group returned, hoping to accost the Bishop Despenser who was striving to suppress the revolt.

River Bure

One record tells of a battle between the monks and the Ludhamites raging all night. However, the Bishop was conspicuous by his eminent absence and the peasants melted away. The following year another lot of peasants revolted in spite of the fact that the Abbey had been fortified: predictably, they were backing a loser. Even if they had reached the Abbey, they would been put down by main force - which by then had been well and truly reinforced. However, they never got that far: they were betrayed and peremptorily executed.

One of the Abbey's best helpers was Sir John Fastolf of Caister Castle and legend has it that he was supposedly Shakespeare's Falstaff - mightily unlikely. The real Sir John built a chapel and he and his wife were buried there. Later, his relatives remonstrated with the monks because there was no memorial to him, in spite of his great gifts. St. Benet's last abbot was William Rugge, made Bishop of Norwich by Henry VIII in 1536. He was charged with running the Abbey and staffing it with no more than a dozen or so monks. It was the only Abbey to escape the Dissolution, but Rugge was not up to his charge, and it went into disrepair - if not indeed disrepute ... with the last monk leaving the place in 1545.

The Abbey then went, not to the dogs, but to local entrepreneurs who made a good trade of its stone, some of which has been unearthed miles away. The estate itself went back to farmland. The remainder of the Abbey buildings, with its 200 year old disused windmill, looks exactly like that; with bits of red brick and falling-down ancient walls hanging on for dear life. From the east, it appears in a more favourable light. However, there is hope yet for devotees, for in 1987 a cross of oak from Sandringham was raised on the site of the main altar - the old religious focal point; and the Bishop of Norwich and acolytes still appear annually to conduct rituals.

Leaving the Abbey, we are now between the tributaries of the Thurne and the Ant, both on the left bank. Our immediate interest, however, lies across the river in South Walsham Fleet Dyke with, at its head, South Walsham Broad. This small broad and its even smaller neighbour, Malthouse just upstream, are renowned as being amongst the most scenic of all the broads; and they are certainly miniature delights. Both Fleet Dyke and South Walsham Broad are dredged to about 4'11"/1.5m. There are good moorings against pilings in the Fleet and at the staithe in the south-east corner. There are also two small islands and some shoal patches, so do check the depth before mooring. The Inner Broad is Private, with the gap between the two having a gravel bottom - all that is left of one owner's attempts to bar the way to infidels by completely filling in the entrance. These days, craft are welcome to enter but mooring, landing, fishing and staying overnight are not permitted. The village with its two pubs and post office is only a short walk away.

Back on the river, the entrance to the Ant is sited on the left bank (we return to the River Ant at p.50) Just past it comes another even more mini-broad: situated at the end of Ranworth Dyke, it is known as Malthouse Broad. Until fairly recently (which in Broads terms means in living memory) it was also dredged to just under 6'6"/2.0m, but is now once more pretty shallow. No good mooring is to be found in the pretty well-treed approach dyke, but there is plenty of choice nearer the staithe - where there are both alongside and stern-to moorings, limited to 24 hours.

Ranworth, a very pretty village, is no distance at all from any of the moorings, all of which are extremely popular. There is a useful information centre here, as well as a post office and pubs. An unusual feature is the availability of electric launches for hire. In addition, the tower of St. Helen's Church, which can be seen for miles, affords a brilliant view of the surrounding landscape (that is, for those hardy souls who are good at ladders). The church is also famous for its painted screen, which, for the less energetic, is to be found at ground level. These 'rood' screens, as they are called, were part of a much more elaborate structure - the main part of which was a cross: (don't miss Jonah and the Whale). The church also has the well-known Sarum Antiphoner; a mediaeval illustrated hymn book written by monks on sheepskin pages. Thanks to the good offices of the church folk, you can get a free guided tour with refreshments. Legend has it there were tunnels from St. Benet's to the village for purposes sacred and profane: proof is a scarce commodity.

You pass Ranworth Broad proper on the way to Malthouse. It is a bird sanctuary belonging to the Norfolk Wildlife Trust. The wooden thatched Ranworth Wildlife Centre is based here; 'based' indeed in more ways than one since it sits on a pontoon constructed on old wherries: 'old wherries never die ... and some don't even fade away.'

After the diminutive charms of these almost twinned minis, the Bure, itself no expansive waterway, appears by comparison to be vast. However, there is no long straight stretch, but bends after more bends, and round each you are likely to find stunning examples of dolce vita architecture. On the right bank, just before urbanity takes over, Cockshoot Dyke leads to Cockshoot Broad, another nature reserve owned by the Norfolk Wildlife Trust which is open to the public everyday all year round. Although most of the dyke is denied to boats, there is a tiny section with free moorings from where you

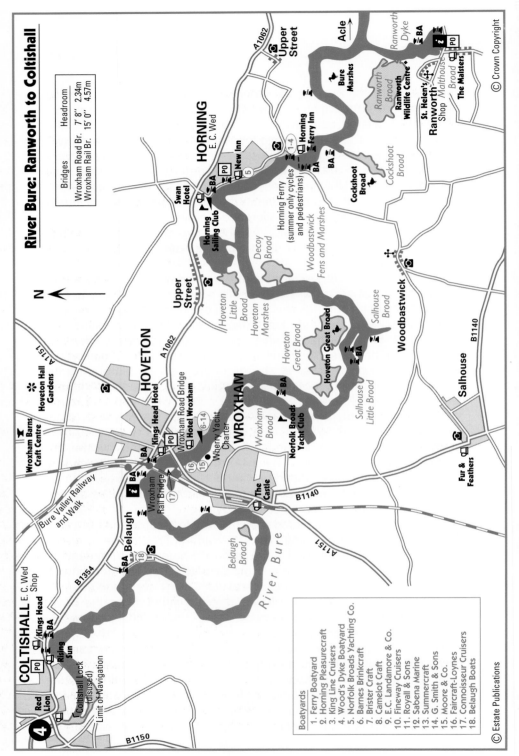

River Bure: Ranworth to Coltishall

Bridges	Headroom	
Wroxham Road Br.	7'8''	2.34m
Wroxham Rail Br.	15'0''	4.57m

Boatyards
1. Ferry Boatyard
2. Horning Pleasurecraft
3. King Line Cruisers
4. Wood's Dyke Boatyard
5. Norfolk Broads Yachting Co.
6. Barnes Brinkcraft
7. Brister Craft
8. Camelot Craft
9. E.C. Landamore & Co.
10. Fineway Cruisers
11. Royall & Sons
12. Sabena Marine
13. Summercraft
14. G. Smith & Sons
15. Moore & Co.
16. Faircraft-Loynes
17. Connoisseur Cruisers
18. Belaugh Boats

© Crown Copyright

© Estate Publications

can indulge in the joys of bird-watching or join the walkway along the bank to the Broad.

Now comes a shift: one small move in boating terms, but a huge leap in culture and civilisation; for this is Horning country. The village itself is divided into two parts: Upper and Lower Street, and the place is often described as the prettiest on the Broads. It is certainly a most popular spot for visitors by road and river alike. However, its appeal must be restricted to those who have a penchant for socialising in style and at length.

There are many boatyards and all domestic facilities very close by; in the one main street in fact. The Swan Hotel, with its grand timber and stucco facade, occupies the prime position on the sweeping bend of the river. It reigns supreme over all it surveys both up and down-stream. Some of the skippers of the commercial trip boats feel they do the same. However, one of them has a most co-operative and appreciative skipper. It is the famous 1974, Broads-built, 'Southern Comfort' paddle boat which, during the summer season, runs public cruises from Horning - perhaps in emulation of its Mississippi mistress.

Horning is famous for its annual August regatta. One of the best-known thrashes is the 'Three Rivers Race' in which all forms and proportions of boats take part. Taking the best part of two days, participating boats sail-race up and down the Bure, the Ant and the Thurne, with and against the prevailing winds and tides. Horning is also known to the many readers of Arthur Ransome's books as the setting of the 'Coot Club' and 'The Big Six'.

The village itself seems to go on for ever; but actually stretches for no more than a mile. It is supposed to have been important in Roman times as well as in The Middle Ages. It is a busy boating spot with much activity from the Horning Sailing Club, just on the bend by the Swan. Particularly well known is the Horning Ferry. There has been a crossing here for over a thousand years: the old chain ferry has long gone, but there is still one for pedestrians and cyclists that runs during the summer. Predictably, there is a Ferry Inn, at which it is often difficult to find a mooring - and impossible to obtain a quiet one. There are Broads Authority moorings immediately opposite the Ferry Inn.

Just after Horning we cease our northerly route and turn to the lusher climes of a southwest mini-cruise before turning north again to head for the contrasted delights of Wroxham and Coltishall. Between Horning and Wroxham, there are three broads to visit. First, just after a big bend in the river, comes Hoveton Little Broad (also known as Black Horse), although it is not so little when you actually come to it

- nor for that matter are you likely to espy a black horse! It is privately owned, but craft may visit during Easter week and from Whitsun to the end of October. Some of it is very shallow, but anchoring is pleasant. The inner broad is chained off, being a shallow bird sanctuary.

Salhouse Broad is another small water, but not, however, as small as its upstream namesake, Salhouse Little Broad. The slightly larger of the two is navigable with care and is prettily wooded - providing acres of good shade for good Broads' summers. There is a charge which is seldom not requested with alacrity. The village is a pleasant, but not insubstantial, walk along a footpath. Spiritual experiences are to be had just for the asking at the 13th century church, and spirituous ones on tap for the usual banter/barter at the Fur and Feathers Public House. You'll find it immediately next the diminutive 'local ales' brewery called Woodforde's - well worth the thirst-making pilgrimage.

On the other side of the river is the unnavigable Hoveton Great Broad with its nature reserve. There is a short nature trail through part of it, which is accessible from the bank where there are special mooring facilities.

Third and last comes what is probably one of the best-known broads of all: Wroxham Broad. In fact, it is really a pretty largish lake, being nearly a mile long and 250 yards wide, giving it an expanse of 80 acres of water. It is the headquarters of the Norfolk Broads Yacht Club. Anchoring and fishing are allowed for a fee, though they are seldom collected. There is little rise and fall of water here, so there is no anxiety about getting hung up, afloat or ashore since the whole area is thoroughly relaxing. Yacht racing takes place during the season, and visitors should neither cruise, anchor nor fish on the course, which is clearly marked. Wroxham is different from most broads insofar as it has its exits and its entrances separate: watch for the traffic signs.

And so to the hub of it all: Wroxham and its over-the-water other half, Hoveton St John. Officially only the community south-west of the river is Wroxham, the north-east side being Hoveton, but generally the two are known as Wroxham.

In the village of Hoveton, there are two Anglican churches and one Catholic. St. John's has a 13th century Priest's Door, and was refurbished in 1640 - with the addition of the square brick tower in 1765. St. Peter's dates from 1624, while the new girl on the block is St Helen's Catholic edifice, built in 1959 - almost hidden by its specially planted mini-forest. Hoveton Hall, no distance from Wroxham Bridge, has gardens of herbaceous borders in the walled and curiously named 'spider garden'; rhododendrons, azaleas and ancient woodland oaks

- as well as sweetly-flowing streams and a lake.

It was from Wroxham, at the end of the 19th century, that boat hiring on the Broads was started by John Loynes from his yard by the bridge. Ever since, this has been the heart and heartland of Broads cruising, and likes to think of itself as the Capital of the Broads. The left-bank houses the famous Broads Shopping Centre. Wroxham boasts two demands for inclusion in the records of the Hall of Fame. The first is its resolute claim to possess the world's largest village stores. Named Roy's, it seems close to taking over the village, being in itself almost a self-contained community. It certainly offers such a wide choice and excellent service that it is difficult to find a truer challenger in the whole of Broadland.

The second claim to fame is its possession of what must be the world's most-bumped-into bridge. This tiny road bridge is known far and wide in Broads cruising circles. There is hardly more than 6'6"/2.0m headroom and 26'2"/8.0m width and the curve of the arch means that practical restricting dimensions are frequently less than this, dependant upon the configuration of the craft. A further complication is caused by the fact that the bridge is not at right angles to the river, so sight lines are not open. A cautious approach and judicious use of the ship's whistle are called for. The stonework has been responsible for more headaches and bruised bumpheads than any other on the circuit. Perhaps it is the proximity of so many hostelries and the general ambience of festive conviviality that distracts the minds of skippers and crew alike. Just to add insult to injury, it is believed that the foundations are slowly sinking due to all the heavy traffic. There is talk of a by-pass - and has been for years ... and no doubt will be for years to come.

Unquestionably it is one of the most popular spots on the Broads, and 'changeover days' for hire craft can be busily grisly. All the shifting from cars to boats and vice versa can make life hectic on the bridge, even for would-be bystanders who may only want to play Pooh Sticks, albeit somewhat perilously, from the bridge. (Actually, such an activity, or even the more passive one of just standing and staring, could be lethal: if the boats don't get you, the lorries will!)

Not only are there some very pretty stretches of river here, but also all the facilities any reasonable cruising family could want (if not indeed, quite a few it could easily live without). In particular, Norfolk Marine and Plain Sailing are two good chandlers - especially useful for a boat owner caught out for a bit of gear. There are plenty of pubs and restaurants in the immediate locality, as well as proper butchers and bakers. Noteworthy is the Hotel Wroxham. With its prime setting it could well be as snooty as some of the Horning establishments which will demand that you cast off immediately from their moorings if you do not instantly book in half a dozen hands for dinner. Hotel Wroxham's singularity is its extreme patience and wish to serve. The rise and fall here is negligible.

To Wroxham belongs the distinction of having opened up the Broads to holidaymakers. Over 150 years ago three Norfolk cronies, led by the adventurous John Loynes of Norwich, handed a small boat on a barrow up to Wroxham Bridge and started the whole idea of Broads Cruising. That mini-odyssey suffused him with such enthusiasm that he opened the very first boatyard at Wroxham.

The same enthusiasm permeates an old book I recently discovered: 'The Best Cruise On The Broads' by John Bickerdyke. It was published in London by Bliss, Sands and Foster, of Craven Street, just off The Strand. There is no publication date inside. I found it so intriguing that I am including some of his choice offerings:

"*This book is to be in some respects more, and in others less, than a guide. The orthodox guide tells one who has built and who has knocked down the ruined castle which formerly crowned the summit of yonder hill; but the friend tells the reader where he can buy mutton, a matter of great moment when one is yachting. Therefore, let me begin by stating the important fact that at Wroxham, our point of departure, and the Cowes of the Broad district, mutton is killed - occasionally. It is some time before one happens upon any more butchers' shops, so I lay considerable emphasis on this fact, and will return to my muttons from time to time.*

With regard to this book acting as philosopher as well as guide and friend, note the advice here given, to grumble not when charged a tri-fling ten per cent more for agricultural produce, bread, and food, than one has to pay in big towns like Great Yarmouth and Lowestoft. It is the proud privilege - possibly the necessity - of the dweller in Districts, the prosperity of which depends upon the summer influx of visitors, to charge a little more for things than is charged in other places. So be philosophical and grumble not.

Not very far from, and on the way to, Wroxham, is Norwich, a quaint old town with a fine cathedral. There anything in reason, required and found wanting in the little village, can be purchased.

One of the necessary essentials of a sailing cruise is a yacht, and of such there are many of all shapes and sizes at Wroxham. As your guide I should now, perhaps, take you down the river, giving you the names and histories of the residences on either side. By-the-bye, I think there is only one, so that would not be difficult. But as your friend, I feel bound to first offer advice on the not unimportant subject of hiring the yacht. This is very much a question of means. The smallest possible thing is an open boat, which can be covered at night by means of an awning, not a bad sort of affair in August for two young men who like to rough it.

A cut above this is a little sailing vessel with a tiny cabin, and abaft the cabin a tiny cockpit. If such a craft is hired and a man or boy engaged, the man sleeps in the cockpit and his employer in the cabin. About the lowest price for a thing of this kind is thirty shillings a week, and one pound or fifteen shillings for the man.

With regard to clothes, there is nothing like flannels. Wear these every day and all day, and if you may possibly wish to pay a visit to Great Yarmouth or Lowestoft, be provided with a white shirt, collars, a neck-tie, and a cloth coat and waistcoat. But flannels are all important - enough for changes in the interests of cleanliness, and one more change in case of a ducking. Mackintoshes or oilers are very necessary, and also a sou'wester head- gear, not one of those flappy things which one buys at a macintosh man's, but a genuine, oiled, sailor's sou'wester.

It is well from the very outset to keep the crew up to his or their work. Let them see that you appreciate smartness, cleanliness, and tidiness. Some of these gentlemen are apt to look upon themselves as the personal conductors of the yachting party. Of course, in all matters of navigation, it is very proper to give way to them, if you do not know the channels and district, but let them understand they are only advisers, and not masters. As a general rule, the yachtsmen of the Broads are very good fellows indeed, and if you treat them well, will return the compliment."

Many things may have changed since those 'halcyon?' days; but one thing remains surely: the man's utterly appealing idiosyncratic approach to boating, to the Broads, to writing and to life itself. Bless him!

If your boat is anywhere near the critical dimensions of Wroxham Bridge, it is important to check the weather forecast before proceeding upstream, since, just as at Potter Heigham, it is possible to become trapped above the bridge if there has been rainfall of any significance.

The river now becomes calmer, quieter and prettier than ever before. The first stopping place above Wroxham is Belaugh, halfway to Coltishall. Between Wroxham and Belaugh, the river is well on its way to becoming an ox-bow lake, such a wide horseshoe bend does it take: only the slow rate of the stream prevents the straight cut off. The Bure is now unostentatiously beautiful and this small, extremely pretty

River Bure

village has an attractive church, the tower of which towers over the whole area. The facilities are basic: aforementioned church, boatyard (Belaugh Boats, the last going upstream, for there is none at Coltishall), telephone and post box.

We are now on the last leg to the head of navigation: Coltishall. I think this straggling village to be one of the most attractive on the Broads. It is often referred to as the Gateway to Broadland. There are simple, quiet moorings available by the common and the riverside pubs, and the village centre is a few minutes walk away. The lock has not been used as such since 1912; and is now in service only as an anti-flood sluice. However, there is plenty of good flowing liquid refreshment to be found in the village; although not quite Pubs Galore, there is plenty of choice. Early in the last century, this tiny village of Coltishall was the major town in the vicinity. The great department store, Roys of Wroxham, started here and, the opposite of the present trend, many folk came to the local malthouses and limeworks to find short-supply work - travelling in, for example, from Wroxham.

While it is possible to canoe above Coltishall, this is the veritable head of navigation of the Bure, which rises much further away at Melton Constable, from where its runs down through Aylsham to Coltishall. We have now travelled over 30 miles/48 km from Great Yarmouth, and have found tremendous contrasts on one river. No two places could differ more in appearance, activities and atmosphere than Great Yarmouth and Courteous Coltishall.

Rive Bure Facilities

Bridges	Headroom	
Acle Bridge	12'0"	3.66m
Wroxham Road Bridge	7'8"	2.34m
(clearance at centre or arch)		
Wroxham Rail Bridge	15'0"	4.57m

Broads Authority free 24hr moorings

South Walsham	Wroxham Broad Island
Ranworth Staithe	Hoveton
Cockshoot Dyke	Hoveton Viaduct
Horning Parish Staithe	Belaugh Staithe
Woodbastwick	Coltishall Common

Boatyards

Great Yarmouth Yacht Station	01493 842794
Great Yarmouth Marina	01493 332285

Acle

Acle Marina (private)	01493 750264
Horizoncraft	01493 750283
Anchorcraft	01493 750500
Bridgecraft	01493 750378

Upton

Eastwood Whelpton, Upton	01493 750430

South Walsham

R &J Russell, South Walsham Broad	01603 270262

Horning

Ferry Boatyard Ltd	01692 630392
Horning Pleasurecraft	01692 630366
King Line Cruisers, Ferry View Estate	01692 630297
Woods Dyke Boatyard, School Road	01692 630461
Norfolk Broads Yacht Co., Lower St	01692 631330

Wroxham

Barnes Brinkcraft, Riverside Road	01603 782625/782333
Brister Craft, The Rhond	01603 783783
Camelot Craft, The Rhond	01603 783096
E.C.Landamore & Co	01603 782212/782213
Fineway Cruisers, Brimbelow Road	01603 782309
Royall & Sons, Riverside Road	01603 782743
Sabena Marine, Marsh Road	01603 782552
G.Smith & Sons, The Rhond	01603 782527
Summercraft, Brimbelow Road	01603 782809
Moore & Co., Staitheway Road	01603 783311
Faircraft-Loynes	01603 782280
Connoisseur Cruisers	01603 782472

Belaugh

Belaugh Boats	01603 782802

River Bure

Places of Interest

Thrigby Hall Wildlife Gardens, Filby
Tel. 01493 369477
landscaped gardens with animals, birds and play area: open daily
1000 - 1700

Stracey Arms Windpump, Tunstall (Norfolk Windmills Trust)
fully restored drainage pump with exhibition of photos and history of
the Broads and windpumps : open Easter to end Sept 0900 - 2000

Candlemaker and Model Centre, Stokesby
Tel. 01493 750242
over 100 varieties of candles and craft: open daily Easter - end Oct
0900 - 1730: tel. for other times

Fairhaven Garden Trust, South Walsham
Tel 01603 270449
174 acres of exotic plants, shrubs and woodland: water trips through the
gardens in a vintage launch: open Apr - end Oct tue - sun 1100 - 1730

Ranworth Wildlife Centre, Ranworth Broad (Norfolk Wildlife Trust)
Tel. 01603 270479
nature trail through woodland and fen: open Apr - end Oct daily 1000
- 1700: admission free

Helska Leisure Centre, Horning
Tel 01692 630392

Hoveton Great Broad
nature trail open May - mid Sept 1000 - 1700 on weekdays

Hoveton Hall Gardens, Wroxham
Tel. 01603 782798
10 acres gardens with woodland and lakeside walks: open Easter -
mid Sept 1100 - 1700 wed, fri, sun & BH mons

Norfolk Rare Breeds Centre, Ormesby St Michael
Tel. 01493 732990
rare breeds of domestic farm animals: tel. for opening times

Bure Valley Railway, Aylsham Station
Tel. 01263 733858
narrow guage steam railway runs 9 miles from Hoveton to Aylsham
with connection to Blickling Hall (N.T.): tel. for train times

Wroxham Barns
Tel. 01603 783762
craft workshop and tearooms: open daily 1000 - 1700

Chandlers

Plain Sailing, Riverside Road, Wroxham	01603 784488
Norfolk Marine, Church Road, Wroxham	01603 783150

Boat Trips

Mississippi River Boats   01692 630262
runs day trips on its replica Mississippi paddle boat 'Southern Comfort'

Shops

Bridge Stores, Acle	01493 750355

riverside store with moorings

Roy's of Wroxham	01603 782131

will deliver groceries to boat or yard if contacted in advance

Wroxham Angling, Station Road	01603 782453

Public Houses

Stracey Arms, Tunstall	01493 651311
Ferry Inn, Stokesby	01493 751096
Reba's Riverside Inn, Acle	01493 750310
Bridge Inn, Acle	01493 750288
White Horse, Upton	01493 750696
Ship Inn, South Walsham	01603 270553
King's Arms, South Walsham	01603 270039
Malsters, Ranworth	01603 270241
Swan Hotel, Horning	01692 630316
Horning Ferry Inn	01692 630259
Fur & Feathers, Salhouse	01603 720003
Hotel Wroxham, The Bridge	01603 782061
King's Head Hotel, Wroxham	01603 782429
King's Head, Coltishall	01603 737426
Rising Sun, Coltishall	01603 737440
Red Lion, Coltishall	01603 737402

Broads Information Centres (open Easter - Oct)

Ranworth Staithe	01603 270453
Wroxham - Station Rd, Hoveton	01603 782281

River Thurne from Thurne Mouth to Horsey Mere and West Somerton
13 miles/21 km

As the mouth of the Thurne is approached, panoramas open all around, with the 14th century church in Thurne village being a landmark. While the Bure turns sharply westward, the Thurne appears to be almost straight ahead as it runs north. The River Thurne rises some miles away near Horsey Mere and Martham Broad which is virtually the head of navigation and is unexpectedly close to Winterton Ness on the North Sea coast. One of the most famous features of this river is the bridge at Potter Heigham, and while that is 3 miles/4.8 km away upstream, it is worth being aware of its problems before setting off in happy ignorance (see p.44).

The first encounter to enjoy is the tiny village of Thurne at the end of the very narrow and shallow dyke, at the entrance of which is a pretty wind pump. Near the Lion pub, all basic facilities are at hand. There are good moorings here, but the tide must be reckoned with hereabouts: it can run fast, with a rise and fall of about 1'7"/0.5m. Next comes the village of Ludham sitting at the head of Womack Water and Ludham Reach Dyke. It is a really comely, characterful village, bursting with vitality in spite of its streets which seem to wend their way purposelessly not only past but also apparently through some of the old residences. The old manor of Ludham was made as an offering in 1019 by King Canute to St Benet's Abbey; consequentially, its church has always had an affinity with the Abbey. The 13th century church is dedicated to St. Catherine, whose death on a spiked wheel is commemorated in the explosions of the annually celebrated eponymous feu d'artifice. A more appropriate reminder can be seen inside the church if you look up to the Catherine Wheel emblem effected in the designs that have been achieved in the roof supports: it also has a wonderful painted rood screen dated 1493. The painter, Edward Seago lived here at Ludham. He was a well known figure about the Broads and several of his paintings used to grace the now ex-Royal Yacht, Britannia.

In sympathy with local feeling, it is appropriate that the ruins of the Abbot's Grange are now farmyard buildings. Indeed, once, there was a causeway from the Abbey gate to Ludham, and finally the church was taken over by St. Benet's in 1220. In the 14th century, Ludhamites, and Potter Heighamites went one night to the Abbey to kill the Bishop who was residing there during his efforts to put down the Peasant's Revolt. Fortunately for him, he was away at the time, and so lived to

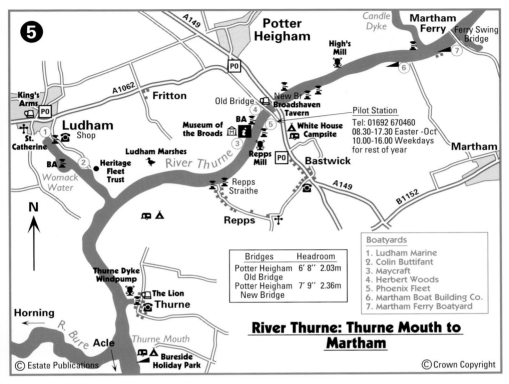

River Thurne: Thurne Mouth to Martham

Bridges	Headroom	
Potter Heigham Old Bridge	6' 8''	2.03m
Potter Heigham New Bridge	7' 9''	2.36m

Boatyards
1. Ludham Marine
2. Colin Buttifant
3. Maycraft
4. Herbert Woods
5. Phoenix Fleet
6. Martham Boat Building Co.
7. Martham Ferry Boatyard

Pilot Station
Tel: 01692 670460
08.30-17.30 Easter -Oct
10.00-16.00 Weekdays
for rest of year

© Estate Publications   © Crown Copyright

fight the good fight another day.

Ludham Dyke Reach has moorings with a good depth of water. The main channel to Ludham Staithe and Womack Water has been dredged, but it is still about a mile of narrow, twisting, and in places, shoal water: In fact, it is a maze of badly silted tiny waterways. The speed limit here is reduced to 4 mph. Secure and pleasant stern-on moorings are available at the parish staithe, free for 24 hours, and there are good, basic boatyard facilities.

The Norfolk Heritage Fleet is based here, at Hunter's Yard on the starboard-hand. It was originally Percy Hunter's hire fleet, and some boats were hired and raced in local regattas. The seven 60 years old mahogany sailing boats have been kept together to this day as a fleet of classic sailing (no engine!) boats for hire.

From the Womack moorings, it is no more than a short walk into Ludham Village for the usual offices and the King's Arms public house.

From Womack Water it is just over 1 mile/1.6 km to Potter Heigham, where the famous mediaeval bridge needs care and attention not only because of restricted sight-lines (it does not lie square to the river); or the near-impossibility of changing your mind or going astern to any purpose; but also because of the even more restricted height; clearance at AHW being 6'8"/2.03m with a width of only 21'0"/6.4m. Then there is the challenge of its special configuration, namely the width and completely circular curve of the arch, which was built to accommodate the trading Wherries with nary a thought to any other craft. Just to make matters more complicated, when there is any wind between south-west and north, there can be a tunnel/funnel effect enough to disturb the passage of slow-moving modest-draught vessels. Newcomers should make use of the professional help that is always available (understandably free of charge to hire boat users: a precautionary courtesy you might say.) You can phone the pilots at the Phoenix Fleet boatyard by the old bridge (tel. 01692 670460). It is wise to check with them about future weather, the possibility of rain and any likely rise of water, since it is not difficult to get trapped upstream of the bridge if your dimensions are at all near the restricting criteria. (An experience that is quite the opposite of being neaped - but just as infuriating!) This is undoubtedly the most tricky of the many tricky Broads bridges, and has in the past wreaked some havoc, with physical harm to person and craft. The new road bridge just upstream is also low (7'9"/2.36m) and is best approached about an hour or so before low water.

Potter Heigham looks very promising from the river. There are those who rave about it; those upon whom it has made no impression; and those who see it as no more than a dump. In itself, it may never have been a dream of Ruskin's, but it does stand sentinel to one of the most beautiful stretches of The Broads. The Romans had a pottery here, and the fact that 'Heigham' is Saxon for 'township' speaks for itself. It is the gateway to the lovely upper reaches of the river, and on to Hickling, Horsey and Martham Broads.

Just downstream of Potter's bridges there are good moorings on both sides of the river. Opposite the Maycraft Boatyard you can tie up securely and enjoy the short mini-pathway walk into the village. There are also many private moorings and those belonging to the boatyard of Herbert Woods. There is a camouflaged water tower, and the yard can charge up electric boats.

We are now moving on into deeply shallow waters as we approach the leg that goes to Hickling, Horsey and Martham, about 1½ miles/2.4km up from Potter. For the first two, you turn to port into Candle Dyke, while to starboard is the route for Martham. Candle Dyke runs through Heigham Sound: its very narrow navigable channel is clearly marked

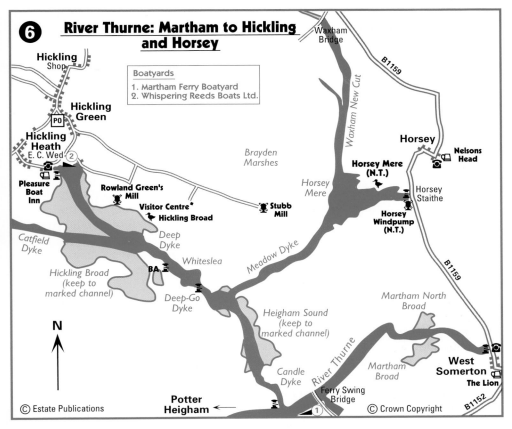

6 River Thurne: Martham to Hickling and Horsey

Waxham Bridge

B1159

Hickling Shop

Boatyards
1. Martham Ferry Boatyard
2. Whispering Reeds Boats Ltd.

Hickling Green

PO

Hickling Heath E. C. Wed 2

Horsey

Nelsons Head

Brayden Marshes

Horsey Mere (N.T.)

Horsey Mere

Horsey Staithe

Pleasure Boat Inn

Rowland Green's Mill

Visitor Centre
Hickling Broad

Stubb Mill

Horsey Windpump (N.T.)

Catfield Dyke

Deep Dyke

Whiteslea

Meadow Dyke

B1159

Hickling Broad (keep to marked channel)

BA

Deep-Go Dyke

Martham North Broad

N

Heigham Sound (keep to marked channel)

Candle Dyke

River Thurne

Martham Broad

West Somerton

The Lion

Potter Heigham ←

Ferry Swing Bridge

1

B1152

© Estate Publications

© Crown Copyright

and it is essential to keep within its limits. Through Deep-Go Dyke and Whiteslea, which is a mini-lake, the course lies straight ahead to Hickling Broad.

Hickling, with its 500 acres of open water, is the largest of the broads; indeed, if its fringe benefits of reed beds and marshes are included, it grows to 1,200 acres. It is well-known and equally well-used for wind-surfing and beach launching. The Broad was created a National Nature Reserve in 1945. There are reedbeds, marshland and woods which constitute a kind of sanctuary to such rare and timid creatures as the upward-beaked avocet; the equally unusual marsh harrier; and the brilliant swallowtail butterfly that lives and breeds on milk parsley. You can take the 'water trail' in an old open 'lighter' boat - complete with an ever present compulsory warden, optional life jackets and obligatory sturdy cloths and clothes.

45

River Thurne

The Broad is quite exposed, with little high ground around and little more than 2'0"/0.6m of water for much of its extent. It is navigable only within the marked channels and is very much nature country. Among other forms of life, it is blessed with the famous Hickling sponge weed. There are some moorings at the Pleasure Boat Inn: at the northern end of the broad, where the siting is most pleasant.

A turn to starboard immediately after Heigham Sound, leaving the black post with yellow stripe to port, will take you to Horsey Mere by way of Meadow Dyke. Then on through the narrow Waxham New Cut and up the shallow gutway to Waxham Bridge, the limit of navigation, although craft drawing much more than 3'4"/1.0m stand little chance of getting this far. Horsey itself is a very small community: one pub, one church and a few houses. It is situate where the Broads come to within a couple of miles of the sea, which has broken through by the Old Hundred Stream at big spring tides, the consequent flooding devastating many thousands of acres. In essence, Horsey, long ago, was no more than an extremely narrow piece of land - no more than a long neck - allowing passage to Roman Caister, and, in fact, Roman coins have been dug up hereabouts.

The speed limit here is 5 mph. The only moorings on Horsey Mere are paying ones at the eastern end of the staithe. The Mere is owned by the National Trust and is acknowledged as an internationally important wildfowl sanctuary: its brackish water makes it particularly attractive to a wide variety of migrating sea birds and waders. During the winter when the migrants are here, navigation and fishing are more or less disallowed. The old Horsey Mill, a working windpump until it was damaged by lightning in 1943, is also in the hands of the National Trust and is open daily in the summer. Here, every bush will hide a bird, and every hide will host a watcher. This is indeed the very living heart of the National Trust Kingdom and its Broads Principality.

Now we go back to the mouth of Candle Dyke and the turn to starboard that leads past the ferry swing bridge, where caution for its movements is necessary. We pass the unnavigable miniature Martham Broad which is owned by the Norfolk Wildlife Trust. The village of the same name is virtually unspoilt, although with all the goings-on of an attractive, but retiring, tourist country village. It has some gorgeous Georgian mansions set off excellently well by the two classics - expansive greens and an even more classic pond - but with the ducking-stool sadly missing. Once upon a time, there was an almighty strange episode; true, most of it more than likely anecdotal if not indeed apocryphal, but nevertheless worth the telling. By the huge tower of St Mary's Church there stands a memorial stone to one female soul by the name of Alice Burraway. The craggy testimonial was erected by one Christopher, her supposed true spouse, mentioning, in passing as it were, that she had been, his 'sister, mistress, mother and wife'. It is claimed that this fellow Christopher was the bastard product of incestuous copulation between his sister and his father. In addition, it is also alleged that he, unwittingly and obliviously actually worked for this female mother/sister. Work led to open-air sexual congress: congress led to bedding and wedding - and discovery. In a 'miraculous' denouement (more important and earnest even, than the archetypal 'Importance of Being Earnest') his lady detected her gentleman's real individuality, identity and personality by, wait for it, the presence of a mole. It is best that history draws a veil over the possibility of their own offspring.

Nearby, is the quiet village of West Somerton, where you can moor by the banks. For seagoing folk, it is only a few minutes' walk from Somerton or Horsey Mere to Winterton Ness.

River Thurne Facilities

Bridges	Headroom	
Potter Heigham (old)	6'8"	2.03m
Potter Heigham (new)	7'9"	2.36m

Broads Authority free 24hr moorings

Womack Water
Potter Heigham
Deep Dyke

Places of interest

Thurne Dyke Windpump
restored windpump, standing close to the St Benet's Level windpump: open May - Sept, sun 1400 - 1700 (also sat, Aug - Sept)

Heritage Fleet Trust, Hunter's Yard, Ludham
Tel: 01692 678263
historic fleet of traditional broads sailing craft - for hire/charter

Hickling Broad Nature Reserve (Norfolk Wildlife Trust)
Tel: 01692 598276
open daily 1000 - 1700: visitor centre open Apr - Sept; water trail in replica reed boat runs from Pleasure Boat staithe: tel. for times

River Thurne

Horsey Windpump (National Trust)
Tel: 01493 393904
4-storey restored mill open daily 1100 - 1700 Apr - end Sept: shop
and refreshments

Boatyards

Ludham Marine, Womack Staithe	01692 678322
Colin Buttifant, Swallowtail Boatyard, Ludham	01692 678066
Maycraft, Potter Heigham	01692 670241
Herbert Woods, Potter Heigham	01692 670711
Phoenix Fleet, Potter Heigham	01692 670460
Martham Boatbuilding & Development Co.	01493 740249
Martham Ferry Boatyard	01493 740303
Whispering Reeds Boats Ltd.Hickling Broad	01692 598314

Pubs

The Lion, Thurne	01692 670796
Kings Arms, Ludham	01692 678386
Broadshaven Tavern, Potter Heigham	01692 670329
Pleasure Boat Inn, Hickling	01692 598211
The Lion, West Somerton	01493 393289

Broads Information Centre, The Staithe, Potter Heigham
Tel. 01692 670779
open Easter - October

The great mill at Breydon: he's the Broad and I'm the High:
we are the University. Look on my works, ye mighty, and despair!

Broads boats and moorings . . . .

Come in all shapes . . .

. . . and sizes.

I saw two swans of goodly hue down along the lee;
Two fairer birds I never yet did see.

The rushes that can be experienced at Oulton Broad Yacht Station . . .

. . . are not of this lovely tranquil order.

Coltishall, at the head of the Bure, asks a little patience of visitors in search of sanctuary . . .

. . . which patience will have been well-earned after such negotiations as these.

Norwich, another head of navigation, claims, with propriety, to be 'A Fine City'.

And Horsey's Head of Navigation claim is simply being next the Great North Sea.

Bridges come and bridges go; and while the Haven Bridge at Great Yarmouth
is closed to hire traffic . . .

. . . the railway swing bridge at Reedham will be opened with alacrity
as oft as possible by its cheerful keepers.

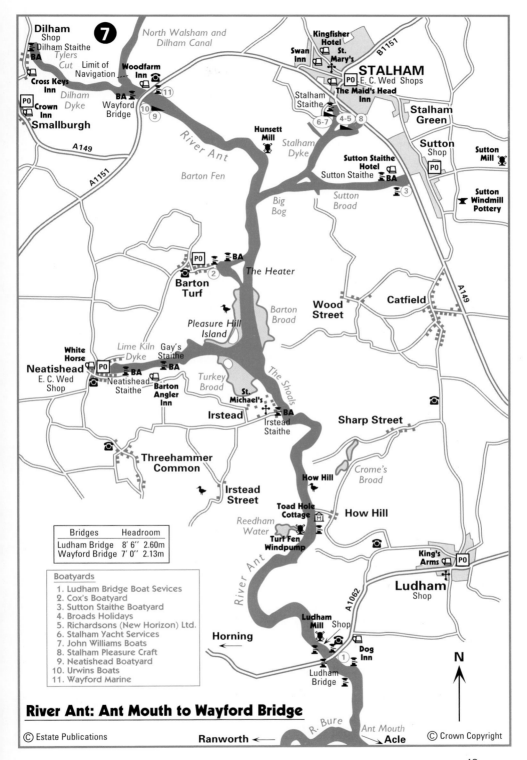

River Ant: Ant Mouth to Wayford Bridge

7

Dilham
Shop
Dilham Staithe
Tylers
Cut
BA
Cross Keys
Inn
Dilham
Dyke
PO
Crown
Inn
Smallburgh

North Walsham and
Dilham Canal
Limit of
Navigation
Woodfarm
Inn
BA
Wayford
Bridge
11
10
9

A149
A1151

River Ant

Hunsett
Mill

Barton Fen

Kingfisher
Hotel
Swan
Inn
St.
Mary's
STALHAM
PO E. C. Wed Shops
The Maid's Head
Inn
Stalham
Staithe
6-7 4-5 8

Stalham
Green

Sutton
Shop

Sutton
Mill

Stalham
Dyke

Sutton Staithe
Hotel
Sutton Staithe
BA
3

Sutton
Broad

Sutton
Windmill
Pottery

Big
Bog

A149

PO
BA
2
Barton
Turf

The Heater

Barton
Broad

Wood
Street

Catfield

Pleasure Hill
Island

White
Horse
Neatishead
E. C. Wed
Shop
Lime Kiln
Dyke
PO
Neatishead
Staithe
Gay's
Staithe
BA
BA
Barton
Angler
Inn

Turkey
Broad

St.
Michael's
Irstead
Irstead
Staithe
BA

The Shoals

Sharp Street

Threehammer
Common

Irstead
Street

How Hill

Crome's
Broad

Reedham
Water
Toad Hole
Cottage
M
Turf Fen
Windpump

How Hill

King's
Arms
PO

Ludham
Shop

Bridges	Headroom	
Ludham Bridge	8' 6''	2.60m
Wayford Bridge	7' 0''	2.13m

Boatyards
1. Ludham Bridge Boat Sevices
2. Cox's Boatyard
3. Sutton Staithe Boatyard
4. Broads Holidays
5. Richardsons (New Horizon) Ltd.
6. Stalham Yacht Services
7. John Williams Boats
8. Stalham Pleasure Craft
9. Neatishead Boatyard
10. Urwins Boats
11. Wayford Marine

Horning

River Ant

A1062

Ludham
Mill
Shop
Dog
Inn
1
Ludham
Bridge

Ludham

N

© Estate Publications

Ranworth ←

R. Bure
Ant Mouth
→ Acle

© Crown Copyright

The River Ant
8 miles/5km

This tiny river comes soon after Fleet Dyke, on the opposite bank. It is the narrowest of the three North Broads rivers, and the one that offers the quietest experiences, the most tortuous channels and the most remote havens in the most beautiful scenery. The River Ant has its source about 2 miles/3.2km to the north-west of North Walsham. In the early 1800's a canal (the North Walsham and Dilham Canal) was dug from Antingham to an area known as the Devil's Ditch: just above the channel to Dilham known by some as the Dilham Dyke and by others as Tyler's Cut. The head of navigation for the vast majority of craft is Wayford Bridge, but small craft can deviate into the Dilham Dyke.

To begin at the beginning: just inside the mouth is Mill Brig Reach, often known as Little Duffers, while about a mile up the river, is Ludham Bridge. When approaching the bridge, it is vital to slow down and sound the whistle, because of the dramatic 'S' bend that precedes it. The average restricting air draught at the bridge is just over 8'4"/2.5m and the rise and fall is a little over 6"/15cm. There are moorings both above and below the bridge. Nearby, small beer can be obtained fom the Dog Inn, as well as most basic domestic and boating needs. Upstream to Irstead, the channel is classically narrow and twisty, with few mooring places and the banks are often foul, but there is a pleasant mooring at How Hill below the fine house of that name. The Broads Authority owns the 353 acre How Hill Nature Reserve and has undertaken the management of what has been described as the 'Broads in microcosm'. There are to be seen stretches of reed and sedge beds still worked in the old manner; and there are marsh meadows with grazing cattle and freshly clean dykes. There is also a fine example of Carr woodland: a dense swamp of a place with alder, sallow (pussy willow) and birch trees - often called a UK tropical rain forest. There are public footpaths through the estate, a walking nature trail, and a water trail on board the Electric Eel, an electric boat. You will also see a tiny thatched cottage called 'Toad Hole' which used to be lived in by the local marshman. It is now an authentic museum of his work, life and family as it would have been about a hundred years ago.

At Irstead the river narrows even further and the bottom becomes gravel, giving this section the name Irstead Shoals: there is a small quay on the left. The river continues to meander in a north-easterly direction and the scenery becomes even more attractive as you cruise through wooded banks, meadows and reed beds with the occasional ruined windmill to add sombre dignity to the locations. Boat progress is more than likely to be well suited to the landscape: slow and easy.

The small village of Irstead comes just before Barton Broad. A left turn, away from the main channel, will take you to the old Lime Kiln Dyke by the village of Neatishead where there is a good staithe: mooring in the dyke is not permitted. The village centre has all the usual facilities, and is only a few minutes up the dyke. There are good moorings also at Gay's Staithe with, close by, the excellent Barton Angler Inn.

If you carry on straight up the river you pass through Barton Broad, where there is an island in the middle, known as Pleasure Hill Isle: boats can pass either side. This Broad is a nature reserve belonging to the Norfolk Wildlife Trust, and is special in two respects: first, others are approached via a dyke, whereas this one has its river running right through it with the shallow patches marked by posts; and second, according to local lore, Nelson learned to sail here. A small channel running westerly at the northern end of the Broad leads to Barton Staithe, also known as Barton Turf. During 1996-99, a major dredging exercise is being carried out on Barton, with vast quantities of mud being pumped out by the Broads Authority to settle in huge lagoons on the farmlands beyond the tree fringe. During this period, yachtsmen are advised to keep well clear of the dredger and to keep a careful watch for the floating pipeline, which must also be avoided.

The entrance to the Sutton channel which branches off to the east is, perhaps affectionately, known as the Big Bog. Sutton itself is situate about a mile south of Stalham, on the other leg, and has a very old corn mill. There is an easily accessible staithe with an attractive hotel at the head of the Broad which can be reached by car or by boat. The Broad itself is little more than a dyke channel, but in the Middle Ages it was much bigger. Over the years, it has become filled in; however, it is still a most pleasing place. Sutton is believed to have been habitable and hospitable since the days of the Anglo Saxons in the 500ADs. It is possible to sit on deck at night and be convinced that hardly anything has changed.

Some special features are to be noted in the Sutton area: the Broad itself is now mightily overgrown with reeds - some of which are reaped for thatching. Some local folk, noting that the reedbeds seem gradually but inexorably to be growing, feel that they are, like Tryffids, about to completely take over. Such a feeling of doom or dread is not likely to be lifted in the Spring by the deep-booming sound, as of a merman's distress horn, of the bittern. Although it is rarely seen, its cry is well known - and much revered. On a clear day, it is possible to espy, from the vantage point of the top of Sutton Mill, churches, light-houses, mills, towers, Horsey Mere and Hickling Broad as well as a goodly stretch of sea-coast. Legend has is that, with its nine floors, it is the tallest still-standing mill in the country. Erected in 1789 it was last used in 1940. All being well, it will shortly be fully working; already, there is a display of machinery, tools, traps and multifarious gadgets.

Off the main route, Stalham Dyke shoots away. Stalham possesses far fewer moorings than one would expect, bearing in mind the many facilities it has to offer. It is a market town with a busy main street and some pleasant Georgian houses. Nevertheless, it is worth trying to find a mooring, since Stalham makes a good centre from which to reach Barton and Hickling Broads as well the previously mentioned upper reaches of the Ant. Domestic needs are met in the town, and moorings and boating needs at the various boatyards.

At one time, the staithe was an extremely important and financially rewarding port of call for wherries landing coal, corn and other produce. St Mary's Church, with a fine 15th century font, stands happily opposite the very old edifice glorying in the appellation of The Maid's Head Inn. Supposedly, it was put up to put up the workers who were somewhat erratically building the church - and even more erratically returning to their lodgings at night. It is said that a tunnel was provided for them so that their rousing carousings should not disturb the wives of the worthies of the town.

Above and beyond Big Bog, the River Ant twists and turns before passing the much photographed mill at Hunsett and then moving on to Wayford Bridge, where there is an eponymous village. There are facilities and moorings here, and above the bridge the North Walsham and Dilham Canal is almost: (take care) navigable (by rowing boats only) for just over 2 miles/3.2km to the first lock at Honing. This canal was constructed in 1825 and originally ran for 8½ miles/13.6km to the source of the river at Antingham Pond. It was built to enable the town of North Walsham to trade with Great Yarmouth. Since it is so shallow and difficult, it should be navigated only by those with an obsession for cruising every last dishcloth-full of water. The legal head of the navigation is the junction with Tyler's Cut, just above Wayford Bridge. After that point, only dinghies are allowed in the waterway. Dilham Dyke is owned by the East Anglian Waterways Assoc. and has about 4'0"/1.2m water: there are moorings at the staithe and a shop and pub in Dilham.

River Ant Facilities

Bridges   Headroom

| Ludham Bridge | 8'6" | 2.60m |
| Wayford Bridge | 7'0" | 2.13m |

Broads Authority free 24hr moorings

Dilham Staithe
Wayford Bridge
Sutton Staithe
Paddys' Lane
Barton Turf
Neatishead
Gay's Staithe
Irstead Staithe

Boatyards

Ludham Bridge Boat Services	01692 630486
Cox's Boatyard, Barton Turf	01692 536206
Sutton Staithe Boatyard	01692 581653
Broads Holidays	01692 581081
Richardsons (New Horizon) Ltd	01692 581081
Stalham Yacht Services Ltd	01692 580288
John Williams Boats, Stalham	01692 580953
Stalham Pleasure Craft	01692 581081
Neatishead Boatyard, Wayford Bridge	01692 580465
Urwins Boats	01692 582071
Wayford Marine	01692 582555

Places of interest

How Hill Nature Reserve (Broads Authority)
Tel: 01692 678763
353 acre Nature Reserve and Environmental Centre managed by the Broads Authority: take a trip through the reserve on the 'Electric Eel' a silent electric-powered launch. There are three windpumps here: the Clayrack windpump has been relocated from Ranworth Marshes; Boardman's Mill is an open-framed timber trestle windpump with turbine in working order: open Easter - May and Oct daily 1100 - 1700 and June - Sept daily 1000 - 1800

Toad Hole Cottage Museum, How Hill
former eel-catcher's cottage furnished as it was in the late19th century open Easter - May and Oct daily 1100 - 1700 and June - Sept daily 1000 - 1800

River Ant

<u>Barton Broad Nature Reserve</u>
170 acres owned by the Norfolk Wildlife Trust

<u>Museum of the Broads, Stalham Staithe</u>
Tel: 01692 630486/ 631181
exhibition of Broads history and boat design through the centuries:
open Apr - end Oct daily 1200 - 1600

<u>Sutton Mill</u>, Stalham
built in 1789 with nine floors, at 75'0"/ 23m high, this is the tallest
surviving windmill in the country: open Apr - Sept daily 1000 - 1800

<u>Sutton Broads Museum</u>
exhibition of domestic, farm and trade tools, bank notes and bygones

<u>Sutton Windmill Pottery</u> Church Road, Sutton
Tel: 01692 580595
large range of hand-thrown stoneware pottery

<u>Pubs</u>

Dog Inn, Ludham	
Barton Angler Inn, Neatishead	01692 630740
White Horse, Neatishead	01692 630828
Sutton Staithe Hotel, Sutton	01692 580244
Maid's Head Inn, Stalham	01692 580200
Swan Inn, Stalham	01692 581492
Kingfisher Hotel, Stalham	01692 581974
Woodfarm Inn, Wayford Bridge	01692 582414

Fishing on the North Broads

Barton Broad

These sheltered waters amount to upwards of 60 hectares; and, within this spread, there are two very preferred posts. The first is near the engagingly named 'Old Gay Staithe', happily finding itself within easy reach of the Barton Lodge Hotel, by the slim dyke near Neatishead village. Here, rudd and roach are to be found, sheltering apart and away from the harshness of high sea tides which can reach this far. Second favourite is via the dyke giving on to Barton Turf Staithe where there are good bream for the tempting - but only from boats. Light cereal groundbait is often used for starters, followed with bread, maggots and worms - the latter especially for the bigger bream and tench. Nights tend to be good for bream; while the winter season is generally poor for pike.

Hickling Broad and Heigham Sound

These two locations of some 700 acres are at their best when well away from the swell and wash of passing boat traffic, although the cruising channel can fish well after dark.
Hickling usually carries masses of roach - with some rudd, perch, tench and pike. When around, the bream can get quite fattish - certainly near Catfield and Deep Dykes ... and where the latter meets Heigham Sound. Near Candle Dyke, roach are good as are pike - all in all, though, best at night. Ironically, boaters being what they are, this area is best fished by boat.

Horsey Mere

Horsey offers fishing that is generally shallow and can be quite clear - although there is lots of weed in the summer. There are plenty of roach, rudd, perch and bream with a goodly number up to 7lb. Horsey in particular is famous for its specimen pike, and few winters pass without a specimen over 30lb being taken. Boat fishing is permitted (by J. Buxton of Horsey Hall) from June 16th to October 31st, after which it is dead water (for conservation of wildfowl) until March 1st, when angling starts until the end of the season. Pike anglers should note that live-baiting is not allowed.

Little Ormesby, Rollesby, Lily, Great Ormesby and Filby Broads

Consisting in all of nearly 1800 acres, these waters are free of leisure craft and so offer grand chances for the small boating angler. Little Ormesby can be pretty deep, and has excellent pike

Martham North Broad, Somerton

The excellent fishing here is pretty well absolutely private.

Ranworth (including Malthouse) Broad

This tidal broad of 100 acres is off the Bure, and is partly a nature reserve. Seasonal fishing brings, firstly, plentiful bream and roach; and in the second season, good fat pike. On the whole, the open parts of the broad are spoiled for the angler by the heavy leisure traffic, so winter angling has to be favourite.

Salhouse Broad

In the main this is also fishing-from-boat territory, with only very limited access from bank sides. Roach and bream are the main candidates - with the usual additions of tench, perch and pike

South Walsham Broad

The inner broad is absolutely private, and the outer fished almost exclusively from boats. Leisure craft are numerous - but, for compensation, the night fishing is very good. Bream, roach and pike are all here.

Womack Water

This is a modest but intriguing waterway. Some smallish bream are to be found, and decent roach are to be encountered - but pike are a rarity. Favourite for food fishing are bread, maggots and worms. Eels abound - and winter is best.

Wroxham Broad

A largish broad at over 100 acres, Wroxham is tidal on the Bure. Some bank fishing is fruitful, but best is to take a small, shoal craft and pursue secrets of secret waters. Very good roach are here, with perch and bream well in attendance - often just of the company of large pike.

Fishing on the North Broads Rivers

The River Ant

Boat business intervenes here quite strongly, but, once avoided, the fishing is good for roach, tench, bream, pike and the omnipresent eel.

Near Stalham, there is some free fishing - and many possibilities of little boats. Autumn is a good time here; where by Barton Broad, there are good chances for bream and roach - not forgetting eels galore ... once again.

The River Bure

The good news is that fishing is free from Coltishall Common, but it is very popular with boaters, and so winter and evenings are favoured.
Towards Wroxham there is good catching from boats, with roach and bream and pike in good numbers. Wroxham itself is one of the busiest spots on the river, and, consequently, in season is to be left severely alone; but in winter the banks burst with happy anglers, with much bream, roach and perch. The occasional tench is to be had, and large pike lurk in the many small dykes and pools.
Downstream for many a mile, the river is given over in season to leisure craft, but out of season and at full night it is excellent, with really good bream - sometimes over 4lb; while near Horning (another boating/boozing centre) roach are ready to be had - accompanied by their fans, the pike.
Near the mouth of the Ant (and, of course St Benet's - though not the anglers' saint) there is usually an abundance of bream and roach - and some do get big around here; while moving downstream, things continue to improve with bream and roach in the majority again. Ledgering with lots of groundbait is favourite on this stretch - and the Stracey Arms is well known to fishermen and boaters alike.

The River Thurne

The Thurne offers lots of free fishing sites. It is a magnet to boaters in season - but also, apparently, to big pike. For example, the 40lb 1oz pike caught here on a dead roach in 1967 by Peter Hancock once held the English record, prior to the stocks being wiped out in the late 1960s. It was nearly four feet long. Bream here are good at night. Near Hickling, bream can be found; and near the famous Potter Heigham bridge the banks are well-used by anglers, with, in general, winter being best for bream and roach.

The coarse fishing season runs from 16 June to 14 March and all anglers are statutorily required to possess an Environment Agency Rod Licence, these can be purchased from post offices and Beccles Information Centre. A fishing permit is also required to fish on certain non-tidal rivers and lakes controlled by the Broads Authority - enquire locally for details. Trout fishing is available on certain stretches, but a special permit must be obtained to fish these.

SOUTH BROADS

Now we retrace our steps to move from the North Broads into the country of the South. There are two ways to approach the South Broads: the first is to negotiate an exit from the River Bure via Great Yarmouth, and cross Breydon Water: this needs caution and good timing (see pages 19-21 for details). The second is to come in from the sea through Lowestoft Harbour and enter the Broads via Lake Lothing and the lock at Mutford (see page 73-75 for details).

Breydon Water

Breydon Bridge stands like a guardian at the mouth of Breydon Water, just as centuries ago did Burgh Castle; and it is intriguing to discover that the word Breydon itself comes from the Danish, meaning a stretch of water broadened from being narrow.

Different from most of the actual Broads, which were originally man-made peat diggings, Breydon Water is the completely natural former sea estuary of the local rivers, before they finally united to rush through the Haven at Great Yarmouth. At low water, it is mainly one large mud flat, but at any state of the tide it is an impressive spread. Nearly 4 miles/6.4km long and over 1 mile/1.6km wide, it is to be compared to an inland sea, although the tourist board PR team likes to promote it as a lake. Consisting of some 2,000 acres of wetness that always look dramatic, it is surrounded by open country leaving it exposed to the elements. The wide, four miles-long channel is well-marked by posts right up to the Berney Arms. But poles do not a lagoon make, nor iron posts a lake: these waters defy all thoughts of both disciplining and confining them. They are pretty impressive in their own right - although it must be said that the area is more frequently gloomy than it is pretty. Rough waters can be experienced; and wind against tide even in these 'sheltered' inland waters can make conditions dangerous for standard Broads cruisers.

The waters are more often grey than blue, but in early morning light, when you are steaming nor-easterly into a low rising sun, they can appear as if possessed of a singular spell and a curious air of mystery. I vividly remember once being alone on Breydon Water: the place was abandoned except for an array of immobile cormorants and shags. In their remarkable wing-drying postures they had perched on the channel markers and were displaying more haughty grandeur than the emblems of a Roman legion, which they uncannily resembled. The notion was all the more potent since we were no more than a cable or so from the old Roman fort of Gariannonum.

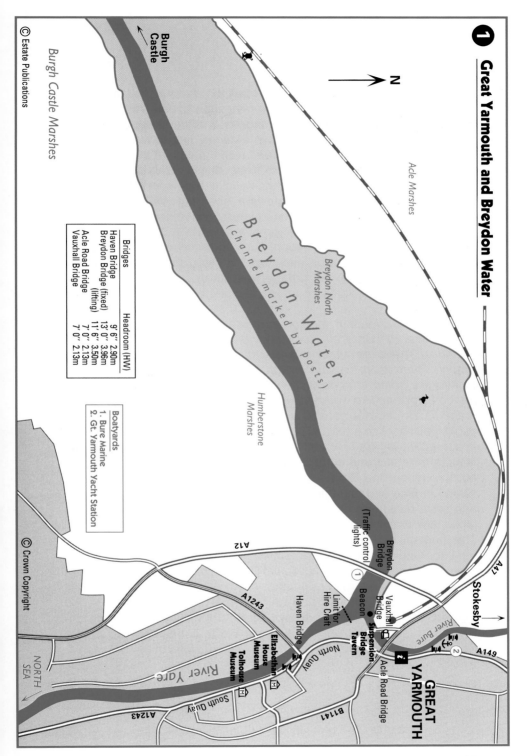

N

Acle Marshes

Burgh Castle

Burgh Castle Marshes

© Estate Publications

Breydon Water
(channel marked by posts)

Breydon North Marshes

Humberstone Marshes

Bridges	Headroom (HW)	
Haven Bridge	9' 6"	2.90m
Breydon Bridge (fixed)	13' 0"	3.96m
(lifting)	11' 6"	3.50m
Acle Road Bridge	7' 0"	2.13m
Vauxhall Bridge	7' 0"	2.13m

Boatyards
1. Bure Marine
2. Gt. Yarmouth Yacht Station

A12

A1243

(Traffic control lights)

Breydon Bridge

Limit for Hire Craft

Beacon

Vauxhall Bridge

River Bure

Stokesby

A47

A149

Acle Road Bridge

GREAT YARMOUTH

Suspension Bridge Tavern

Haven Bridge

North Quay

Elizabethan House Museum

Tolhouse Museum

River Yare

South Quay

A1243

NORTH SEA

B1141

© Crown Copyright

59

Breydon Water

Nowadays, clearly numbered stakes mark the channel in standard red and green, and there are plenty of warnings to skippers not to deviate. Nevertheless, lots of boats still manage to find the sticky bottom and have to wait for a pluck (if in luck) or a decent tide to wash them off. And all this in spite of the recommendations that have been issued in the brochures for at least 25 years: 'Keep strictly in the channel, don't cut corners outside the line of posts even at high water. Don't follow the other fellow who thinks he knows a 'short cut', we've seen three cruisers who did that being left 'on the putty' for 12 hours because the 'leader' was a stupid know-all. Keep at least 20'0"/6.0m inside the line of posts. Before crossing Breydon, have your anchor (or mud weight) ready to drop and the rope secured to a cleat, then in the event of engine trouble you will not drift between the posts onto the mud. If you have to anchor, leave room in the channel for coastal vessels to pass.'

As one of the Broads Inspectors once said to me: *'On one occasion there were 20 boats all stuck on the mud down the sides of the channel. The deep water channel between them was completely empty. There wasn't a boat in sight where they should have been. It looked like some strange layout for a maritime board game with all the boats poised like watery chessmen before the first move has been made.'* Talk about a gambit; it was certainly an opening move that might well sacrifice a piece!

It is true that we are now well and truly inland, and the influence of the tides is not the same as in the North Sea or next the Haven Bridge; but throughout the Broads you will find you can make a substantial saving in time and fuel and at the same time you will have smoother and more hassle-free trips, if you work the tides in your favour. Tide tables are available at most of the mooring points.

The mud spit at the junction just before the Berney Arms extends well out into the river and since there can be as little as 4'0"/1.2m of water here it is only sensible to decide well in advance which route you are going to take. The turn to port takes you into the River Waveney, past Burgh Castle, St Olaves and on to Oulton Broad, Lowestoft and Beccles. While the starboard turn leads to the Berney Arms on the River Yare and to the first of the many windmills that are, sad to say, for the most part, literally littered over some sections of the Broads.

The River Waveney
22 miles/ 35km

Let us travel the shorter river first. A well-marked and staked-out channel leads to the first stopping place on the port hand where there is history all round: many Roman coins, pottery and Saxon relics have been found here in the past. Here, on a commanding site above the river, stand the imposing remains of the Roman Saxon shore fort of Gariannonum, with walls of flint and brick surrounding six acres. This fortress was vital to the defence of Caister near Great Yarmouth. It was a working garrison, with a troop of African cavalry until the Romans left in the 5th century AD. In the 7th century AD St. Fursa came to the area and with the help of the East Anglian King Sigebert, established Christianity hereabouts; and a monastery was set up in the ruins of Burgh Castle. Fursa died in 650AD, but his monastery at Burgh Castle may well have survived until the 9th century AD when invading hordes destroyed abbeys and monasteries - and much more as well. It was certainly mentioned by the Venerable Bede in 731AD. Come the Norman Conquest, it guarded the river route to Norwich. Like many of the abbeys and monasteries it suffered ruination at the hands of those who did good business in the transport and sale of flints and stone. There is now a marina for modest-draught craft here (Burgh Castle Marina) and some riverside moorings. It is a popular spot, so space on the river bank is usually restricted. The facilities are only basic for food, drink and singing in unison, but absolutely first rate for all boating needs.

The river then continues a placid winding course on to St Olaves near the junction of the River Waveney with the New Cut. Before this is reached, however, just downstream, by Bowling Alley Reach, is Belton, with the interesting round-towered church of All Saints. Nearby are the elongated marshes that bear the village's name. Before we reach the final stopping place in this region, the river takes a huge horseshoe bend to the north round Fritton Marshes, finally arriving at the important feature on this stretch: St Olaves. This is a small community - pretty, self-contained but yet managing to keep itself to its charming rustic self without being unwelcoming. It bubbles with the kind of village life in which everyone knows or wants to know who is who and what is what. It is certainly a nice enough spot for a couple of nights with better than basic facilities for pubbing, grubbing and messing about in boats. It is, however, not over-blessed with sophisticated mooring arrangements, and some bankside depths have less than 3'4"/1.0m. A metre is also just about the size of the

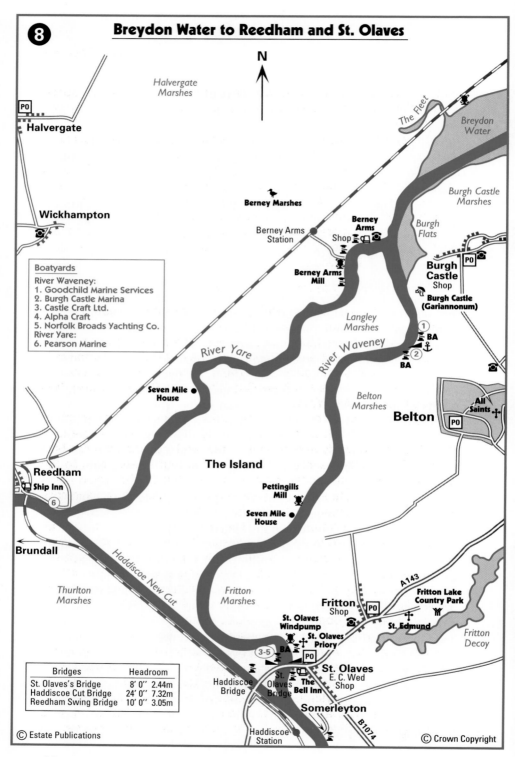

N

Halvergate Marshes

PO

Halvergate

The Fleet

Breydon Water

Wickhampton

Berney Marshes

Burgh Castle Marshes

Berney Arms

Berney Arms Station

Shop

Burgh Flats

PO

Burgh Castle
Shop

Burgh Castle (Gariannonum)

Berney Arms Mill

Boatyards
River Waveney:
1. Goodchild Marine Services
2. Burgh Castle Marina
3. Castle Craft Ltd.
4. Alpha Craft
5. Norfolk Broads Yachting Co.
River Yare:
6. Pearson Marine

Langley Marshes

River Waveney

1
BA

River Yare

2
BA

Seven Mile House

Belton Marshes

PO

Belton

All Saints

PO

The Island

Pettingills Mill

Reedham
Ship Inn

6

Seven Mile House

←
Brundall

Haddiscoe New Cut

Thurlton Marshes

Fritton Marshes

A143

Fritton
Shop

PO

Fritton Lake Country Park

St. Edmund

Fritton Decoy

St. Olaves Windpump

St. Olaves Priory

PO

BA

3-5

Haddiscoe Bridge

St. Olaves Bridge

St. Olaves
The Bell Inn

E. C. Wed
Shop

Somerleyton

B1074

Bridges	Headroom	
St. Olaves's Bridge	8' 0''	2.44m
Haddiscoe Cut Bridge	24' 0''	7.32m
Reedham Swing Bridge	10' 0''	3.05m

Haddiscoe Station

© Estate Publications

© Crown Copyright

rise and fall of the tide. Unexpectedly, there are one or two spots, especially near the bridge, where local currents are much endowed with eddies.

The Priory, which was founded in 1216 is near the famous bridge, and is open all the year. St Olaves' Bridge, with its bow-girdered construction, is a listed building. Fritton, just across the river, is famous for its Decoy: a pretty lake surrounded by trees once used as an entrapment for wild ducks. During the war, the RAF used the area for experiment, and much was the talk of experimental firing: bursting, blasting and detonation. Today, it is much more serene. Now a Country Park and nothing more than a lake with gardens and trees, it is difficult to imagine there might ever have been any kind of threat here.

The River Waveney to Beccles and Geldeston

With the bridge of St Olaves behind us, we come to the junction where there is an important choice to be made: northwest for Norwich or southeast for Beccles. More or less straight ahead (tending only a little to port) keeps you still on the River Waveney, while the alternative is the hairpin bend to starboard into The Cut, which for some locals is what is still known as the New Cut, and so to Reedham and then Norwich via the River Yare.

Taking the Beccles route, we first pass Herringfleet Mill which is unique in the Norfolk and Suffolk Broads. It is the only timber-built smock drainage windpump left in the area, and those windpumps built in the 1750s looked similar, with cloth sails that swept down to the ground. These were tended by a hardy marshman who would come out in all weathers to turn the characteristic boat-shaped cap and sails into the wind. Somerleyton Staithe, where there is a convenient mooring just downstream of the railway swing bridge is next. Charles Dickens is supposed to have been inspired on a trip to Somerleyton Hall after seeing the signpost to Blundeston. Indeed, this is supposed to be the Blundestone where David Copperfield was born. Cromwell had some troops at Somerleyton Hall. The owner was a Staunch Royalist, so was made to feed them all, and their horses: he was also fined and had his goods and chattels confiscated.

Somerleyton is a pretty estate village. The village, the school and Somerleyton Hall were the work of Sir Morton Peto. He made his fortune from railways and is responsible for much of the building at Lowestoft Harbour and for much of the rebuilding of the Houses of Parliament. Somerleyton Hall was rebuilt in 1846, by Peto, to combine magnificence with a modest fireside-homely feel. The clock was designed by Vulliamy in 1847 and intended for the Houses of

River Waveney

Parliament, but when it proved too exorbitant a purchase for the Government, Peto, no doubt embarrassing all the Members of the Parliament of the day, decided to buy it for Somerleyton - leaving Westminster to content itself with Big Ben. Coming down to earth, there are some excellent gardens - and for those who are not content just to stand and stare, there are also a trail, a maze and a miniature railway.

South of Somerleyton, the river continues its marshy way through very ordinary scenery until we reach the parting of the ways with Oulton Dyke which leads to Oulton Broad and Lowestoft. We shall return to Oulton, Lowestoft and this other way from the Broads to the sea on page 73.

The River Waveney is tidal as far as Beccles, 23 miles/37km above its mouth, and is accessible to craft with no more than 6'0"/1.8m draught. The first edifice to catch the eye after passing the Oulton Dyke fork is St Mary's Church, with an eponymous reach and a staithe, where mooring is not easy because of shoaling banksides. The church is a rather strange long and narrow building with an unlikely thatched roof which was built towards the end of the 14th century. Its brick and flint tower must be unique, resembling, as it does, a construction from children's building blocks: although started around the end of the 16th century, it was not actually completed until the end of the 18th.

The river here is, in the main, a very quiet stretch, but almost immediately after turning into it there is one of the most popular spots on the Broads and an unusual one in an area which is generally given over to gentle cruising and the not always so gentle wild life. Decreed as a pleasure dome by its owners, it is known as the Waveney River Centre. There is a large mooring basin, where craft go stern to: there are plenty of riverside moorings, a shop, restaurant, leisure centre and boatyard. Quite large craft are to be seen moored and jilling around the Centre where there are all the facilities that a country-loving but socialising family could hope for. It has grown over the years; and into a better not merely a bigger place. More strength to their combined elbows. The actual village of Burgh St Peter is tiny and located about a mile away in a pretty, isolated spot

It is now about seven miles to Beccles. Just a short distance upstream from the River Centre, by Castle Mill and Reach, there is a much quieter spot for those who want peace rather than a piece of the action; but care must be taken not to be caught out by thinking there is always deep water at the banksides. Reeds frequently disguise silt and a foul bottom. And so the river continues right up to Beccles:

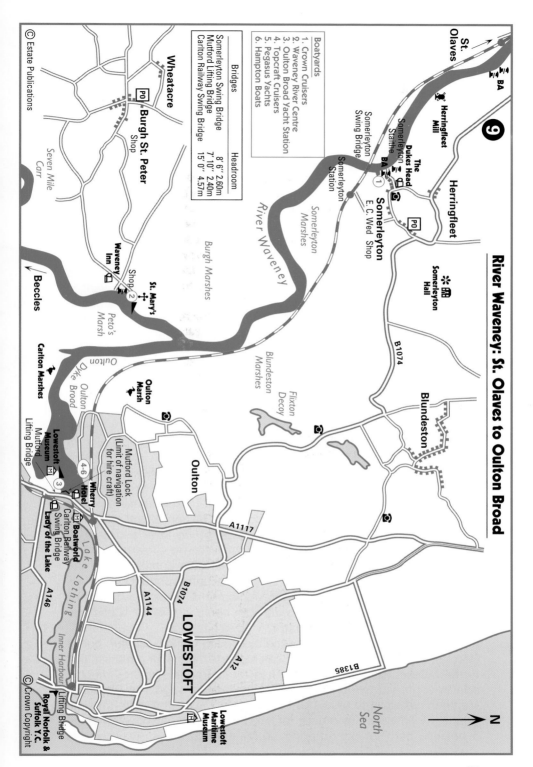

River Waveney: St. Olaves to Oulton Broad

9

Boatyards
1. Crown Cruisers
2. Waveney River Centre
3. Oulton Broad Yacht Station
4. Topcraft Cruisers
5. Pegasus Yachts
6. Hampton Boats

Bridges	Headroom	
Somerleyton Swing Bridge	8' 6"	2.60m
Mutford Lifting Bridge	7' 10"	2.40m
Carlton Railway Swing Bridge	15' 0"	4.57m

© Estate Publications

Wheatacre

P0 Burgh St. Peter
Shop

Seven Mile Carr

St. Olaves

BA 1/4 1/4

Herringfleet Mill

Herringfleet

The Dukes Head
Somerleyton Staithe
BA
Somerleyton Swing Bridge
Somerleyton Station
1
P0
Somerleyton
E. C. Wed Shop

Somerleyton Hall
B1074

Blundeston

River Waveney

Somerleyton Marshes

Burgh Marshes

Waveney Inn
Shop
St. Mary's
2

Peto's Marsh

Beccles

Carlton Marshes

Oulton Dyke

Oulton Marsh

Oulton Broad

Blundeston Marshes

Flixton Decoy

North Sea

Lowestoft Museum
4-6
3
Wherry Hotel
Mutford Lock
(Limit of navigation for hire craft)

Mutford Lifting Bridge

Boatworld
Carlton Railway Swing Bridge
Lady of the Lake

Lake Lothing

Outon

A1117

A1144

A146

A1144

A12

LOWESTOFT

B1074

Inner Harbour

A146

Lifting Bridge
Royal Norfolk & Suffolk Y.C.
Lowestoft Maritime Museum

B1385

N

© Crown Copyright

65

quiet, peaceful, remote and just the spot for those fishing families who do not like to be disturbed too much.

The environs change little even for the last run into Beccles, where there are all-round services and facilities, including a heated outside swimming pool, plenty of corporation utilities, a 5 mph speed limit and deep-water moorings that are more of a pleasant boat park really. The A146 crosses the river here, with a restricting air draught of 6'6"/1.9m at ordinary High Water at the Old Bridge. Craft of up to 6'0"/1.8m draught will have little difficulty with regard to water depth. The tidal stream runs hard through Beccles Old Bridge and there is a rise and fall of about 1'7"/0.5m.

It is decidedly difficult to imagine that Beccles was once a famous fishing port. Nowadays, it is the kind of place where you will want to spend a few days just meandering around. In a small café, I overheard, 'We came here on holiday and just fell in love with the place'. The marina staff in particular go out of their way to be, as they themselves describe it, 'available for service'.

A short trip up the river will show that St Michael's Church (with its bell tower actually inside the structure and not atop it) looms over all, towering above the area and proclaiming the status that Beccles once had as a centre of agriculture and business. It is worth exploiting the church's commanding position and mounting the steps for the splen-did view. Another, though modest, claim to fame is that Lord Nelson's parents were married in this church in 1749.

Beccles Museum (grade 1 listed building in flint and brick) is a joy: it was previously the 1631 Sir John Leman School. It is of general appeal, containing an intriguing representation of Beccles as it was in the middle of the 19th century with miscellaneous agricultural costumes and other offerings telling the historical tale of the town and area. A more specialised treat is in store at the William Clowes Printing Museum. Opened in 1984, it celebrates the 400th anniversary of the Charter of Beccles. It has since become a prime printing museum, hosting well-preserved machinery, equipments various, wood-cuts, and many books - all from the early 19th century. It offers a compre-hensive history of the printing industry up to I.T.

Because of the limited height of the old bridge going upstream out of Beccles, it is only smaller craft that can navigate the further 4 miles/6.4km to the derelict lock at Geldeston. It is, of course possible by dinghy, and is a pleasant trip in clement weather through the Barsham Marshes, with plenty of hostelries en route. Geldeston is an amiable village, much visited by artists, tourists and anglers, all of whom have a positive bent for gongoozling. If, for nothing more, the cruise is

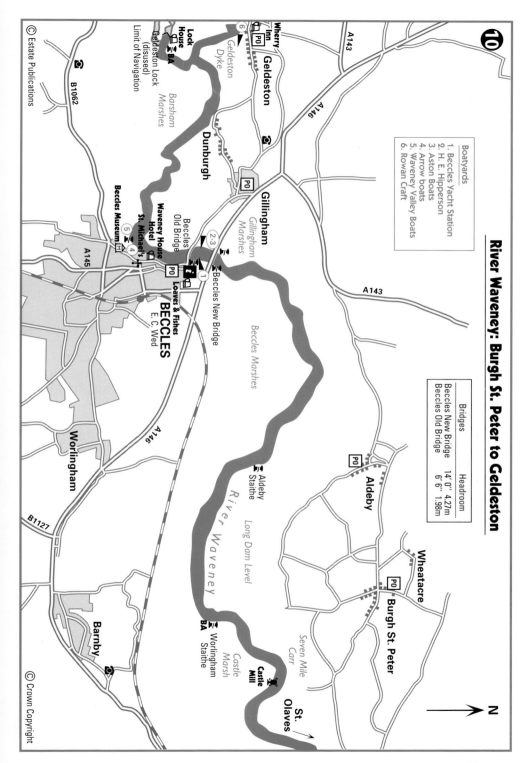

River Waveney: Burgh St. Peter to Geldeston

10

Boatyards
1. Beccles Yacht Station
2. H. E. Hipperson
3. Aston Boats
4. Arrow boats
5. Waveney Valley Boats
6. Rowan Craft

Bridges	Headroom	
Beccles New Bridge	14' 0"	4.27m
Beccles Old Bridge	6' 6"	1.98m

Wherry Inn

Geldeston

Geldeston Dyke

Lock House

Geldeston Lock (disused)
Limit of Navigation

Barsham Marshes

B1062

Dunburgh

Gillingham

Gillingham Marshes

Beccles Old Bridge

Beccles Museum

Waveney House Hotel

St. Michael's

BECCLES

Loaves & Fishes
E. C. Wed

Beccles New Bridge

Beccles Marshes

A145

A146

Worlingham

B1127

River Waveney

Long Dam Level

Aldeby Staithe

Aldeby

Wheatacre

Burgh St. Peter

Seven Mile Carr

Worlingham Staithe

Castle Marsh

Castle Mill

Barnby

St. Olaves

A143

A146

N

© Estate Publications

© Crown Copyright

67

worthwhile because of the old watermill and ever intriguing and quaint Lock House pub by the old lock and the Wherry Inn just up the cut. It is possible, with light craft capable of portage, to go still further up the river, for the Waveney actually goes as far as Bungay.

This quaintly named place is well over ten centuries old, and it still uses Saxon words in some of its official town business. There are ruins of its 12th century Bigod family castle to be seen: imposing twin towers, with what were once enormous flint walls. They are now ruins only, since, once the castle was no longer occupied, round about 1750, the crafty indigens procured the stone for their own purposes - believing in spreading the wealth. In better repair, but still with an eye on the main chance, is the famous Butter Cross, right in the centre of the town. The octagonal edifice was host to those local farmers and market women who used to sell their eggs and butter from its steps. It wasn't always a happy place, for, at one time, there used to be a cage and dungeon here to restrain prisoners. It was rebuilt after the Great Fire in 1689.

Since Bungay is, in a way, almost the end of culture, history and everything; and since Beccles is the head of navigation for all but low-ceiling floaters, we now return to the junction with Oulton Dyke and move on the other way.

River Waveney Facilities

Bridges

Bridges	Headroom	
Haddiscoe Bridge (New Cut)	24'0"	7.32m
St Olaves	8'0"	2.44m
Somerleyton Swing Bridge	8'6"	2.60m
Beccles New Bridge	14'0"	4.27m
Beccles Old Bridge	6'6"	1.98m

Broads Authority free 24hr moorings

Burgh Castle
St Olaves
Herringfleet
Somerleyton
Worlingham Staithe
Aldeby
Geldeston Lock

Boatyards

Goodchild Marine Services, Burgh Castle	01493 782301
Burgh Castle Marina	01493780331
Castle Craft Ltd, St Olaves	01493 488675
Alpha Craft, St Olaves	01493 488254
Norfolk Broads Yacht Co.	01493 488469
Crown Cruisers	01502 730335
Waveney River Centre	01502 677343/677217
Beccles Yacht Station	01502 712225
H.E.Hipperson, Gillingham Dam	01502 712166
Aston Boats, Beccles	01502 713960
Arrow Boats, Puddingmoor	01502 713524
Waveney Valley Boats, Puddingmoor	01502 712538
Rowan Craft	01508 545208

Places of Interest

Fritton Lake Countryworld
Tel. 01493 488288/488208
250 acres of wood, grassland and formal gardens with a 170 acre
lake for watersports etc. open daily Apr - Sept 1000 - 1730

Somerleyton Hall and Gardens
Tel. 01502 730224
Victorian mansion built around original Tudor House by Sir Morton
Peto in 1846: 12 acres gardens with a maze and miniature railway:
tel. for opening time

St Olaves Windpump
Tel. 01493 488230
tiny boarded windpump open daily: key from Bridge Stores

St Olaves Priory
Tel. 01493 488609
remains of 13th century Augustinian Priory open daily: key to vaulted
brick undercroft from Priory House

Beccles Museum, Ballygate
Tel. 01502 712941
exhibition of local industry and farming, domestic implemets etc. open
Easter - October 1430 - 1730, closed mons

River Waveney

Otter Trust, Earsham
Tel. 01986 893470
collection of otters in natural surroundings: open daily 1030 - 1800
Apr - end Sept

William Clowes Print Museum, Newgate, Beccles
history of printing in Beccles: open June - Aug, mon - fri 1400 - 1630

Broads Information Centre, The Quay, Fen Lane, Beccles
Tel. 01502 713196
open Easter - Oct

Pubs

Fisherman's Bar & Restaurant, Burgh Castle	01493 780729
Bell Inn, St Olaves	01493 488249
Duke's Head, Somerleyton	01502 730281
Waveney House Hotel, Beccles	01502 712270
The Locks, Geldeston	01508 518414
Wherry Inn, Geldeston	01508 518371

Oulton Dyke to Lowestoft

In order to reach Mutford Lock, we return to the parting of the ways with the River Waveney and move into Oulton Dyke; the stretch of water that leaves the river halfway between Somerleyton Railway Bridge and the Waveney River Centre. It must be one of the busiest stretches on the Broads. and it is not really suitable for mooring, although it is pleasantly situated. Indeed, from the deck it can appear that you are marooned in the middle of vast marshes.

After a short mile, it leads to what might be described as one of the Biggest and Broadest experiences of them all: Oulton Broad. This is one of the best known and largest of the lake-like expansions that are to be found on the Broads. It covers about 130 acres and apart from one or two clearly obvious shoal patches it is all navigable.

It is also one of the busiest of the Lakeland centres, managing to combine some of the charms of rurality with access to enough socialising to satisfy even the most convivial of crew members. All facilities are close to hand, with plenty of places to moor; and, of course, all the attractions of Lowestoft are nearby. It is particularly well-known as a motor speedboat-racing centre - which activity reaches the heights of its crazed manoeuvrings at the height of the summer season - summer madness in the silly season indeed! Predictably, Oulton Broad is not suited to serious cruising or sailing since it is so busy and crowded; although it is a pleasant enough spot for young persons' water sports.

Oulton Broad Yacht Station is the last possible halt on the Broads-side of Mutford Lock. The increased traffic created by the improvements in locking has made it so much more popular than before, that it is frequently necessary to book a place well ahead of arriving. This is not always easy, even though the Harbour Master and staff have up-to-date telecommunications. Those of us who phone ahead, most frequently encounter the answer-machine that seems to get used if not wisely then perhaps too well - but certainly too much. This is one of the few fully-equipped marina facilities on the North or South Broads, and is deep in the heartland of Hire Boat Land - or Heartwater, perhaps.

Oulton Broad is accessible through Mutford Lock (although not to hire craft), with no attendant hazard, at most times of the day. It boasts all the facilities that any cruising family intent on a Good Time on Holiday could possibly desire, crave or pine for.

Mutford Lock has been refurbished and now affords an easy and inexpensive access to the Broads from the sea. It used to operate once a week - and then erratically ... and only with much telephoning

River Waveney: St. Olaves to Oulton Broad

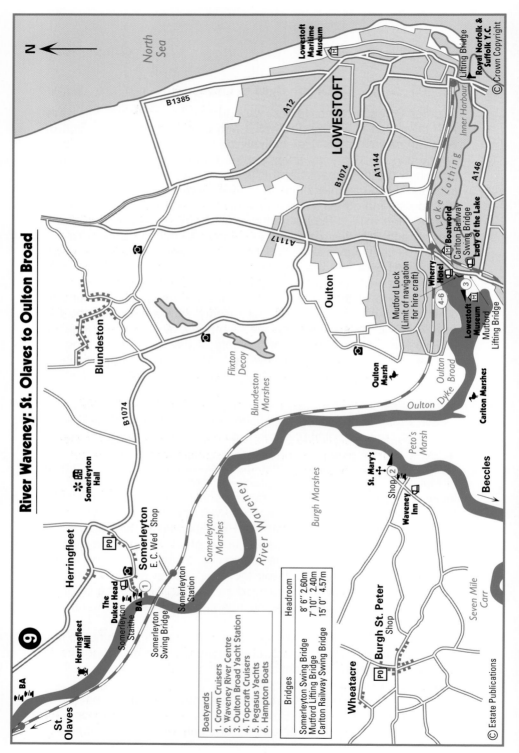

N ←

North Sea

B1385

Lowestoft Maritime Museum

LOWESTOFT

A12

A1144

B1074

A146

Lifting Bridge

Royal Norfolk & Suffolk Y.C.

Inner Harbour

Lake Lothing

Boatworld

Carlton Railway Swing Bridge

Lady of the Lake

Wherry Hotel

Mutford Lock (Limit of navigation for hire craft)

Mutford Lifting Bridge

Lowestoft Museum

4-6

3

A1117

Oulton

Oulton Broad

Oulton Dyke

Oulton Marsh

Carlton Marshes

Blundeston

B1074

Flixton Decoy

Blundeston Marshes

Somerleyton Hall

Herringfleet

Somerleyton

E. C. Wed   Shop

The Dukes Head

Somerleyton Staithe

BA

1

Somerleyton Swing Bridge

Somerleyton Station

Somerleyton Marshes

River Waveney

Burgh Marshes

Peto's Marsh

St. Mary's

Shop   2

Waveney Inn

Beccles

Wheatacre

Burgh St. Peter

Shop

PO

Seven Mile Carr

Herringfleet Mill

BA

9

St. Olaves

PO

Boatyards
1. Crown Cruisers
2. Waveney River Centre
3. Oulton Broad Yacht Station
4. Topcraft Cruisers
5. Pegasus Yachts
6. Hampton Boats

Bridges	Headroom
Somerleyton Swing Bridge	8' 6'' 2.60m
Mutford Lifting Bridge	7' 10'' 2.40m
Carlton Railway Swing Bridge	15' 0'' 4.57m

72

and form filling; but now the hassle has been taken out of the system and it is a small joy to pass through. It is used to provide access between the hardly-ever-threatening Broads and the frequently-grey-and-turbulent North Sea.

Approach from the sea

Approaching from this seaway, Lowestoft Harbour's traffic controls through the entrance and Lake Lothing are still as properly strict as they should be, but the Harbour Master's staff are friendly and co-operative, so it is not often that a yacht is held up very long waiting for the town bridge to open. For those who do not like jilling around, there is the Royal Norfolk and Suffolk Yacht Club which welcomes visitors and can usually offer a berth, and their berthing has now become nearly a calm water paradise thanks to the improvements afforded by the new constructions. Since Lowestoft is a mass of leisure and pleasure for land-grabbers and sea-pirates alike, a few days spent exploring its milieu is not a penance.

Associated British Ports, Lowestoft: General Information
(Abstracted from the Harbour Master's instructions)

Information for the guidance of small craft and yachts using Lowestoft Harbour and seaward approaches to Mutford Lock

1   Approaching, departing and transit craft must make every reason-able effort to establish and maintain contact with the Lowestoft Harbour Control on VHF Channel 14.

2   Any vessel without radio contact must give particular attention to the harbour control lights and navigate with extreme caution in the vicinity of structures, which may mask their presence.

3   ALL vessels must observe the international port traffic signals located on the South Pier.
    Three vertical red lights - vessels shall not proceed.
    Green, white, green vertical lights - a vessel may proceed only when it has received specific orders to do so.

3(a) For small craft and yachts without VHF communication the green, white, green signal may be considered in favour of proceeding with extreme caution and navigational courtesy.

3(b) Mariners should note that port control (located at the harbour bridge) and departing vessels within the Outer harbour basin have extremely limited vision to the north of the entrance piers and should conduct their navigation accordingly.

Oulton Broad

4   The Lowestoft Harbour Bridge (between the Outer and Inner harbours) will only be opened on demand for commercial shipping.

4(a) Commercial shipping is discouraged from passage: 0815 - 0900 hours, 1230 - 1300 hours and 1700 - 1730 hours.

4(b) Small craft and yachts may use a bridge opening for commercial shipping provided that prior arrangement has been made with Lowestoft Harbour Control - VHF Channel 14, telephone 572286 or personal visit.

4(c) In addition to 4(b) and subject to prior notification of at least twenty minutes, small craft and yachts may be given a bridge opening at the following times:
Monday to Friday 0700, 0930 1100, 1600, 1930, 2100
Saturday, Sunday, Bank Holidays 0745, 0930 1100, 1400, 1730, 1900, 2100

5.   Navigation in the bridge channel is controlled by VHF advice with additional amber and green traffic lights when the bridge is operated.

NOTE: Long bridge openings make it difficult to preserve the facility from pressures of road traffic and in consequence bridge keepers are instructed not to wait for stragglers.

6   Small craft passing under the bridge have a clearance of 2.2 metres at mean high water springs (approximately 2.4 metres on the tide gauge) with a reduction of 0.5 metres for the arch sides.

7   The maximum permitted speed in the harbour is 4 knots.

Lowestoft Harbour Control tel 01502 572286 VHF Ch 14

Mutford Lock and Opening Bridges

Transit bookings are advised: by telephone 01502 531778 Lock or 01502 523003 (W.D.C. Office Hours).

Mutford Lock, connecting the Lowestoft Inner Harbour with Oulton Broad, is operated daily under the direction of the Broads Authority and provides a point of access to approximately 120 miles/75km of navigable inland waterways. The lock, with safe usable dimensions of 70'0"/22.0m x 20'0"/6.5m, has a water depth of 6'6"/2.0m plus tidal variations and should only be used by craft suitable for the water depths of Oulton Broad. Non-local craft with a draft exceeding 5'6"/1.7m should seek advice from Mutford Lock staff and consider the Oulton Broad tide, which is approximately three hours after Lowestoft with a mean range of 2'4"/0.7m.

Mutford Road Bridge, adjacent to the Lock, has a clearance of 6'10"/2.1m at mean high water springs (approximately 7'10"/2.4m on the Lowestoft tide gauge) and it is therefore advisable for all craft requiring an opening to make an advance booking and to be prepared to wait. Such bookings will automatically include the Railway Bridge located close eastward.

VHF Channels 9 and 14 are monitored on an occasional basis by Mutford Control, which is attended daily in response to bookings and at the following times: 0800-1100 and 1300-1600 British Summer Time. 0900-1200 Standard Time.

NOTES:

1 A charge of £6.00 is levied for each lock transit or day return.
2 Broads tolls are payable in addition to the inward lock transit depending on length of stay.
3 Craft entering with a fixed air draft of more than 24'0"/7.3m are confined by fixed bridges to the River Waveney.
4 Local maps and publications are recommended.

Oulton Broad

Oulton Broad Facilities

Bridges	Headroom	
Mutford Lifting Bridge	7'10"	2.40m
Carlton Railway Swing Bridge	15'0"	4.57m

Boatyards

Oulton Broad Yacht Station	01502 574946
Topcraft Cruisers, Oulton Broad	01502 563719
Pegasus Yachts, Oulton Broad	01502 585631
Hampton Boats, Oulton Broad	01502 574896

Chandlers

Jeckells, Bridge Road	01502 565007
Frithvale Chandlers, Battery Green Rd	01502 517992
Lowestoft Yacht Services, Harbour Rd	01502 585535

Places of interest

Boatworld, Oulton Broad
Tel. 01502 574441
working exhibition of boat-building skills, bookshop and tearoom

Lowestoft Museum, Nicholas Everitt Park
Tel. 01502 511457
exhibition of local history and Lowestoft China

Lowestoft Maritime Museum, Sparrows Nest Park
Tel. 01502 561963
exhibition charting the history of fishing and seafaring: open daily
Apr - Oct 1000 - 1700, Nov - Mar 1000 - 1600

Pleasurewood Hills, Lowestoft
Tel. 01502 508200
American theme park and miniature railway

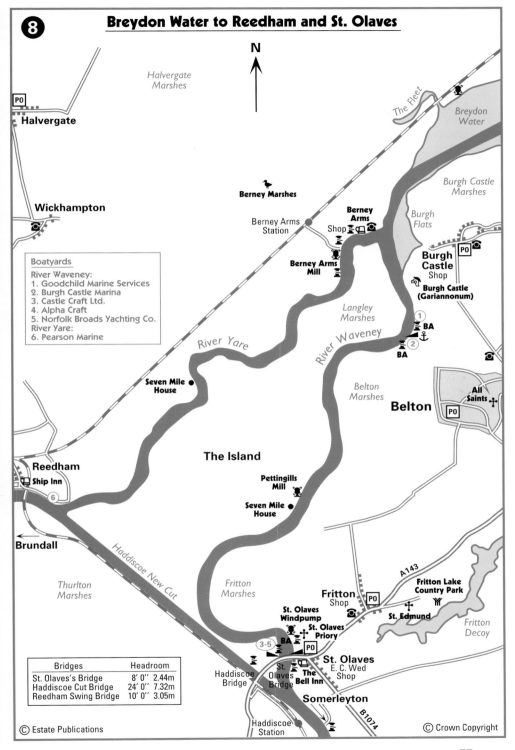

N

Halvergate Marshes

PO

Halvergate

The Fleet

Breydon Water

Burgh Castle Marshes

Berney Marshes

Wickhampton

Berney Arms Station

Berney Arms
Shop

Burgh Flats

Burgh Castle
Shop

PO

Boatyards

River Waveney:
1. Goodchild Marine Services
2. Burgh Castle Marina
3. Castle Craft Ltd.
4. Alpha Craft
5. Norfolk Broads Yachting Co.
River Yare:
6. Pearson Marine

Berney Arms Mill

Langley Marshes

River Waveney

Burgh Castle
(Gariannonum)

1 BA

2 BA

River Yare

Belton Marshes

Belton

All Saints

PO

Seven Mile House

The Island

Pettingills Mill

Seven Mile House

Reedham

Ship Inn

6

Brundall

Haddiscoe New Cut

Thurlton Marshes

Fritton Marshes

A143

Fritton Lake Country Park

Fritton

Shop

PO

St. Edmund

Fritton Decoy

St. Olaves Windpump

St. Olaves Priory

3-5 BA

PO

St. Olaves

E. C. Wed Shop

Haddiscoe Bridge

St. Olaves Bridge

The Bell Inn

Somerleyton

B1074

Bridges	Headroom	
St. Olaves's Bridge	8' 0''	2.44m
Haddiscoe Cut Bridge	24' 0''	7.32m
Reedham Swing Bridge	10' 0''	3.05m

Haddiscoe Station

© Estate Publications

© Crown Copyright

The River Yare to Reedham

There are no fixed bridges on the Yare until the new Postwick Viaduct just before Norwich is reached, thus making this comparatively wide river accessible to many coastal craft as far as Norwich.

Situate at the apex of the Rivers Yare and Waveney, at the mouth of Breydon Water, is the famous Berney Arms Mill. These ancient and old-fashioned (but suddenly, now extremely fashionable) power sources can be seen all over Norfolk; but this is perhaps the most famous. Indeed, it carries the mark of an ancient monument in the care of the Secretary of State for the Environment. It can be seen for many miles around, not only because of East Anglia's flat landscape, but because it towers seven floors and 69'0"/21m high; thus standing out as a spectacular example of the genre. It was designed to grind cement clinker, made from chalky mud which was dredged from the river. Towards the end of its life, it was put to work draining the marshes. A vast wheel worked a scoop, and is still to be seen, although the mill ceased its active life around 1880. It stands, a solitary sentinel and a salutary reminder of so much of what we have lost; not only in aesthetic terms but also in the way of sensible and danger-free engines of power.

The nearby pub, the Berney Arms is a much-used staging post. The small community here consists of a telephone kiosk, a shop and pub. The Berney Arms doesn't even try to compete with the grandeur of the next-door wind-swept monument that is the Berney Arms Mill, although it is itself quite old and occupies a site that probably makes it unique as a pub in the UK, for it cannot be reached by road; only by boat or by rail ... and then, finally, on foot. In days past, the beer used to be delivered by boat.

The sprawling village of Halvergate lies almost equidistantly from the Berney Arms, The Stracey Arms, Acle and Reedham. The round saxon tower of St Mary's Church has a remembrance for Jan Piers, the Dutchman who undertook many of the local drainage schemes. For those with a penchant for longish walks, Halvergate village is a good starting point for a marshland odyssey taking in not only the nearby Berney Arms Mill but also the Stracey Arms Windpump, with its photographs of local drainage and windmills. The marshland, which was laboriously reclaimed from the sea, is sectioned into dyked areas. Traditionally, there is an annual grazer's auction 'The Grass Sales' here, when graziers put up their hands for parcels of the Waveney Marshes grazing for their cattle.

In the summer, fat cattle are all round, but out of season the whole-most is taken over by snipe, wild duck, curlew and heron. Cattle have been reared here for centuries, and the local markets have grown equally fat by selling thin cattle to the fatteners and fat cattle to the butchers. I am indebted to John Seymour's 'East Anglia' for introducing me to the 1723 words of Daniel Defoe:

"These Scots runts, so they call them, coming out of the cold and barren mountains of the Highlands of Scotland feed so eagerly on the rich pasture in these marshes, that they thrive in an unusual manner, and grow monstrously fat; and the beef is so delicious for taste, that the inhabitants prefer 'em to the English cattle, which are much larger and fairer to look at. Some have told me there are above 40,000 of these Scots cattle fed in this country every year, and most of them in the said marshes between Norwich, Beccles and Great Yarmouth."

Halvergate Marshes consist of grazing meadow between the Bure and Yare. They were once an outlet to the North Sea. After the reclamation they started to dry out, shrinking and sinking to below sea level; so river flood-banks had to be built. The drainage windpumps were needed to take the water up from the low-lying dykes into the (highflowing if not highflying) raised-up rivers. The cattle and sheep now safely graze 'protected' from untimely slaughter by the network of dykes. These dykes supply the crystalline water that is needed if the delicate wild flowers are to survive: namely, the water violet, the contrasting water soldier accompanied by the arrowhead and the ever curious bladderwort - with the habits of the Venus fly trap. The dykes also provide good cover and living ground for pewits, red shanks, snipes and wagtails. The marshlands provide superb cover and 'hides' with their lush growth of rich grassy vegetation.

Haddiscoe Cut joins the River Yare just below the swing bridge at Reedham, less than a couple of miles upstream. This straight section was dug by the Victorians as part of the Lowestoft to Norwich navigation. Joining the rivers Yare and Waveney between Reedham and St Olaves, it considerably shortens the journey from Norwich to Beccles, as well as avoiding the strongish tides that can be encountered by Breydon Water. Rather like the EEC funded 'New Cut' on the 'Old' Sheffield and South Yorkshire Navigation, it never caught on, and was soon superseded when the Yare was properly dredged, thus providing a better route from Great Yarmouth to Norwich. In the New Cut, you should keep well clear of the banks where there are some nasty submerged piles. Craft drawing more than 2'5"/0.75m will have difficulty getting through the cut at Low Water. The range is about

River Yare

3'0"/0.9m on Neaps and 4'6"/1.4m on Springs.

Where the New Cut joins the Yare you should watch out for shoal patches on the spits and coasters coming round the bends. Reedham is almost 'protected' by the railway bridge below it and the chain ferry above; certainly they mark the boundaries well. The bridge is something of an antiquity and is operated by characters, who are also gentlemen, with more than a touch of old-fashioned spirit, enjoying nothing more than swinging their beloved bridge. Eminently capable, they believe in the personal touch, and will do anything they can to help waterborne navigators, be they regular coaster skippers or first-time cruisers.

The bridge will open for seagoing yachts and high motor cruisers. Skippers should signal three long blasts: two red flags on the flag pole indicate "Bridge Off Service" while one red flag means "Bridge In Service - Will Open."

Recent causes of the bridge not opening were (a) being struck by lightning and (b) being overcome by an autumn heatwave! On such occasions a keeper will come out personally to signal and shout the news with relish. Skippers should also keep an eye on the 'minutes' boards, but note the "Bridge Will Open" sign is fixed and is displayed even when the two red flags are up signifying that the bridge is out of action. Confusing? Yes! Surely we can do better than this for the second millennium!

Between bridge and chain ferry sits the village of Reedham. It is a truly splendid place and I always try to make sure I spend a few days there whenever I am near. Although it is a tourist-busy spot with comprehensive facilities, it somehow manages to absorb us all without losing its quiet charm. It is divided, like Caesar's Gaul, into three parts: the horticulture, husbandry and locals' shops of the top village by Witton Green; the boating-cum-tourist mélange of the waterfront; and those relics of the industrial revolution, the railway station and chain ferry which lie to the west. It is a place dear to my heart: a Victorian village basically centred upon its riverside, where there are good, free, public moorings. Sandersons' boatyard keeps its old interest in wooden boats; the Broads Chief Navigation Officer has his boat nearby and there is usually a friendly member of staff to help with mooring. There are three pubs in the village, two shops, a tea-room restaurant and a chip shop. At the Lord Nelson on the quay, folk music and singing is almost nightly, and the Chief Navigation Officer might even give you a song! Caution however: the tide runs strongly past the moorings and private boats are at risk of collision from inexperienced hirers who get into hair-raising muddles in the tideway.

The famous chain ferry upstream of the village is also extraordinary and usually busy with its loads of holidaymakers in, on and around motor cars. It is more than wise to wait upon the movements of this monster, for its pleasure is to grind slowly and, like the wheels of God, it could grind you exceeding small if you crossed it or its path. It has all the puissance of an African Queen and is just as inexorable.
Part of the village is at sea level: riverside on the waterfront; and part on the high rise behind. No visitor should leave without taking a walk up the short hill-lanes to the upper village of Witton Green, where you will find an almost separate community. Wherever you wander, you will hear the mellow melodious tones of mannerly Norfolk contrasting with the accents of visitors.
Sanderson Marine Craft boatyard is a place for a good chat. They are boatbuilders of the old school trying to survive in the new school without losing skills or integrity. While they are no longer building wooden boats, they are always happy to while away the moments talking wood'n'boat, and indeed taking your booking for a holiday hire boat which is nowadays their main work. It is a family business, and they have a sense of humour that can take you unawares. They seem to be pleased with all their clientele. I don't know how they manage it. (The true secret is that Colin, the principal with first rate principles is an affable, easy going friendly sort of chap with a diesel pump!)

The River Chet to Loddon
3¹/₂ miles/5.5km

After Reedham, the tiny River Chet a few cables up on the port hand leads to the tiny haven of Loddon. By the junction of the rivers is the famous Hardley Cross (1676AD) on the bank. It marks the lower boundary of the city of Norwich and stands as a reminder of all the ancient disputes between Norwich and Great Yarmouth; not forgetting those that still persist. It is said to have been the place where the officials met to resolve their annual differences.
Loddon is a fine and easy place to visit in a shoal-draught craft, and always accessible for craft of around 3'4"/1.0m draught, but at 6'6"/2.0m you must needs await good tides and work them properly. The Chet can also be tricky for craft with a LOA of more than 32'0"/10.0m, for it is narrow and has some very tight bends. It is not always possible to see what is coming round the corner, and turning is hopeless. In addition, there are the Hardley Marshes to beware of: they used to be well-drained but now they flood, and cross-currents can be set up. In spite of these obstacles however, the market town of

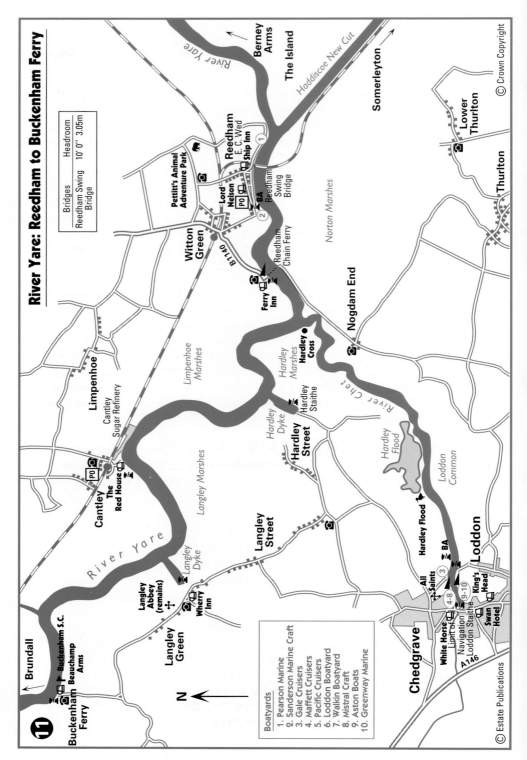

River Yare: Reedham to Buckenham Ferry

Bridges	Headroom
Reedham Swing Bridge	10' 0'' 3.05m

Boatyards
1. Pearson Marine
2. Sanderson Marine Craft
3. Gale Cruisers
4. Maffett Cruisers
5. Pacific Cruisers
6. Loddon Boatyard
7. Walkin Boatyard
8. Mistral Craft
9. Aston Boats
10. Greenway Marine

© Estate Publications

© Crown Copyright

N

Loddon is worth the hassle, for it is a small treasure of a place. The staithe is situate on one side of a mini-marina; it is possible to moor along some pretty stretches and there are boatyard facilities nearby. The buildings in the town, apart from offering food and drink, goods and chattels, are attractive in their late 18th century styles.

There are in fact two choices of village life to be reconnoitred, for as far as Loddon is from one bank of the river, so far is Chedgrave from the opposite. Although they are very close, Loddon and Chedgrave grew up quite separate and independent, both having been, in their time, under liege law of the Normans. Loddon first obtained the right to hold a market and fair, and in the 15th century one James Hobart, Henry VII's Attorney General, not only built Hales Hall but also put up the Holy Trinity church. In the 18th century, shops, farms, workshops and public houses went up in and around the small town - as did numerous fine examples of Merchants' Houses ... if not indeed mansions. A very well-known and fine example was Loddon House, near Farthing Green. It suffered something of a fall from grace when, in 1786 it was transmogrified into a 'private madhouse'.

The main Chedgrave folk were known as the Proctor Beauchamps, and they built a splendid hall landscaped by none other than Capability Brown. They also installed a stained glass window from Rouen Cathedral in All Saints Church.

In the 19th century, Loddon and Chedgrave had between them a sufficiency of services: shops, school and craftsmen were to be found at Chedgrave, while Loddon had solicitors, surgeons, vetinerary surgeons and land surveyors. Between the two villages, they also hosted banks, insurance agencies, police and registrars: there was also a basic fire service, as well, as time went by, a post office, telegraph and telephone exchange. They were important enough for their waters to be deepened so that wherries could reach the staithe.

The River Yare to Brundall and Norwich

Now we move back on to the River Yare and up to Brundall and Surlingham. Hardley Dyke, just downstream of Cantley, is a miniature waterway, marked by a long line of masts. The entrance bears the forbidding notice of foreboding: `Hardley Dyke. No facilities. Difficult to turn. 3 mph.' Clearly territorial rights are exercised strongly in this neck of most attractive backwoods and waters.

In keeping with the picturesque ambience just before you get to the Cantley Bends, there is a small reminder of riparian undertakings at their proud best. There is a modest group of private boat berths on the bank, backed by verdant gardens that in turn front a classic red brick country cottage. Setting off the scene stands a Victorian street lamp standard and a lion rampant in white stone.

At the end of the stretch is something quite else: being the Landscape Blott of the Cantley sugar beet factory that dominates the surroundings: smell, sight and sound, it has the lot. In the sugar beet season, the near-nauseating odours advertise its presence more effectively that any placard ever could. This sugar beet is a most important East Anglian crop. Prettily, in the summer a beet field looks like a green sea; but the downside comes in the autumn when lorry loads of these roots litter the roads.

Nor is this near-neat-dead-beat factory alone in ugliness: there could hardly be a greater contrast between the cared-for spruceness of Hardley Dyke and the sad remnants of a once-splendid windmill and other derelict farm buildings. As a relief, right on the bend is The Red House pub: it occupies a magnificent site, commanding views up and down the river.

Shortly after comes another contrast: Langley Dyke, a shallow, quiet spot with easy mooring at the entrance, and an entirely ungrand legend indicating the presence of the appropriately named Wherry Inn. Langley Dyke, Langley Staithe and the ruins of Langley Abbey, very close by are all intriguing in their peculiar ways.

The most popular spot in this stretch is the site of the old Buckenham ferry, for which there is a large sign but no sight. So, the extinct ferry is not the reason for the attraction; that honour going to the Beauchamp Arms. It will hove into view as a relatively mini-mansion, heralded by the masts of the Buckenham Sailing Club where there is a small lay-by and a large hard-standing boat park. The Beauchamp Arms also has a useful lay-by and a neat stretch of good moorings put down to strong grass. However, they do not drain as efficiently or as quickly as they might and you may have to recourse to wellies. Nearby, there is plenty of good fishing and good pub grub; and you don't have to catch your own for it to be fresh!

Rockland Broad is a miniature affair consisting of Short Reach as one way in and the Fleet Dyke as the other. The former is also known as Short Dyke - a much more appropriate description. The Broad is liable to silting, and there is not a lot of water to be found anywhere around. There is a 3 mph speed limit. The channels across it are marked with buoys on the outside (or even on the inside at Low Water): beware there is precious little depth! It is worth crossing the broad however to get to Rockland Boat Dyke with a lovely public mooring basin at the head and the very real pleasure of the New Inn hard by.

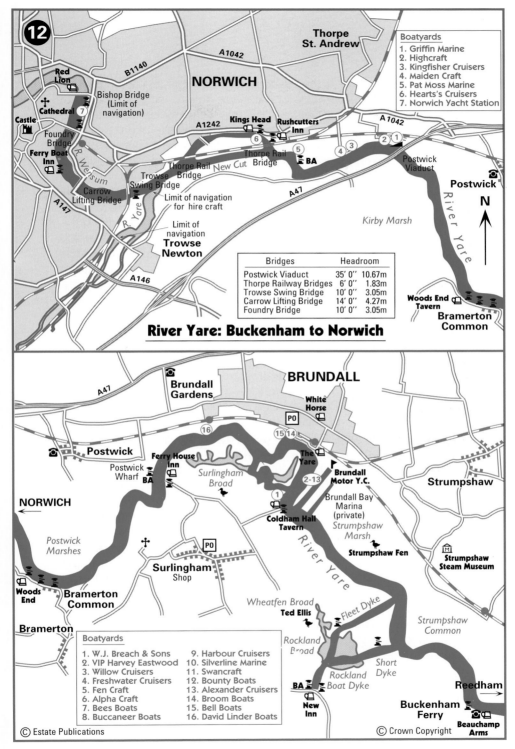

River Yare: Buckenham to Norwich

Boatyards
1. Griffin Marine
2. Highcraft
3. Kingfisher Cruisers
4. Maiden Craft
5. Pat Moss Marine
6. Hearts's Cruisers
7. Norwich Yacht Station

NORWICH

Thorpe St. Andrew

Red Lion
Bishop Bridge (Limit of navigation)
Cathedral
Castle
Foundry Bridge
Ferry Boat Inn
Carrow Lifting Bridge
Trowse Swing Bridge
Thorpe Rail Bridge
New Cut
Limit of navigation for hire craft
Limit of navigation
Trowse Newton
Kings Head
Rushcutters Inn
BA
Postwick Viaduct
Postwick
Woods End Tavern
Bramerton Common
Kirby Marsh

N

Bridges	Headroom	
Postwick Viaduct	35' 0''	10.67m
Thorpe Railway Bridges	6' 0''	1.83m
Trowse Swing Bridge	10' 0''	3.05m
Carrow Lifting Bridge	14' 0''	4.27m
Foundry Bridge	10' 0''	3.05m

BRUNDALL

Brundall Gardens
White Horse
PO
Ferry House Inn
Postwick
Postwick Wharf
BA
Surlingham Broad
The Yare
Brundall Motor Y.C.
Brundall Bay Marina (private)
Strumpshaw
Strumpshaw Marsh
Strumpshaw Fen
Strumpshaw Steam Museum
NORWICH
Postwick Marshes
Coldham Hall Tavern
River Yare
Surlingham Shop
PO
Woods End
Bramerton Common
Bramerton
Wheatfen Broad
Ted Ellis
Rockland Broad
Fleet Dyke
Strumpshaw Common
Short Dyke
Rockland Boat Dyke
BA
New Inn
Buckenham Ferry
Beauchamp Arms
Reedham

Boatyards
1. W.J. Breach & Sons
2. VIP Harvey Eastwood
3. Willow Cruisers
4. Freshwater Cruisers
5. Fen Craft
6. Alpha Craft
7. Bees Boats
8. Buccaneer Boats
9. Harbour Cruisers
10. Silverline Marine
11. Swancraft
12. Bounty Boats
13. Alexander Cruisers
14. Broom Boats
15. Bell Boats
16. David Linder Boats

River Yare

Canoeing is permitted in the reaches although it is a nature reserve. You will meet lots of barnacle and canada geese and grebe; and, of course, the omnipresent Coot & Co. Unlimited. Rockland Broad and the dykes are mainly remote encounters; quite different from Brundall, which is the next big port on the agenda. But before it takes over, the Strumpshaw Steam Museum is not to be missed. In particular, its old chimney and weathered brick outbuildings are magnificent.

A little further upstream, way-marked paths and hides encircle nearby Strumpshaw Fen Nature Reserve which has five miles of mown footpaths through woodland, grazing marshes, and reedbeds all along the river bank. A special hide overlooks the Buckenham Marshes which are used by the United Kingdom's largest flock of bean goose. This is an excellent place to see Broads wildlife - flowers, birds, dragonflies, and the swallowtail butterfly. Among the birds nesting here are the marsh harrier, bearded tit, gadwall, reed warbler and water rail. Bearded tits, warblers and reed bunting are often seen in the reedbeds, where they nest and feed. Other birds which you'll see on the grazing marshes include redshank, snipe and lapwing (peewit). They use the large tufts of grass to make their nests in and to hide from predators. Look out for naturalised Chinese water deer, and grass snakes swimming in the dykes.

The first proper hint of Brundall is the imposing edifice of the Coldham Hall Tavern on the port hand on the way up. It is a good old pub, with good old free moorings. Its environs are made up of a large marquee, small waterside boathouses, modest wooden buildings and trim sailing craft. Nearby, a black and yellow board shows the flow of the tide, for the motions of the North Sea, distant as they may seem from this inland retreat, still reach effectively, though not disturbingly, up here.

Brundall itself, afloat or shoresides, is a sophisticated and urban, if not entirely urbane locale, extremely well suited to its preoccupation with expensive bungalow sites, mooring plots and GRP cruisers, the best known of which are the famous Brooms. Nor can you miss the large notice advertising Brundall Bay Marina: 'Private moorings … berths available' and nearby the massive picture of a heron on a board.

Brundall does not have one focal essence; it has two. One is generated by the majority of the buildings which are waterside homes, with their near-permanently fixed living sculptures of ducks. Sets of China Ducks flying up walls may be the unacceptable sign of kitsch but ducks on the front lawn (no back parlour insults here), apparently tethered like geese for foie gras, hint at the upwardly mobiles.

Sooner or later you will encounter the Broom-Brooms, afleet, in harness or just plain solo: except that Brooms tend not to come plain, certainly not penny plain. Nor for that matter is there prospect of tuppence coloured either: their owners are all in the Upper Income Bracket. They always seem very much at their ease when rounding the downstream corner approach to their birthplace and Valhalla. The big bend is dominated by a film-location type of mansion which fittingly overlooks, apparently in blessing, the expensive craft that pass beneath.

Central to Brundall, and just off the fairway, is the long, low wooden building of the fuel station, supermarket and Yare Boatique chandlery. I first went there nearly two decades ago and was immediately impressed by their range of goods, goodies, necessities and desirables (whether they be for domestics, socialising, boating or angling). In addition, their warm, courteous and witty service is an unexpected bonus.

The island offers a dramatic contrast to the village with its almost untouched but equally unbuilt upon natural glory. The route is through the soft underbelly of Brundall, as it were, entering just after the Coldham Hall Tavern and coming out on the other side at Postwick. There used to be a ferry plying its trade here: predictably it no longer exists. Equally predictably there is a Ferry Inn which is a pleasant spot with good food and beer. The moorings are stern-to.

Close by is Surlingham. It is situate on a pleasant stretch of the river near two sharp bends. It has a small broad, most of which is too shallow for navigation, but there is a channel that leads to Bargate Water which is a nature reserve.

A little further up the river comes one of the prettiest, sleepiest settings on the river: Bramerton Woods End. The first views of it come complete with manse-like mansions in the hills; and, at the water's edge, 'desirable properties in rural surroundings'. The houses seem to get better year by year. It is tranquil, with sandy hills and trees. People tend to keep their own counsel on this stretch with the result that few come calling unless invited. It is a particularly attractive and popular spot with usually enough room along the free parish staithe for all those who want to stay. Some people prefer to moor a little further along, to be that much nearer the convivial local, the Woods End Tavern, only a few cables upstream.

After Bramerton Woods End is the (new in 1992) Norwich Southern Bypass Flyover (Postwick Viaduct) which carries the traffic on the A47 over the River Yare. If you can't scrape under but want to visit the fine city of Norwich, it is best to return to Brundall and take the train from the station which is very close to the riverside and the marinas.

River Yare

Then a surprise: on the outskirts of Thorpe St Andrew there is a mini-marina with an intriguing assortment of craft from midget runabouts to large seagoing vessels, power boats and all kinds of genuine sailing vessels. Next door are the contrasts of the dark and sinister shapes from the commercial barge yard and a dainty cottage complete with rose-bedecked door. Opposing it all is a popular picnic site with easy road access, ensuring a constant flow of single-person, hand-propelled floats of all kinds.

We are now not far from Norwich. But before its pleasures are to be enjoyed there are two impediments and one attraction to be negotiated. The attraction is the tiny community of Thorpe on the narrow old river course. The New Cut was dug so that the railway could cross the river twice without the need for bridges. Thorpe is a small, nearly self-contained boating community with plenty of facilities and charm, both quaint and vulgar. It is popular with those smaller boats who can negotiate its narrow waterway without difficulty so it's not always possible to get a berth for more than a very short stay. Sadly, Thorpian pleasures are denied to all except those who can drop their overall height to 6'0"/1.8m to pass under the railway bridges.

After Thorpe's small twinned bridges Norwich proclaims itself, or is proclaimed, by towering pylons, huge chimneys and the legend, `Welcome to Norwich. A fine city. Yacht station half a mile ahead.'

However, there are bridges to be passed before we arrive there and we also here leave the Yare which turns south at Trowse, and join the Wensum for our passage into the city. The first bridge is a railway bridge (Trowse Swing Bridge) and the second the Carrow Road Bridge. Both bridge-masters keep a listening watch on VHF Ch 12, but while the keepers are more than efficient and user-friendly, the system itself can be capricious. Openings of the British Rail bridge are regulated by what are known in the authorised jargon as 'windows of opportunity'. Men and boats alike are required to wait upon what seem to be the caprices of BR hands on. It is worth a call on VHF, well ahead of your approach, to check the next opening times or you could be in for a long wait. You could anyway, because the bridges are prone to sticking. It must be the wrong kind of grease, but they haven't cracked it yet. With regard to Carrow Road Bridge, the keepers need notice in order to be able to call out the engineers for the lifting. You can contact them on 01603 625091 at the Broads Authority River Control Centre. The longer notice you can give them the better, and you may have to wait anything from half an hour upwards - although they do the very best they can not to keep boaters waiting. That is, if it be deemed that it is necessary for the bridge to lift. The regime is as follows: if gear can be lowered, then boaters must lower it and not ask for a lift - and this applies equally to wherries; if, by waiting for Low Water, the bridge can be negotiated, then this is also to be done; if, however, these conditions cannot be met, then the bridge will be lifted - by arrangement. It is worth noting that Colman's riverside factory buildings have overhangs that can seriously damage the health of masts and rigging.

Visitors can no longer find a secure berth upstream of Carrow and below the main road bridge, since, just round the bend and the turning bay for the commercial coasters, where there used to be good moorings, there is now an embargo enforced by the City Fathers. (It is not without relevance that the Norwich Yacht Station is just upstream) You are then surrounded by the massive structures of the station, the hotel and Foundry Bridge.

This will be the head of navigation for many: remember, the river is still tidal at this point. Close by is the refurbished railway station: it is splendid in its re-found, restored glory. It is good to be able to note that the Norwich Yacht Station, of which I have been critical in the past, has much improved its welcome and its facilities. Although there is no mains electricity, water is in plentiful supply. The Harbour Master and his staff are more than tolerant of the problems they have to solve on the narrow waterway. In particular, they go to some lengths to make sure that seagoing craft are given enough space in which to manoeuvre; thoughtful of them. The street lights are decorated with masses of flowers in season. You don't have to travel far for food: there is actually a rather good corner restaurant at right angles to the railway station.

You can reach the head of navigation on the River Wensum and the old pumping station in the very heart of Norwich but only in a dinghy, and even then you need to be cautious, for there are all kinds of nasties on the bottom and round the edges. It is also possible to go further upstream on the River Yare. In fact, its source is in East Dereham, some 12 miles/19km north of Norwich. When it reaches the city, it is joined at Trowse by the Wensum before it flows through the centre on its way to the sea.

The City Fathers advertise the virtues of Norwich by erecting on the roadside at each entrance the same legend: 'NORWICH: A FINE CITY', and it is treated as the capital of East Anglia. The custodians and guardians have transported their city into the 20th century with a balanced mixture of restored old edifices and heritage-aware new ones that produces an architecture that is both tasteful and functional. In particular, the many red brick features of Norwich are splendiferous

River Yare

to behold, and come in so many shapes and sizes that eyes, mind and spirit need almost a full cruising holiday if they are all to be properly appreciated. Not only are there the predictable facilities you would expect from a city of the size and status of Norwich; but there are also many useful contacts for seagoing yachtsmen that you would certainly not expect to come across so far inland.

Visitors who approach Norwich along the Yare turn into its tributary, the Wensum, on the south-eastern outskirts of the city. They pass the ruins of mediaeval boom towers, between which a boom or chain could be stretched across the river, and make for the yacht station just above Foundry Bridge. The Wensum reaches this point after winding through Norwich, in whose defence it once played a useful part, forming a natural boundary in the north-west and east when other parts of the city were enclosed by great walls in the 13th and 14th centuries. Remains survive at Carrow Hill, Barn Road and elsewhere.

On the western side of the Wensum, just over Foundry Bridge which is close by the yacht station, a riverside walk leads to Pull's Ferry and one of the most historic parts of Norwich. At Pull's Ferry, where John Pull was ferryman and innkeeper early last century, stands an arched Watergate. Restored and re-roofed in 1949, this 15th-century gateway spanned a narrow canal (now filled in) along which boats carried supplies, including materials used in the construction of the cathedral and priory. The house adjoining the gateway, formerly the ferryman's house and inn, dates from the 16th century.

Norwich, the capital of Norfolk, is an ancient and gracious city of which Sir Nicholas Pevsner once remarked, 'Norwich has everything.' Until about 200 years ago, it was one of the richest and most populous towns in the country, and in the late seventeenth century it was second only in size to London. Today, Norwich has all of the amenities one would expect of the capital of England's fastest-growing region combined with a compactness that enables its residents to feel very much at home. It has managed to preserve the best of its historical and architectural heritage while meeting the demands of a modern commercial, financial and shopping centre. The visitor would do well to explore the city on foot as so many of its finest buildings are tucked out of sight down narrow, cobbled alleys such as Elm Hill, a beautifully restored mediaeval street.

Apart from such fine buildings as the cathedral and castle, Norwich is also an excellent shopping centre, with many of the shops centred around the market-place area, although there are also delightful shopping areas in St Benedicts and Pottergate. There are several fascinating museums including the Stranger's Hall Museum with rooms representing various periods; St Peter Hungate, exhibiting ecclesiastical art; and the Bridewell Museum which features local industries. The 'Castle Mall' may be merely a shopping mall beneath the castle, but as an example of ingenious design and stylish realisation it has few equals.

A Little History

The Romans settled at Caister and the Anglo-Saxons by the River Wensum. The latter was known as Northwic and it grew into a very large mediaeval walled town which, by the 17th century, was known as Norwich and was England's largest provincial city.

In 1066, it was among the topmost communities in the land, possessing its own mint. Business, trade and commerce by water was well under way, with pots from the Rhine, Scandinavian and Russian skins, Flanders wool and - predictably - good old North Sea herrings.

The city's castle was a Norman flourish courtesy of King William, with a timber castle atop a motte, surrounded by a bailey. Predictably, soon after the military came the other estate in the form of a cathedral and priory. Fifty years later, presbytery, transepts and most of the nave were finished, although there was to be no consecration until 1278. By mediaeval times there were 56 churches within the city walls.

But things temporal were not overlooked, and from the middle of the 12th century the standing of the city was enhanced by walls, with towers and bastions. Twelve monster gates controlled exits and entrances; while an iron chain was hung across the river at Carrow to curtail arrival by water. The city actually became a city in 1194, thanks to Richard I's Charter.

In 1349, the Black Death reduced the population of 6,000 by nearly 50%; but, no more than thirty years later, the numbers were back again. Less than a century later, Norwich was the main worsted centre in the country; and by the beginning of the 15th century, the city had grown to such a substantial size that it was granted permission for a mayor, two sheriffs and twenty-four aldermen (replacing the previous bailiffs).

In March and June 1507, two mini-infernos razed street after street of Tudor timber and thatch houses. All in all, over a thousand houses were burned - after which it was decreed that new buildings should be tiled.

The Peasants' Revolt wrought considerable havoc, until the warlike bishop formed a private army to protect his worldly goods and chattels - an act which later precipitated attempts to put matters to rights by arsoning churchmen's properties. In 1534, the prior threw in the sponge and renounced his claims over the city. Not long after, Robert Kett led 20,000 yeoman farmer rebels, to take over the city, complaining of high rents and commons enclosures. They were put down by royal troops after a six weeks resistance: Kett and 48 of his troupe being hanged.

A little later, another 'invasion' took place with the resettling of refugees (many of them weavers) from the Netherlands. After a short time, they made up about a third of the population. Prosperity prospered: the rich grew richer - and, predictably, the rest, already poor, grew poorer, until towards the end of the 16th century, one mayor outraged his contemporaries by declaring that His Fine City of Norwich was alive with tramps - and was giving sanctuary to about 3,000 souls who were on charity.

It was not long before the place became the centre of high life for the local nobility, who poured in to shop, to play cards, to dance - and generally to besport themselves. One monkey parade became known as 'Gentleman's Walk'. Perhaps as a result of all this socialising (or the clear water and the best barley in the area being exploited by the clearheaded best businessmen) brewing grew, and by the beginning of the 19th century there were half a dozen big breweries. Banks were born; and in 1792 Thomas Bignold founded what was to grow into Norwich Union. Solid building was keeping pace, with the Bethel lunatic asylum; the Assembly House; a theatre and a library; and the Norfolk and Norwich Hospital. But, even so, conditions in the 19th century were not a bundle of fun: no fresh/clean water - and numerous epidemics of cholera and similar mortal afflictions; so a new cemetery was dug and a waterworks built. At the same time, the Jenny Lind (Swedish Nightingale Soprano) Infirmary for Sick Children was founded from money she had enabled to be raised. Also at this time, Norwich was to be host to three railway stations (but only Thorpe endures today) while much refurbishment was undertaken on houses and shops - and, of course, Victoria's religiosity assisted in getting under way in 1892 the Church of St John the Baptist, later the Catholic cathedral. But perhaps more remembered for his building and his works was one Jeremiah Colman and his mustard mill at Carrow; while enthusiasts for boating guides will recognise the name of John Jarrold who has printing works at Whitefriars.

Sadly, much of the brilliant building that had been achieved over the centuries, was destroyed or severely damaged during the 1939/45 war, when the city was bombed more than forty times (suffering two of the infamous 'Baedeker Raids') and more than 30,000 houses and 100 factories suffered as well as churches and shops. The post-war rebuilding was not without contention: the new library and the buildings of the University of East Anglia prompted heated discussion (rumpus on the campus, as it were); while the later Sainsbury Centre for Visual Arts occasioned many altercations - but most agreed that the benefits to pedestrians brought about by the city centre regime was worth the inhibiting of motor traffic by the new one-way regimes. All in all, after many long years of growth, decline, re-growth and development, it must be said that old and new live cheek by jowl in Norwich: if not exactly happily married, then certainly in contented alliance.

River Yare Facilities

Bridges	Headroom	
Reedham Swing Bridge	10'0"	3.05m
Postwick Viaduct	35'0"	10.67m
Thorpe Railway Bridges(2)	6'0"	1.83m
Trowse Swing Bridge	10'0"	3.05m
Carrow Lifting Bridge	14'0"	4.27m
(VHF 12 Tel 01603 625091)		
Foundry Bridge	10'0"	3.05m

Broads Authority free 24hr moorings

Reedham Quay
Chedgrave Common
Loddon Basin
Rockland Staithe
Bramerton Common
Postwick Wharf
Thorpe Green
Whitlingham (Commissioners Cut)

Broads Information Centre, Bridge Stores, 41 Bridge St, Loddon
Tel. 01508 520699
open Easter - Oct

River Yare

<u>Boatyards</u>

Pearson Marine, Reedham	01493 700288
Sanderson Marine Craft, Reedham	01493 700242
Gale Cruisers, Loddon	01508 520663
Maffett Cruisers, Chedgrave	01508 520344
Pacific Cruisers, Chedgrave	01508 520321
Broadland Riverine Broadcraft, Loddon	01508 528735
Greenway Marine, Loddon	01508 520438
Aston Boats, Loddon	01508 520353
Walkin Boatyard, Chedgrave	01508 520649
W.J. Breach & Sons (Coldham Hall Boatyard)	01508 538203
VIP Harvey Eastwood	01603 713345
Willow Cruisers, Brundall	01603 713952
Freshwater Cruisers, Brundall	01603 717355
Fen Craft, Brundall	01603 712057
Alpha Craft, Brundall	01603 713265
Bees Boats, Brundall	01603 713446
Buccaneer Boats, Brundall	01603 712057
Harbour Cruisers, Brundall	01603 712146
Silverline Marine, Brundall	01603 712247
Swancraft, Brundall	01603 712362
Bounty Boats, Brundall	01603 712070
Alexander Cruisers, Brundall	01603 715048
Broom Boats, Brundall	01603 712334
Bell Boats, Brundall	01603 713109
Brundall Bay Marine	01603 716606
David Linder Boats	01603 714330
Griffin Marine	01603 433253
Highcraft, Thorpe	01603 701701
Kingfisher Cruisers, Thorpe	01603 437682
Maidencraft, Thorpe	01603 435173
Pat Moss Marine, Yarmouth Road	01603 702424
Heart's Cruisers	01603 433666
Norwich Yacht Staion	01603 622024

Places of Interest

Berney Arms Mill (English Heritage)
Tel. 01493 700605
largest windpump in the country. built 1870 it was in use until 1951 and now houses a permanent exhibition: open daily 0900 - 1300 and 1400 - 1700 end Mar - end Sept

Berney Marshes(RSPB)
Tel. 01493 700645
boat trips through these remote marshes are available

Pettitt's Animal Adventure Park, Reedham
Tel. 01493 700094
crafts and tame animals and birds: bus picks up from outside Lord Nelson pub: open Easter - Oct 1000 - 1730 (closed sat, except BH)

Hardley Flood Nature Reserve
area of marshes and alder carr flooded in 1920s: now area of lagoons and reedbeds with walkways

Strumpshaw Fen Nature Reserve (RSPB)
Tel. 01603 715191
4 miles of mown nature trails and walks through 120 acres meadow: open daily 0900 - 2100 or dusk if earlier

Strumpshaw Hall Steam Museum
Tel.01603 712339
collection of steam engines including a fairground organ: open Easter 1100-1600 and mid July - Oct 1st 1100 - 1600 except sun

Ted Ellis Nature Reserve, Wheatfen Broad
open fen, reed beds and 3 mile nature trail

Norwich Castle Museum
Tel 01603 223624
12th century castle built to replace the early wooden Norman castle: now a museum of regional art / archeology and natural history open mon - sat 1000 - 1700 and 1400 - 1700 sun

Bridewell Museum, Norwich
Tel. 01603 667228
built 1325 of squared flints now a museum of local industry: open Apr - end Sept 1000 - 1700, tue to sat

River Yare

Mustard Shop, 3 Bridewell Alley, Norwich
Tel. 01603 627889
19th century-style shop housing displays illustrating the history of
Colman's mustard: open all year mon - sat 0930 - 1700

Sainsbury Centre, University of East Anglia
Tel. 01603 456060
collection of works by Picasso, Bacon, Henry Moore etc.: open all
year tue - sun 1100 - 1700

St Peter's Hungate Museum, Norwich
Tel. 01603 667231
15th century church with fine hammerbeam roof and brass rubbing
centre: open Apr - end Sept, mon - sat 1000 - 1700

Chandlers

Yare Boatique, Brundall	01603 715289

Pubs

Lord Nelson, Reedham	01493 701239
Ship Inn, Reedham	01493 700287
Ferry Inn, Reedham	01493 700429
King's Head, Loddon	01508 520330
Swan Hotel, Loddon	01508 520239
White Horse, Chedgrave	01508 520250
Red House, Cantley	01493 700801
Wherry Inn, Langley Green	01508 528427
Beauchamp Arms	01508 480247
New Inn, Rockland	01508 538395
Coldham Hall, Brundall	01508 538591
Ferry House Inn, Postwick	01508 538227
Woods End Tavern, Bramerton	01508 538296
Rushcutters, Thorpe	01603 435403
King's Head, Norwich	01603 433540
Red Lion, Norwich	01603 623300

Fishing on the South Broads and Rivers

Rockland Broad

This smallish broad is a tidal 40 acres with much weed, many water lilies and some good roach and bream. The weeds also favour tench - but they do not prosper as do some flounders and eels. Rudd and perch are well sought after, but the main target is pike - especially in winter. In general, fishing is best from boats.

The River Waveney and Oulton Broad

Near Beccles, the River Waveney is pretty deep and fairly narrow. Its thickly-swelling reeds play host to many roach and some quite large bream - a few even magicking the scales up to the unlikely figure of 4lb and more. In addition, pike are to be found ... both large and small. Happily, fishing is free throughout these Beccles Marshes, and good roach and dace are to be found. After this stretch, bank fishing is impossible, but, since boats and fish happily and temptingly mix, the mandatory response is to visit the hire centres at Beccles and get yourself a boat.

Moving down past Aldeby Staithe and on to Worlingham Staithe, Castle Marsh, Mill and Seven Mile Carr, fishing tends to be pretty good throughout the whole stretch. However, it is not long before the tidal influence begins to make its presence felt more strongly and consequently the waters are prone to much muddying - a kindly factor for the fish since they offer good shelter for the plenitude of bream, roach, eels and flounders that inhabit them. Experts recommend ledgering, good leads, lots of tough groundbait and plenty of bread. However, it has to be said that maggots are always firm favourites in winter.

Perhaps unexpectedly, the area round Oulton Broad offers much good recreation. Oulton Dyke, winds through lonely marshlands, before it reaches Oulton Broad itself from its southern bank and there is excellent sport to be had here, particularly at night during the summer months. Indeed, it is one of the best bream spots to be found in Broadland.

Much of Oulton Broad, especially at the weekends, is taken up by pleasure craft, hydroplane and water-skiing enthusiasts - but there is still enough water for the angler. From October onwards he has virtually the entire broad to himself. Perch and roach of more than modest proportions are unlikely here - as is the specimen tench; but bream are favourably found ... and there always flounders and eels at the ready for maggots and worms. Mullet also exist here, but they are as skilled at existing and avoiding disaster at the hands of humans here as they are anywhere - and occasionally a big fellow of a pike will find his way in from the outer reaches.

The River Yare
Near Trowse, the clear water shows carp, roach and chub; and in general in the area of the city, there is good fishing for roach, chub, bream, pike and dace. Boat fishing can bring good pike and roach in the winter. A little downstream, by Thorpe railway bridge and island, there are roach and bream. A favourite spot just downstream is Bramerton ('free' for boaters as well as anglers - and where, for once, there seems to be harmony between all parties .. except of course the fish) where there is a race for dace and the roaching is for poaching.
On the stretches between and near Surlingham and Brundall, there is good sport - on the river as well in the mini-broads and dykes for roach and bream. Winter pike are good; while downstream, the sport gets better by the mile right down to Cantley (where noisomeness takes over) … winter and summer alike - although the boats are often more numerous than the fish.

The River Chet
In Loddon, we find another favourite spot for anglers and boaters both; with plenty of shoresides sport for the latter and roach and bream for the former.

The River Wensum
In the Norwich area there is free fishing from the banks, with good chances for roach, bream and pike; a hundred yards below Carrow Bridge, bank access ceases, and there is just another half-mile of the Wensum before it joins forces with the Yare. This last section can fish particularly well during the winter for pike, roach and bream - but angling is by boat only

The coarse fishing season runs from 16 June to 14 March and all anglers are statutorily required to possess an Environment Agency Rod Licence, these can be purchased from post offices and Beccles Information Centre. A fishing permit is also required to fish on certain non-tidal rivers and lakes controlled by the Broads Authority - enquire locally for details. Trout fishing is available on certain stretches, but a special permit must be obtained to fish these. Fritton Lake is private water, where both a permit and licence are required and boats are available for hire by the day, half day or hour.

THE FENS

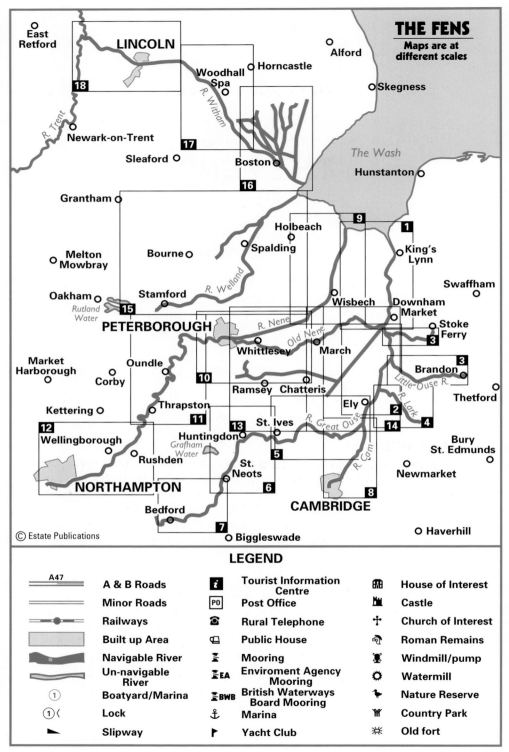

THE FENS
Maps are at different scales

East Retford

LINCOLN

18

Horncastle

Alford

Woodhall Spa

Skegness

R. Trent

R. Witham

Newark-on-Trent

17

Sleaford

Boston

16

The Wash

Hunstanton

Grantham

Holbeach

9

1

Spalding

King's Lynn

Melton Mowbray

Bourne

Swaffham

Oakham

Stamford

R. Welland

Wisbech

Downham Market

Stoke Ferry

Rutland Water

15

PETERBOROUGH

R. Nene

Old Nene

3

Market Harborough

Oundle

Corby

Whittlesey

March

3

Brandon

Little-Ouse R.

10

Ramsey

Chatteris

Thetford

Kettering

Thrapston

R. Lark

12

11

Ely

2

4

Wellingborough

Huntingdon

R. Great Ouse

14

Bury St. Edmunds

Grafham Water

13

St. Ives

Rushden

St. Neots

5

R. Cam

Newmarket

NORTHAMPTON

6

8

CAMBRIDGE

Bedford

7

© Estate Publications

Biggleswade

Haverhill

LEGEND

A47	A & B Roads	ℹ️	Tourist Information Centre	🏛️	House of Interest
	Minor Roads	PO	Post Office	🏰	Castle
	Railways	☎	Rural Telephone	✝	Church of Interest
	Built up Area	🍺	Public House	🐎	Roman Remains
	Navigable River	Mooring		🪟	Windmill/pump
	Un-navigable River	EA	Enviroment Agency Mooring	⚙	Watermill
①	Boatyard/Marina	BWB	British Waterways Board Mooring	🦅	Nature Reserve
①‹	Lock	⚓	Marina	🎪	Country Park
►	Slipway	⚐	Yacht Club	※	Old fort

100

MAPS FOR THE FENS

Area covered   page

	page
1 River Great Ouse: The Wash to Denver	112
2 River Great Ouse: Denver to Ely	116
3 River Wissey and River Little Ouse	119
4 River Lark	122
5 River Great Ouse: Ely to Hemingford Grey	128
6 River Great Ouse: Hemingford Grey to Little Barford	131
7 River Great Ouse: Little Barford to Bedford	136
8 River Cam: Popes Corner to Cambridge	147
9 River Nene: The Wash to Guyhirn	153
10 River Nene: Guyhirn to Alwalton	156
11 River Nene: Alwalton to Ringstead	159
12 River Nene: Ringstead to Northampton	163
13 Middle Levels	170
14 Middle Levels	171
15 Rivers Welland and Glen	183
16 River Witham: The Wash to Scrub Hill and Witham Navigable Drains	204
17 River Witham: Scrub Hill to Short Ferry	210
18 River Witham: Short Ferry to Torksey	215

River Authorities

The Great Ouse, Nene, Welland and Glen Rivers all come under the jurisdiction of the Anglian Region of the Environment Agency. All recreational craft using these waters must be registered and licensed: details from the Agency Tel. 01733 371811. Information on the method of working the locks in use on these waterways should also be obtained: note that keys are required to operate the locks on the Rivers Great Ouse and Nene.

The River Cam between Bottisham Lock and Byron's Pool in Cambridge is controlled by the Cam Conservancy.

The Middle Levels are under the jurisdiction of the Middle Level Commissioners: no licence fees or tolls are levied but all boats entering the system are required to register on entry with the lock-keeper at Stanground Sluice or Salters Lode.

The River Witham and Fossdyke Navigation comes under the jurisdiction of British Waterways: all craft must be licensed and/or registered.

THE FENS

The Fens are a more-or-less silted-up extension of that vast East Coast inlet from the North Sea known as The Wash. Sometimes called 'Fenland', but more usually known as The Fens, this strange locality consists of an amazing 800 square miles that stretch at their maximum about 70 miles/112km from north to south and 35 miles/56km from east to west. Low, flat, wild, windswept places they are with hardly a tree to be seen. The only strong vertical growth comes in the shape of windmills (some of which date back to the 17th century) and the dramatically perched temples of Ely and Lincoln Cathedrals and Boston Stump. Just as important, though not so upstanding, are the few 'islands' (the Isle of Ely being a prime example) that go to make up those dollops of firm ground that cannot be described as 'sceptr'd isles' but are nevertheless close to a 'blessed plot, this earth'.

If you yearn for religious supervision, you are in luck: there is a good chance that you will never be out of the surveillance of one of the three major religious buildings of the area: Lincoln Cathedral, Ely Cathedral and the more intriguingly named Boston Stump - the Church of St Botolph. Physically, spiritually, symbolically and metaphorically they dominate these low-lying if not low-living wetlands.

The Fens once reached the North Sea in what must have seemed like a vast lagoon, extending, as it did, westwards unto Peterborough. Even today, the land seldom reaches up to 164'0"/50m above sea level, while parts of the Bedford Level are now below sea level. The sediment carried by the feeding rivers was dropped en route to the North Sea, slowly treating The Wash to what all east coast rivers persistently experience: silting up. The Wash today is only a shadow of its former self - and like all its east coast counterparts, is shrinking day by day. The shrinkage has been aided and abetted by the hand of man, for The Fens, as they now exist, are almost entirely factitious, consisting, in the main, of fully reclaimed and/or reconstituted marshland. Before the reclamation, the indigens lived mainly by fishing, fowling, fleshing and good red herringing; cutting peat for fuel and reaping the sedge for thatching. The marsh/bogland, when reclaimed, turned out to be A100 production class at Lloyds - and not only for agricultural fodder for Fenmen, but also excellent provender for cattle and sheep. So, how did all this goodness and richness come about?

Until the middle of the 17th century the Fens were pretty well water-logged, with only a few of the previously mentioned islands and highlands in evidence. The Romans tried their hands (or rather the hands of the locals) at draining parts of Lincolnshire (including their excellent creation of an inland waterway route from The Wash to York - known as The Grain Run) and also built causeways. But when they left, the Fens went back to back-waters and the Fenmen back to back-woods-men; and so it remained an inhospitable swamp for centuries. The first shot after the Romans, was from the hands of John Morton, Bishop of Ely, in about 1500 (see Morton's Leam). Others had folies de grandeur after being tempted by experimenters with pseudo-tech-nological procedures, and even Charles I had a go; but it was not until the 4th Earl of Bedford imported the Dutch engineer Cornelius Vermuyden and put him to work from 1632 to 1653 that anything noteworthy actually occurred. He managed to reclaim nearly 100,000 acres, an area that is known as the Bedford Level.

However, Vermuyden's work was not wholly successful: after his drainage, the peat (not surprisingly) shrank, and there were renewed threats of inundation. Windpumps had to be used to prevent the flooding - after which came steam, diesel and electricity. Drain after drain was created to form a diversion into another (perhaps existing) waterway which was used to sluice off the excess - which would be well contained and confined between high banks. Other water courses (including river stretches) were deepened or had their channels shifted. This brought into being that maze of wet mystery and magic that is now known as the navigable Fen Drains and its Middle Levels.

A Little History

The first and foremost of the Fennites were the Iceni. Their queen, Boudicca who died in 60AD, was tortured and beaten, her daughters raped, and her tribesmen put to slavery. She got together an army and did severe damage to the Romans - killing as many as 70,000 according to some authorities. Eventually, the Romans defeated her - and in defeat she poisoned herself. However, her legacy is still to be encountered in the will and spirit of the locals - for example the Lineham family, mentioned elsewhere.

Later, in the 7th and 8th centuries the high ground 'islands' were taken over by the religious and reverent for the service of God and Mammon - for then as now there was no conflict between the two. In 673AD, Ely was set up as a Benedictine Abbey and went on to flourish and to flaunt its affluence; but the majority, the penniless locals, had to fight to survive, wringing no more than a minimal sustenance in living conditions that attract the description 'durance vile'. It was a basic living at subsistence level, in a community that was completely removed from any of the small social advances that were being made at that time. Even their feeble attempts at moving around the country-side had to be undertaken on stilts. They became known as 'Slodgers', and their way of life continued (almost unbelievably) well into the 20th century.

In 1070, for a time, Hereward the Wake, based his opposition to the Norman William at Ely (then known as Eel Island). He was well supported by the locals, as were the leaders of the Peasants' Revolt of 1381. They also shared the Pilgrimage of Grace in 1536 and stood by Oliver Cromwell. This was not the end of their tribulations: they also opposed the 'legal' enclosures that were thrust upon them once the land was usefully drained. (Please see mention of these martyrs of Littleport in the chapter on the Ouse p.120.)

Whether afloat in The Wash or adrift in The Fens, it is not difficult to imagine what life was like centuries ago: bleak it was - and bleak it still is ... yet possessed of seductive charm reinforced by an irresistible, and probably elemental, magnetism.

The Great Ouse
75miles/120km

Approach from the sea

Decades ago, the main channel to King's Lynn was what is now known as the Old Lynn Channel, to the west of Roaring Middle and Thief Sand. In 1966, a training wall was built to prevent the severe scouring caused by the power and swiftness of the tide, and it served its purpose well. Partly as a result of this artifice there are still semi-secret channels across the sands at High Water to Wisbech - for those in the know. Namely those on whom the mantle of wisdom sits and who, therefore, like London taxi drivers, have 'the knowledge'.
Recently the channel was through Cork Hole from the Roaring Middle light float. A straightforward south-easterly route is easy to follow and has no navigational hazard. The pilot boats used to wait around the area of the tide gauge, a great help to visiting yachtsmen. The buoyage was well-laid, and if followed exactly, with no corner cut, was problem free. When the tide was out, some of the buoys could be seen sitting on the very edges of the banks, high and mighty above the channel itself. Close encounters were not unknown; and, to improve the shining hour, the tide was swift and strong - reaching, at times, more than two knots. This channel was used for many a year.
But, in late summer 1995, Captain Garside (Tugmaster and Harbour Master to King's Lynn Conservancy Board) and his staff re-routed the approach back to the old Teetotal Channel. During the autumn, some sad souls who had not seen the notes to mariners, found themselves in trouble by just following their old ways or their uncorrected charts. Even with the new buoyage, it is still wise to call Lynn Harbour on VHF Ch 14 for advice on traffic movements, and to take any appropriate instruction. Once the buoys have been spotted, they serve extremely well and there is little chance of any watchful skipper getting into error.
Ignoring any wilful foolhardiness, the time to start from the Wash for King's Lynn and in all probability Denver Sluice, or to leave the Great Ouse for The Wash will depend upon your draught, air-draught, speed and destination. There is no point in steaming faster than the rate of the flood tide, for that will only bring about an encounter with the bottom. Conversely, it is unwise to be late if you are en route for the lock at Denver Sluice, since the question of air-draught and headroom under the many bridges on the Great Ouse is paramount

(see page 113). This is a matter for some study, and prospective navigators should contact the lock-keeper at Denver (Tel. 01366 382340) on VHF Ch 16/17 and/or a local pilot who will advise and/or assist.

I was originally told to let the flood run for about an hour before even trying to begin to make my way inland, and I still find nothing wrong with this counsel. True, some local fishermen do set off earlier, but they all know the shifting grounds well, and not many of them draw as much as the 6'6"/2.0m that some of the Boston boats do. Unless you personally know who is in front, it is better not to follow. On the whole I think it is best to consider access as being no better than half-tide from outside and two hours to High Water (HW - 2) from the mouth.

I can still remember one of my earliest visits to The Wash and King's Lynn. It is imprinted on my memory, so I hope you will forgive my indulgence in nostalgia. I was anchored towards the southeast corner of the Wash near the Sunk Sand waiting for the tide into the Ouse. I reported my position and my intentions to King's Lynn Harbour Radio and relaxed. As usual, I pretended to fish. 'Pretended', that is, as in 'pretender: one who makes baseless, false or insupportable claims'; for I am successful in the piscatorial stakes only when mackerel are shoaling like crazed Gaderene, with their fishy eyes fixed on tackle for self-immolation. Even then, my hooks, lines and sinkers are more perilous to me than to the fish. As if to confirm my inefficiency and lack of intimidation to surrounding life, wild or otherwise, I was closely encountered by three seagulls, all of a particularly impertinent bent. For a long time, I thought I could hear them in telecommunication with a band of seals, letting them know how pathetic this human was. In keeping with this wheeling indifference, I was solicited, or so I thought, by a solo seal; but all he/she did was to sidle close to Valcon's stern and wallow off after a massive show of indifference.

It was relaxing to be in waters where every buoy was on station with a name that could be easily read and a light that showed at the advertised times and intervals. Up to that moment the Wash had disclosed nothing of its inmost nature and little of its deep-seated disposition. It had been a trouble free inland sea. Not wanting to overtake the young flood, for I wasn't really late on the tide, I tried to glide slowly and effortlessly along with it, looking to discern something of its special qualities.

As I moved slowly through the narrow channel, the still exposed banks of mud unfolded to each side in sad but splendid grandeur. The ribbon of the rising tide showed me the way as clearly as ever did the Yellow Brick Road to its four arcane space travellers. It led me on through an apparent maze of undulating contours where steep mounds and elongated humps lay like the carcasses of prehistoric amphibians. As the setting sun slanted on the banks and the relatively motionless waters, it seemed to sculpt mountains emerging from a slow stream of lava.

Occasionally, the shriek of a seagull or the baying of a seal would filter through the slight mist to add yet another aspect of other-worldliness to my circumstance. It was a vast vista; the whole scene majestic and compelling. I only wish that all my entrances to the Great Ouse could have been so mild and wonderful.

I was jolted back into the other world of the Wash only by a timely VHF call from King's Lynn Radio wanting to know why I wasn't on the move and telling me that if I didn't get up there soon I would lose the light. Captain Garside and his staff are more caring than they have need to be, especially when they are busy with big ships on the tide. Of course, there is no doubt an element of self-interest in their solicitations, wanting no trouble from leisure craft - but I am convinced it is, in the main, the gentle co-operative art of humane mariners.

Once having negotiated the new channel, features to note in particular are the West Dump yellow buoy and the cardinal West Stones which mark the long training wall that goes all the way into Lynn Cut from that point on the west side, and from the new cut itself on the east. After the first mile of the training wall, which is virtually southerly, the channel tends to the southeast when approaching King's Lynn, and the route is straight ahead for the docks, the port and the town.

King's Lynn

King's Lynn itself has not yet made up its mind whether to stay plebeian or to take on the more up-market Lynn Regis as its nomenclature. Since there is a North Lynn and a South, as well as a West Lynn, it is ironic that there is no sign of the best known of all: East Lynn.

However, there is more to this argument than Kings and Cardinals (no matter how pointed), since before 1537, the area was called 'Bishop's Lynn', after Herbert de Losinga, one of the Lords Spiritual. He had an eye not only for the Three Estates, but also for Real Estate, and bought himself into the top drawer by bribing King William II to give him the office and title of Bishop of Norwich. When Pope Paschal II got to know of this at the opening of Norwich Cathedral (1101) he compelled the bishop to build priories and churches all over the place. One of the biggest was by Great Yarmouth on the sand: " ... and the rain descended, and the floods came, and the winds blew and beat upon that house; and it fell: and great was the fall of it." The other huge affair was Holy Mary Magdalene and St Margaret, and All Holy Virgins: only marginally better sited, it was erected on salt-marsh on one of Herbert de Losinga's own plots at an encampment known as Linn - Saxon for a small lake. The fact that it already had a church was as nought; and to seal the matter and his ego at one fell swoop, the town became 'Bishop Losinga,' later turning into Bishop's Lynn - with one of the prized markets. There is more: another Bishop, Turbe of Norwich, envied Herbert, and tried to outsmart him by building a completely new town just to the north, merely in order to be able to erect a church (St Nicholas) - and have a market. So came about two towns and two markets. King John chartered two markets in 1204 and so united the two towns.

King's Lynn suffers from a major drawback: while the town has many and manifest attractions, it has no facility for leisure craft. The problem is twofold: King's Lynn Port and Docks are extremely busy with commercial shipping traffic; and there are huge tides, the rise and fall of which make the idea of quayside berthing a difficult proposition. It is almost impossible to envision how, without a major and massively expensive excavation and building scheme, the situation could ever be improved for visiting yachts. Tradition has it that alongside the quays there are 'barges' that stay afloat at all states of the tide and against which a yacht may moor without fear or favour and free of fee. This is not the case! The barges do not stay afloat; the bottom in that region is foul in the extreme; leisure craft are not permitted to moor there; and since no berth exists, it can be neither f.o.c. nor paying. Yachts may safely moor there just as sheep may safely graze in the company of wolves.

Tradition also informs that you may berth free of charge in front of the very Customs House; and finally that you can 'arrange something' with the fishermen who use Fisher Fleet, Purfleet and Mill Fleet. More likely, they will 'arrange' something with you; and to their advantage! As T. S. Eliot says, 'tradition without intelligence is not worth having.' In this case, certainly, intelligence can often be the better part of tradition. There are some isolated sunk concrete buoys below the road bridge but they are all in private or port hands. Even if prior permission can be obtained, it is not easy to pick them up as many of the lines and markers are pulled under by the strength of the tide - and it can be a patience-exhausting activity to wait for settled conditions or to make the most of it and have a go. The tide rip is indeed a thing of wonder, since the rise can easily achieve 25'0"/7.6m - and has been known to exceed that. For a single-handed skipper, it is fraught with complications and adversity. Recent changes have brought modest

improvement with mooring buoys; but even so, visitors should start to make enquiries about a possible booking well ahead of their expected arrival.

Should you, by the greatest of good fortune, get allotted one of the Port Authority moorings within hailing distance of the East/West Lynn ferry, you will find that the ferrymen are more than pleased to help you across.

I know some of the brazen souls who have tried for a berth with the fishing brethren in Friars Fleet. They regretted it only slightly less than those reckless enough to leave their boats at Boal Quay, failing to think of local 'trespassers' and completely ignoring (or being in ignorance of) the rate, rise and fall of the river.

Just below the road bridge, GOBA maintain three moorings of their own strictly for their members, while the Denver Cruising Club similarly have two. There is also one noticeable yellow Harbour Authority buoy, and use of this requires even more prior organisation and permission than those of the Association and the Club. King's Lynn Port Authority officers (Tel. 01553 773411) will advise about tide heights and times (and of course help in emergencies); and in any case it is always a good idea to let them know what you are doing and to request a traffic report from them.

Sad, since King's Lynn is such a pleasingly built, welcoming community, as soaked in history as were King John's jewels in the Wash. There are many buildings of great historical and architectural importance in the town. In addition to the famous Custom House on Purfleet Quay, which was built by Henry Bell in 1683, there are two medieval Guildhalls (one now housing the Art Centre), the 12th century Church of St Margaret and the 15th century Hanseatic Warehouse, the only surviving remnant of the Hanseatic League in Britain. There are also a number of museums and other attractions such as the 'Tales of the Old Gaol House', where stories of local criminals are recreated in the original cells.

Before we move on upstream, let us consider the procedure for leaving King's Lynn for the Wash. It makes no difference where you are heading for, you will still need to leave with the ebb and anchor in the Wash to await the flood for one of the other three ports. If for any reason you should quit King's Lynn on the flood, don't be surprised to notice that people walking on the banks are likely to overtake you! It is only the river doing its usual stuff.

There are many who boast of making the passage from the Great Ouse to Boston Grand Sluice on one tide. The two requisites are that you should know exactly where you are going; know exactly what you are doing; and have a craft that can move at a great rate of knots. It is over 40 miles/64km from Denver Sluice to Boston Grand Sluice, and about 30 miles/48km from King's Lynn to Boston. Simple arithmetic gives an idea of the Speedy Gonzales cruiser needed for such a project. Surely, far better to plan for decent weather and enjoy the peace of a leisurely trip and, if predictions should fail to meet your best desires and expectations, the protection of the sandbanks at Low Water will help you make the best of the disappointment; and if the weather is fine, you can crop and reap the mussels which abound in many of the stretches en route.

It is possible to make one inter-port trip without the need to anchor off. This is the passage between Boston and Fosdyke; but even so, you still need to have your speed and draught in the right combination. As for the rest, they are routes used over the centuries by fishermen, pirates and smugglers. The buoys or marks (if there be any at all) are not easy to see or locate; and even when spotted it is no mean task to read their meaning and direction. Many there are who have come to grief trying these so-called `short cuts' over the sands and in the final resort have achieved merely a thoroughly long-drawn-out and boring haul. Some rash skippers have even found themselves stranded on one of the training walls. It is well to remember that in some places there is a vertical drop on one side of the wall, and a long, gradual slope on the other; no oozy mud berth into which to sink softly.

So, having safely quitted the Lynn Cut, the next step is out through the Teetotal Channel to the No.1 cardinal buoy and from there to your favourite sandbank. The Wash is completely exposed to north-easterly winds and when the wind is against the ebb even the best found boat becomes uncomfortable in the nasty conditions that can arise in as little as a Force 3. Shelter is to be found in the protection of the sandbanks at low tide and these are the places to make for even if you have to sweat it out in lumpy conditions before they top out. The Freeman Channel and its famous Roger Sand are popular for this manoeuvre because they are central, and also afford the best shelter.

King's Lynn to Denver Sluice

The river deserves its adjectival Great, being long, strong and tortuous, with its deep water at the extreme edges of some of its very tight bights, where unfortunately the bottom can be foul. It floods for between two and three hours, consequently ebbing for all of nine to ten. The Admiralty Pilot quotes the streams at 4 knots but at times I have been able to make only minimal headway against a spring flood; and Valcon's Parson's Pike twin 56hp diesels, will, at full throttle, push her at 7+ knots.

At a few specified places in King's Lynn it is safe to moor to the wall for a time if you need to wait for the tide for any reason, but permission should have previously been obtained and there must always be competent crew on board. For most skippers, the plan is to pass through King's Lynn so that the tide will get you safely to Denver for the locking. The following must be considered: the tides, their rise and fall and thus the amount of water below you in the river and the amount of air above you under the bridges.

Bridge heights are critical on the Great Ouse between King's Lynn and Denver, for there is nowhere to moor on that stretch of potentially dangerous river and it is not a place to get caught out. The following tabulation was promulgated by the Environment Agency and should

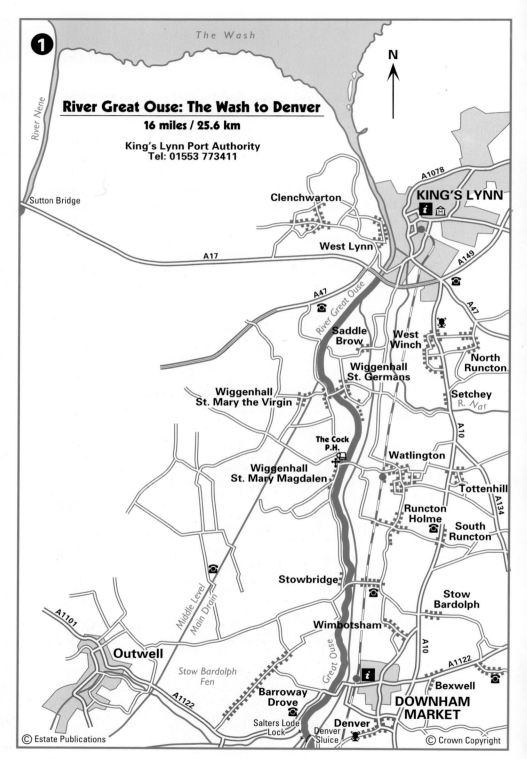

River Great Ouse: The Wash to Denver

16 miles / 25.6 km

King's Lynn Port Authority
Tel: 01553 773411

© Estate Publications

© Crown Copyright

help. There are also some overhead pipelines, but they are high enough not to be a problem.

Bridge	Headroom			
	Springs		Neaps	
	HW	LW	HW	LW
Downham Market	2.6m	7.5m	3.6m	7.0m
Stow	2.3m	6.5m	3.7m	6.6m
Magdalen	2.3m	7.3m	3.7m	7.1m
St Germans	2.5m	7.6m	3.9m	7.4m
Free	2.8m	8.7m	4.2m	8.0m

Departure times will depend upon the individual measurements of the craft; but in general, it is not a good idea to move past King's Lynn until the flood has been running for about two hours. The intention being to achieve a smooth trip, no encounter with bed or bridge, and to arrive at the lock when there is plenty of water all round and the flood is beginning to lose its ferocity. As usual, good advice can be obtained not only from the Harbour Master at King's Lynn but also from the lock-keeper at Denver Sluice and the marina at Ely. Above Denver, the waters are no longer tidal, and it is a delight to cruise slowly up to the splendid cathedral at Ely and find a really well cared for stretch of the river under its mighty shadow.

An extra caution is necessary, particularly at springs, and not even big ones: if you are navigating early on the tide, the young flood is up your stern. (As in the famous Dad's Army line: "They don't like it up 'em, Captain Mainwaring; they don't like it up 'em."). Should you dig into a mud bank or just catch an unexpected hillock in the channel, you can be keeled over with the wheel snatched out of your hands and the boat suffering scouring in minutes. In such cases, fast and expert action is essential: for to run aground under such circumstances is to risk the possibility of the loss of the vessel.

Moving upstream from the Harbour Master's office and West Lynn, we pass the infamous Boal Quay, where many have been tempted to moor in the past - but where it can still be hazardous for anything more than a short time. Nowadays, it is in constant use by professional fishermen, and with their consent, skippers may find it possible to arrange for an alongside stay, perhaps overnight, so long as there is always competent crew on board. By leave of the Harbour Master, it is sometimes possible to stay on South Quay for a short time - or to hang on to the side of one of the big ships. There are those who have hopes of a marina development on the river - but that is, as ever, in the pipeline ---- or more realistically, a pipe dream.

The Great Ouse

Moving on, we prepare to pass under the first of the many bridges before Denver. It is known as the Free Bridge, since in the early days, when it was first erected in 1821, in wood, it was necessary to pay a toll to use it. Now it looks hardly any different from its neighbour, the A47 bypass road bridge. After Eau Brink Cut and its relief channel are pylons and pipelines that cause no headroom problem. The first of the bridges that requires special consideration becaus of restricted headroom is known as St Germans Bridge, from the nearby village of Wiggenhall St Germans. Just before it, on the starboard hand going upstream is the entrance to the Middle Level Drain. It was also a wooden toll bridge, but once again has been brought into the present times and style. Before the next bridge at Wiggenhall St Mary Magdalen, (known in its shortened eponymous version as The Magdalen) there are two outstanding features: the 15th century church and the public house called The Cock. Between them, they present a pretty picture of riverbank life. Just after, power cables pass high overhead and once more there is little to see on the banks other than the occasional house or clump of bushes and trees. Next comes Stow Bridge, which was also originally wooden, followed by another high power cable. There is a nasty double bend after this bridge, and on one occasion I had to pass so close to the port bank that I was afraid of seriously bruising the boat along its side. But the flood water rushes round and has gouged out a deep water channel very close in. The bottom is foul and the bank immediately above is encumbered so much that with a big spring tide all kinds of detritus will be brought into the mainstream.

The last bridge before Salters Lode Lock, the Old Bedford River, the New Bedford River (called by some the Hundred Foot) and Denver Sluice is Downham Market Bridge. It goes back more than five centuries and like all the others was originally made of wood.

Salters Lode Lock is the key to the Middle Levels system and is still a dramatic reminder of centuries gone by. Nothing much has changed here - certainly not the skill you need to negotiate a passage if conditions are not entirely in your favour. It is essential to book a penning well in advance with the lock-keeper (Tel. 01366 382292). It is High Water at Salters Lode just over an hour after HW King's Lynn or one and a half hours after Immingham. In general, at neaps, locking is possible for craft to be penned through from -2hrs HW to + 2hrs HW; but at springs it is seldom more than 30 minutes either side - and may indeed be less. Entry from the tidal river can be difficult if there is a strong current or wind. Restricting dimensions are: LOA 80'0"/24.4m, Beam 12'6"/3.8m. There are no facilities at Salters Lode

Lock (see p.169 for futher information on the Middle Levels).

It is a much easier proposition to go from Denver to King's Lynn than it is to do it the other way round. If you need a pilot at all for this river, it is only to take you up. The Denver lock-keepers have a tradition of helping to sort all boaters in and out and, like many of their vocation (yea verily, for it is an eccentric calling) they are often to be found working well beyond the normal demands of duty. 1990 saw Denver Bert retire after 42 years; and all users and Ousers still remember those days well and carry grateful thoughts. In my experience, the majority of lock-keepers seem to be called Bert; but God bless all lockies, Bert or no!

The community at Denver is an interesting one and while there are only the basic facilities of food and drink and water, there is pleasant shopping to be found not far away at Downham Market. Things have changed at Denver since my first visit; the full refurbishment of the lock has been completed, and guillotine locking is smooth and easy. Nevertheless, I am confident that Denver will never succumb to the rat race or be a centre of la dolce vita; although there is an hospitable pub (the Jenyns Arms)with noisy peacocks for company. There are EA 48hr moorings along the northerly bank, but there is shoaling at the sides. All in all, Denver Sluice guards its secrets too jealously for any chance visitor to find himself there at all. In fact, Denver is best visited only if you are going on to Ely and beyond, otherwise the difficulties tend to be out of proportion to the gain.

There is a six-storey grinding windmill at Denver (built in 1865), and nearby is Denver Hall with its 16th century east gable and pretty 1570 gatehouse. It also has Denver Sluices, old and new. The Old Sluice was built by Vermuyden in 1652 to limit the run of the sea tides up the Great Ouse. It was unpopular with sailors when they found they could make only half the trips they used to make with coal to Cambridge; and it was destroyed not very long after completion by a group of near-pirates known as the Fen Tigers, who were living off the seals and wildfowl - which would, of course, no longer be available after drainage.

The sluice was 'blown up' again by a high tide in 1713, and there was loud rejoicing by its opponents. But it was rebuilt again, and then again in 1748-50 - much bigger and stronger - by Sir John Rennie, who also built Old Waterloo Bridge. Since Rennie's time it has been remodelled and has had steel gates fitted. It will be noticed that it is a double lock - that is, that at low tide a vessel passing through it goes downhill from south to north, but at high tide uphill.

In addition, it is worth noting that you can get neaped at Denver! With

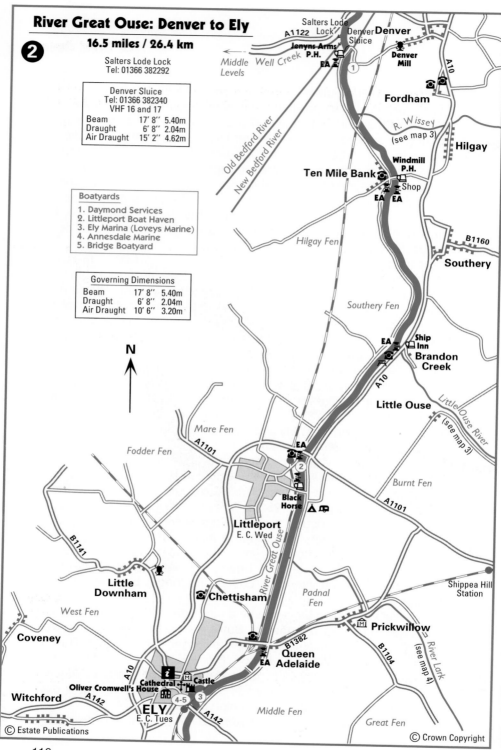

River Great Ouse: Denver to Ely

16.5 miles / 26.4 km

②

Salters Lode Lock
Tel: 01366 382292

Denver Sluice
Tel: 01366 382340
VHF 16 and 17
Beam   17' 8''   5.40m
Draught   6' 8''   2.04m
Air Draught 15' 2'' 4.62m

Boatyards
1. Daymond Services
2. Littleport Boat Haven
3. Ely Marina (Loveys Marine)
4. Annesdale Marine
5. Bridge Boatyard

Governing Dimensions
Beam   17' 8''   5.40m
Draught   6' 8''   2.04m
Air Draught 10' 6'' 3.20m

N

Salters Lode Lock
A1122
Denver Sluice **Denver**
Jenyns Arms P.H.
EA
Denver Mill
A10

Fordham

Middle Levels   Well Creek

R. Wissey
(see map 3)

Hilgay

Windmill P.H.

Old Bedford River
New Bedford River

Ten Mile Bank
Shop
EA EA

B1160

Southery

Hilgay Fen

Southery Fen

EA
Ship Inn
Brandon Creek

A10

Little Ouse

Little/Ouse River
(see map 3)

Mare Fen
A1101

Fodder Fen

EA
②

Burnt Fen

A1101

Black Horse

Littleport
E. C. Wed

Shippea Hill Station

B1141

Little Downham

Chettisham

Padnal Fen

River Great Ouse

West Fen

Prickwillow

Coveney

B1382
EA
Queen Adelaide

B1104

River Lark
(see map 4)

A10

i
Cathedral Castle
Oliver Cromwell's House
A142 ④-⑤ ③
Witchford A142

ELY
E. C. Tues

Middle Fen

Great Fen

not more than 6'0"/1.8m draught, it is possible to get to Ely, cruising the long straight stretch of the enjoyable non-tidal section; but first comes a choice of waterways.

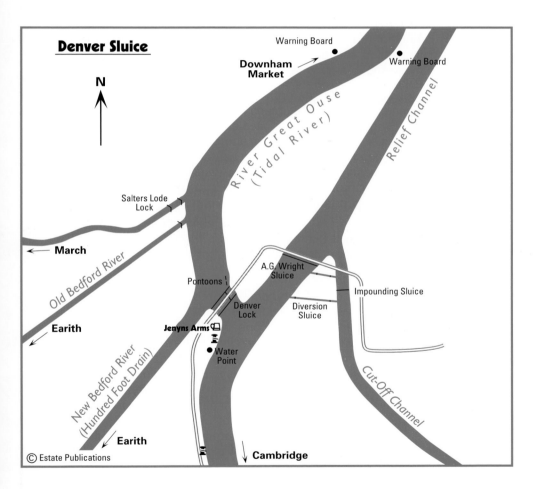

River Wissey
10 miles/16km to Stoke Ferry - no locks

The entrance into the narrow River Wissey, just about a mile above Denver, is a difficult one: the turn is sharp and the entrance is narrow with a tight bend almost immediately after. There are 10 miles/16km of river for cruising, and in one place the course has a small 'broad' all of its own.

The village of Hilgay is the first (and very popular) stop. There are moorings here and also basic facilities: chemical toilet disposal; toilet pump-out, toilet and water. Some of the church goes back to the 14th century and George Manby's grave is there. He was born at Denver and actually went to school with Nelson. He was deeply shocked and sorrowed by seeing a large vessel go down near Great Yarmouth; but he was also inspired, for soon after he invented his famous mortar and the even more famous rocket - used by lifeboat men and coastguards to fire their life-saving lines to stranded ships and their crews.

Upstream, past a few moorings, comes the potentially noisome Wissington sugar-beet factory. It is after this point that the marked channel leads to the south of the island and to the lake. At the head of navigation, Stoke Ferry was at one time a thriving river port, but now is accessible only by modest-draught craft. In the 19th century, coal was brought from Newcastle right up to the quay at Stoke Ferry. No doubt they enjoyed the pub, that is to hand, as much as present day leisure adventurers. Just upstream again are the GOBA moorings - only just below the head of navigation - after which only portered ships can proceed further.

Back on the Ouse, and after the junction with the Wissey, we next come to the old Ferry Boat Inn, HQ of the Denver Cruising Club; it is soon followed by another hostelry, the Ship Inn, where there are EA moorings and a picnic site which also lies at a river junction, that of the Little Ouse.

Little Ouse River
14 miles/22.4km to Brandon - 1 lock

This branch line is also known as Brandon Creek and is navigable to Brandon for craft with up to 3'3"/1.0m draught. The first hamlet (but only just!) is suitably called Little Ouse, where there are some moorings. Moving upstream brings some intriguing names: Osier Holt, Botany Bay sluice and Hockwold-cum-Wilton. The head of navigation is the

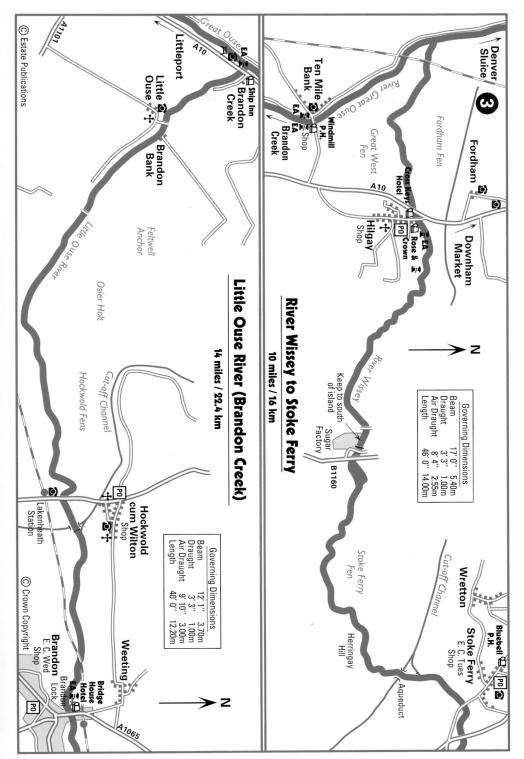

© Estate Publications

Littleport

Little Ouse

A10

Great Ouse

A101

Ship Inn
EA

Brandon
Creek

Brandon
Bank

Little Ouse River

Feltwell
Anchor

Osier Holt

Cut-off Channel

Hockwold Fens

Little Ouse River (Brandon Creek)

14 miles / 22.4 km

PO

Hockwold
cum Wilton
Shop

Lakenheath
Station

Weeting

Brandon
E. C. Wed
Shop

Brandon
Lock

Bridge
House
Hotel
EA

A1065

Governing Dimensions

Beam	12' 1" 3.70m
Draught	3' 3" 1.00m
Air Draught	9' 10" 3.00m
Length	40' 0" 12.20m

N →

© Crown Copyright

Denver
Sluice

River Great Ouse

Fordham Fen

Fordham

❸

Ten Mile
Bank

Windmill
P.H.
EA EA
Shop
Brandon
Creek

Great West
Fen

A10

Cross Keys
Hotel

Hilgay
Shop

PO
Crown
EA
Rose &

Downham
Market

River Wissey

Keep to south
of island

Sugar
Factory

B1160

River Wissey to Stoke Ferry

10 miles / 16 km

N →

Governing Dimensions

Beam	17' 0" 5.40m
Draught	3' 3" 1.00m
Air Draught	8' 4" 2.55m
Length	46' 0" 14.00m

Stoke Ferry
Fen

Herringay
Hill

Cut-off Channel

Wretton

Bluebell
P.H.

Stoke Ferry
E. C. Tues
Shop

PO

Aqueduct

staunch just below Brandon Bridge, where the river is really quite shallow. It is unwise to go past the moorings. There are EA 48hr moorings above the railway bridge at the landing stage below the lock.

The small town of Brandon is interesting because it is the centre for flint knapping - and consequently, there are some first rate flint buildings. The 'new' bridge (built 1953) is prettily dressed with local flint. The church of St Peter has a 14th century font and two turrets, and at one time a lantern shone to guide pilots. Grimes Graves, not far away, is the name given to the shafts from which flint was extracted -as it still is in nearby areas.

Great Ouse

Back on the Ouse, we have one more stop to make before we reach Ely: this is at the small community of Littleport on the northerly bank, with the well-known and even better patronised Black Horse pub. At Littleport Boat Haven, you will find an astonishingly fresh and spirited welcome from young Gary Andrews who has not been there as long as many of the Fens boat folk. He is obliging and can fit you out or up with almost anything small-boat-wise. He is known for not turning craft away.

Littleport is a location specially remembered for its martyrs. In 1816 there was widespread hunger in the Fens owing largely to the Enclosure of common land. When their children were starving, the unemployed farm workers of Littleport were obliged to watch trains of Fen Lighters being loaded in their village with the grain that would have kept them alive - grain grown in their own parish and being sent away to London to make profits for the already extremely wealthy farmers. Wages, for the few that had any, were 9s a week: wheat was £5 5s a quarter. They rioted. They marched to Ely armed with billhooks and scythes, and covered by a predecessor of the tank: a farm wagon on which were mounted four great punt-guns. They fired no shot, killed nobody, and after some window-breaking and lawlessness retired home. The military were sent for, and infested the district; after weeks of searching and interrogating, eighty men were arrested and taken to Ely to be made an example of. They were tried by judges selected by the Bishop of Ely, for in this 'Liberty and Franchise' he had this power. Five men were publicly hanged (with great difficulty, for the Bishop could not for a long time get anybody to lend him a cart for the job), five were transported for life, and the rest imprisoned for long periods. The bishop then marched into the cathedral in a great procession with fifty men of Ely carrying white wands, his sword being borne before him by his butler, and everybody singing 'Why Do the Heathen Rage?' This miserable exhibition was the last exercise of temporal power by the Bishops of Ely.

The River Lark
10 miles/16 km to Judes Ferry - 1 lock

Next comes another parting of the ways, in the shape of the River Lark, which is navigable to Isleham for craft drawing no more than 4'0"/1.2m draught. Two miles upstream brings into view the village of Prickwillow, situate in what are known as the Black Fens: wetlands for centuries fit only for fish, fishermen, fowl and wildfowlers. Like a few other places on the east coast, the houses were perforce built on stilts: above the water level and theoretically safe; for example, the church and the old school - with the old vicarage now having ten steps to its door instead of the one it had to start with in 1876.

Many folk stop at this intriguingly named community, where there are EA moorings between the two bridges, not because it is as pretty as its name suggests; nor to fathom the unfathomable depths of its ever-shrinking peat; nor for its St Peter's piled church (which actually contains a surprise in the form of a real oddity: the exquisite white marble font from Ely Cathedral presented by Dean Spencer in 1693); but to inspect the 1922 Mirrlees diesel in the Drainage Engine Museum - surrounded by engineering intricacies and some excellent pictures. Most boaters will be making for Isleham. The river trip becomes less attractive for this, but once there you find a recently completed leisure development of private domestic residences with boat spaces. There is occasionally, and by grace and favour, a space for a visitor. (It helps your entrée if you are an honourable member of GOBA who are more persona grata here than most others - and 'most others' includes hire boat crew doubled in spades!)

Isleham Priory has a Norman chapel, set up by Benedictines and deserted by them in 1254. The chapel is plain, while the church is anything but, with its gabled south porch, tall clerestory and a decoration of angels. Totems of the Peytons abound; but since the family built the lot over the years, that is not surprising. Perhaps this is the real Peyton Place? Moving up to West Row (also known as Judes Ferry) the river gets prettier again. The bridge is the head of navigation for most craft, as the rest is shallow -with no channel except for portaged craft.

In 1932 some fascinating items were unearthed at nearby Thistley Green from a Roman habitation. A pottery, and hypocaust were found. Pottery is pottery, but a hypocaust is something else: a precursor of

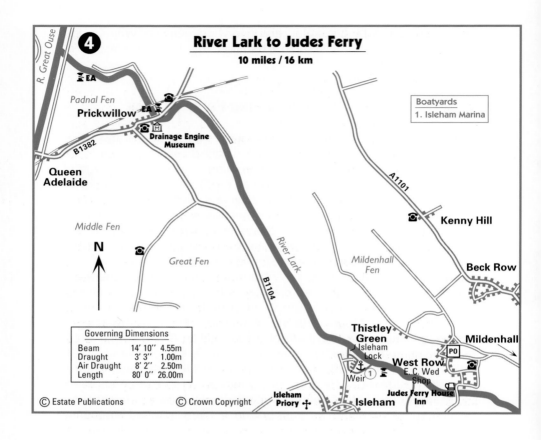

River Lark to Judes Ferry
10 miles / 16 km

R. Great Ouse

EA

Padnal Fen
Prickwillow EA

Drainage Engine Museum

B1382

Queen Adelaide

Middle Fen

N

Great Fen

River Lark

B1104

Boatyards
1. Isleham Marina

A1101

Kenny Hill

Mildenhall Fen

Beck Row

Mildenhall
PO

Thistley Green
Isleham Lock

West Row
E. C. Wed
Shop

Weir ①

Judes Ferry House Inn

Isleham Priory ✝

Isleham

Governing Dimensions		
Beam	14' 10''	4.55m
Draught	3' 3''	1.00m
Air Draught	8' 2''	2.50m
Length	80' 0''	26.00m

© Estate Publications   © Crown Copyright

central heating, it is a hollow space under the floor into which hot air was sent for warming up a room or a bath. (The Latin 'hypocaustum' comes from the Greek 'hupokauston' meaning 'a place heated from below'). 'Hot as Hell' seems to have some significance here! Ten years later a veritable hoard of Roman silver was also unearthed, this time by the workings of a plough.

Not far away, the small town of Mildenhall is blessed with an over-abundance of establishments: it has one church, St Mary's which can be seen for miles, and is embellished with angels all round; a Wesleyan, a Calvinist and a Baptist chapel - the latter having members devoted to total immersion … no doubt a tempting experience in mid-winter in the waters of the local - what a Lark! Finally, it has given its name to the vast spread of the great Mildenhall USAF air base.

Great Ouse to Ely

So, back on the Great Ouse, we now approach Ely: the place about which there is so much talk with the tongues of angels and even more sounding brass and tinkling cymbals. Legend has it that when St Dunstan arrived here, he found most of the monks living, if not in sin, then at least in pleasure, and such was Dunstan's consternation (holy or wholly envious) that he turned the fornicating fellows into eels - and there have been eels there ever since. Hence Eel Island ... Eel Isle ... Ely.

Etheldreda (630-679AD) was another soul with a sexual hang-up and she it was who founded the nunnery at Ely; appointed herself Abbess; and decreed that there should be monks there as well.

As a lass, Etheldreda was sent to Whitby Abbey in the care of her Aunt Hilda; and it was there, avoiding the perils of Dracula, she got religion. Back in the Fens she was married off to one Prince Tonbert, of the ruling local tribe, the Girvii. Although his Queen in many ways, she didn't let him lord it over or under her; nor, after his death, did she permit any intimacy with her next husband, Egfrid, King of Northumberland. After more than a decade of sexless marriage, Etheldreda took the veil under Bishop Wilfrid of York and vowed to be sanctimonious ever after.

Back at Ely, she stuck her staff in the ground and it miraculously took root and put forth branches. After her death (attributed by some to throat cancer caused by wearing too many necklaces as a teenager - Oh, vanity!) Etheldreda was canonised and became very famous. Firstly because of her great virtue; for example, when Danish warriors plundered the town in the 9th century and one of them tried to break into her tomb, his eyes somewhat improbably fell out of his head. Secondly, her name got shortened to 'St Audrey' and fairs were held all over the place where baubles or icons in the form of her necklaces were sold. Much of what was sold was inferior rubbish, namely 'shoddy'; but in this case, becoming even more namely when abbreviated through common usage to 'tawdry'. In 'A Winter's Tale', Shakespeare has it thus: 'Come you promised me a tawdry lace and a pair of sweet gloves.' (Let it be known that the nearby market place offers contemporary bargains of all kinds, but few that are tawdry.)

During the Norman Conquest of 1066, Ely was the centre of Anglo-Saxon resistance led by Hereward the Wake. The foundations of the present cathedral were laid by William 1 after the conquest. After the Norman tower collapsed in 1322, the local-boy-made-good, Alan of Walsingham, wandered as if in a dream to the mounds of fallen stone, stood mindlessly for a while - and then came to life with God's decision: he was to build a huge Octagon onto the square tower, and cap it with a wooden lantern. It seems his thought was instantaneous, but the building took a little longer: 26 years; but its eight palm-leafed pillars that apparently hold up the great eight-sided lantern (legendary weight 400 tons) create a portentous effect.

Alan of Walsingham did better than 'tawdry' for this is in brass over his grave: "These things are of note at Ely, the Lantern and Chapel of Mary, A windmill too, and a vineyard that yieldeth wine in abundance. Know that the Choir before ye exceedeth all others in beauty, Made by Alan our brother, Alan the wise Master Builder; Alan the Prior, forget not, here facing the Choir lyeth buried. He, for that older Tower which fell one night in the darkness, Were erected, well-founded, the Tower that ye now are beholding." Walsingham House was built for him in 1335.

The present Ely Cathedral Order has learned a lot from Margaret Thatcher, and possesses a clear understanding of the phrase, 'Charity begins at home'. You will find a host of religious goodies (and perhaps even some flummery) on display - and most of them for sale at prices that indicate that the powers that be understand very well the price of everything but appreciate the value of very little. Their commercially competitive nous strikes you the moment you cross the threshold ... Plus ça change!

So; this then is the capital of the Fens: a settlement encompassing all the sophistication of marina-cum-cathedral life to be enjoyed in a city with a population doing its best to keep at the 10,000 mark - an eccentric, fascinating and beautiful place. Of its many contrasts, the one I found most appealing was the market on the hill and the boating centre below with the threateningly competitive name of Babylon. The marina has now gone one better, for it calls itself Lovey's! Their berths are amongst the most pleasant I have thrown a bowline at, and their proximity to first rate hostelries and the excellently restored Maltings, an example of picture book architecture, makes a stay there an attractive proposition.

The riverside Maltings were built in 1868 for a local brewery, but were burned down in 1967. However, Phoenix-like, a decade later, a public hall was opened with good general facilities; and what could whet the appetite more than the nearby Cutter Inn with its bankside moorings. It is something of a long haul up the hill to the Cathedral and market place, but the architectural delights, the comprehensive range of shops and the friendliness of one and all make the climb worthwhile. In particular, the chandlery (Ely Boat Chandlers) is especially welcoming, efficient and no more expensive than they have an absolute right to be, considering the services they offer and the quality of their goods. It comes as quite a surprise to find such a first rate chandlery so far from the sea and so thoroughly well equipped for big boats in what is, after all, no more than a smallish boating centre.

Ely to St Ives

The next leg to Popes Corner, takes us deep into Fenland, where the legendary Fish and Duck pub stands sentinel at the junction of the Old West River and the Cam. To enjoy its ambience, it is best approached by boat, and you will find good moorings set aside. The Old West is the old channel of the Great Ouse, before Vermuyden dug his rivers to cut out the big bends; just as Morton famously did with his Leam and the corners of the Nene. The Old West is as charming as is the Old Nene, both still navigable, and both offering a course of natural wandering in an area of mainly dead-straight cuts. The River Cam leads on to the lock at Bottisham, pronounced locally by those who know as 'Bo'isham', and then into the heart of Cambridge; and we look at this romantic prospect on p.148.

Having left the Ely Ouse behind, the first place on the Old West River (but still really the Great Ouse) is Stretham, which is mainly of interest because of its remarkable Old Pumping Engine. Installed for £400 by the Commissioners in 1831, it is a beam engine built by Butterley's of Derbyshire. Driven by steam and, taking 30,000 gallons of water from the lower Fens up into the higher level Old West, it soon put many windmills out of business. The engine still works as well as ever, but is in retirement - having handed on the baton to diesel. The engine is as good to look at as is a piece of sculpture.

Just up the river comes Stretham Ferry Bridge and the Lazy Otter Inn, which provides food for all, but specialises in goodies for boaters who are made welcome at their overnight moorings. There is a marina and pub just below the next bridge - Twenty Pence Bridge.

The small village of Wilburton is a short walk away from the Twenty Pences (past Australia Farm, nevertheless). It is of interest for "Burystead", a 17th century isolated red-brick manor house; and a number of saintly souls now departed but muralled on the church walls: Saint Christopher, Saint Blaise, and Saint Leodegar.

Three miles upstream, there are GOBA moorings just after Aldreth road bridge. It was from here that William the Conqueror laid down the first of the Fen causeways - with this one going to Ely.

It is another 3 miles/4.8km or so upstream, above Hermitage Lock and marina to the Crewe of the Fens: Earith, being a great meeting

place of the waters; where as you would expect, there is much to distract and to entertain. It is essentially a working business kind of place, but it does have some pretty cottages. Somewhat unexpected, is the short, sharp stretch of tidal river, between Hermitage and Brownshill Locks where the rise and fall can get well on its way towards 3'3"/1.0m at springs and with big freshets. Earith is basically a work-horse of a community, reflecting its past importance as a centre for Fen drainage and water transport; indeed, at one time it was a busy inland port - specialising in timber. From here, the Old Bedford courses its straight-as-a-dye 21 miles/33.5km to Salters Lode Lock. The Founding Fathers, not content with their achievement decided to build another one parallel to it - which they did two decades later. This was, predictably, the 'New' Bedford which runs, almost straight, to Denver Sluice. The 'Old' has no tide, being sluiced below Denver Sluice; while the 'New' is tidal, causing the rise and fall mentioned above. The filling of the sandwich created between the 'Old' and the 'New' is known as the Ouse Washes, and it takes up the overflow when necessary. At their junction with the Ouse, is the famous Bulwark, fortified earthworks built in the Civil War period. There are two marinas here, Hermitage and Westview and the Quiet Waters Boat Haven also has moorings.

Before leaving Earith for the great trek up the Upper Ouse to Bedford, it is worth noting that within a few (land) miles there are some interesting religious locations worthy of minor pilgrimages. The first is Over (hardly a mile from the river) with St Mary's Church that boasts gruesomely sprouting gargoyles which spout amazingly when in full flow. We have come across the famous Barnack Stone elsewhere in the area. Here, the church seems to have had more than its fair share of it - but the end product surely justifies it. The turret holds a sanctus bell - quite a rarity in a non-Papist establishment - and there is much delicate carpentry inside the main body.

The next candidate is the larger village of Willingham. Its church has a great hammer-beam roof, and inside there are many examples of True Decorated Style at its best. Nearby is the fortified mound known as The Hill of Belsar; he who was William the Conqueror's general, responsible for the building of the Isle of Ely causeway.

It was in tiny Swavesey, just south of Over, that Alan de la Zouch (as in Ashby de la Zouch) founded a Benedictine Priory, but of it nothing remains. The church, like its sister at Over, is another example of the lush life of lords of the neighbourhood. Cedars and larches set off the outside, while the windows with (more) Decorated tracery and the Perpendicular porch and nave with splendid bench-ends, are a

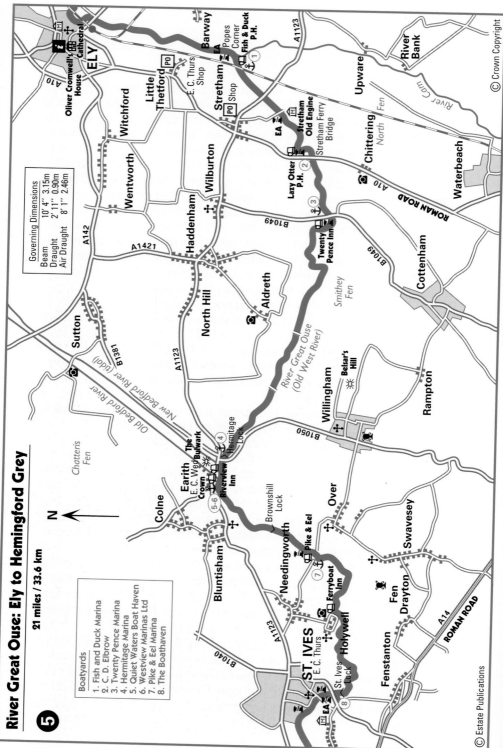

River Great Ouse: Ely to Hemingford Grey

5

21 miles / 33.6 km

N ←

Governing Dimensions
Beam	10' 4" 3.15m
Draught	2' 11" 0.90m
Air Draught	8' 1" 2.46m

Boatyards
1. Fish and Duck Marina
2. C. D. Elbrow
3. Twenty Pence Marina
4. Hermitage Marina
5. Quiet Waters Boat Haven
6. Westview Marinas Ltd
7. Pike & Eel Marina
8. The Boathaven

© Crown Copyright

© Estate Publications

128

delight to see.

Last on this mini-circuit, Longstanton presents us with two exemplary churches: St Michael and All Saints. The first is Early English with a Victorian re-made chancel; and one of its intriguing possessions is an oak chest from the 12th century. The church of All Saints is basically Decorated style, with many tributes to and reminders of the Hattons, the influential local family who did a deal with Queen Elizabeth for their manor after she had done down the Bishop of Ely and taken it from him under threat of de-frocking.

Back nearer to the river, the village of Bluntisham has a number of choice buildings, including the Non-Conformist Meeting House (rebuilt 1874) and the 18th century farmhouse across the street. The Parish Church of St Mary's has an unique 14th century chancel which ends in a triangular format; while nearby, is the old rectory (1720) which was once the home of Dorothy L. Sayers.

And now, actually back on the river, we move along first to the Pike and Eel, a spot where there used to be a busy crossing. It is now absorbed with its hostelry and its marina; both of which, together with GOBA offer moorings. No more than 1 mile/1.6km upstream we reach the village of Holywell. It is a small, picturesque place, with parts set actually on the banks. Some very attractive timbered cottages nestle near the 13th century church, with a 16th century stone tower (created out of bits from Ramsey Abbey) that used to be a beacon for approaching vessels. Underneath, is to be found the spring of the 'Holy Well' of the eponymous village.

The old Ferry Boat Inn marks the disused crossing to Fen Drayton on the other side, where Hereward the Wake is supposed to have crossed when fleeing from William the Conqueror. For those for whom dry land may have an appeal after a day on the water, there is a pleasant walk to be had back to the Pike and Eel Inn. It is claimed that the Ferry Boat Inn (and the ferry the innkeeper ran) is down in the records as having been selling beer as, far back as 1068 - thus challenging the Nottingham 'Trip to Jerusalem' pub; and indeed it is mentioned in papers from 980AD. There is also a sad tale to be told: one Juliet Tewsley topped herself by a most unpleasant hanging from a tree on the banks of the river on 17th March, St Patrick's Day, 1050AD. She did not wish to go on living after Thomas Zoul, a woodcutter, failed to respond to her charms, her arms, her bosom or her flowers as she proffered all to him as he passed by returning from work.

We now move on to something quite different: the refinement of St Ives. Its name is said to derive from one peripatetic Persian bishop who died at Slepe in 600AD, and was called St Ivo. At that time, St. Ives was known as Slepe: the name being in the Domesday Book and in current use as in Slepe Hall Hotel - and Cromwell farmed at a place called Old Slepe Hall. The town is particularly famous for its six arched 15th century bridge with a chapel on its centre span and eccentric formation of pointed and blunt ends. The chapel is a national monument - one of only four of its kind. The bridge is closed to the generality of traffic.

Boaters need to know that the only safe passage through the bridge is the marked arch on the town side of the chapel. The Quay has very pretty views of the river and a good sight of the bridge and mediaval chapel. Ramsey Abbey promoted the bridge chapel and also gave the town its name, for when the Ramsey outpost monastery was founded in the 11th century, legend has it that the bones of an obscure Persian saint were found: one St Ivo. An ancient custom is still practised here: Dicing for Bibles. Six Bibles are diced for by children of the parish as part of the May Festivals.

The town has a good museum of local history and there are tempting markets. The 15th-century parish church of All Saints with its soaring spire stands close to the old fording point to Hemingford Meadow. In the centre of the town there is a statue of its golden boy: Oliver Cromwell, who, amongst other things, farmed the area and was a churchwarden at All Saints. St Ives is also known to many boating folk as the HQ of Imray, Laurie, Norie & Wilson, publishers of Imray charts and many pilot books.

Upstream comes a veritable run of settlements with moorings abounding. The first hint of habitation, comes with the charmingly named Hemingford Meadows, after which come Hemingford Grey and Hemingford Abbots. At Hemingford Grey, the waterside church of St James', perched on the very edge of the river bank provides one of the most memorable views of the Ouse. It dates back to well before the 14th century, although almost all of its spire went to a watery grave in the river in the gales of 1741. There are more grand chateaux in the vicinity: the 1150AD Norman Manor House and its moat, reputed to be among the oldest inhabited houses in England, and once home to one Miss Gunnings, an 18th century socialite; Hemingford Grey House, the red-bricked former Rectory (1697) with its huge plane tree going back to 1702; and the old River House, where lived the painter Sadler in the early 1900's.

Hemingford Abbots, centred on the 13th century St Margaret's Church and the 16th century Manor House is the upstream version of the pair, and, not surprisingly, during its past it was part of the great Ramsey Abbey estate. Church spires are landmarks on this stretch of

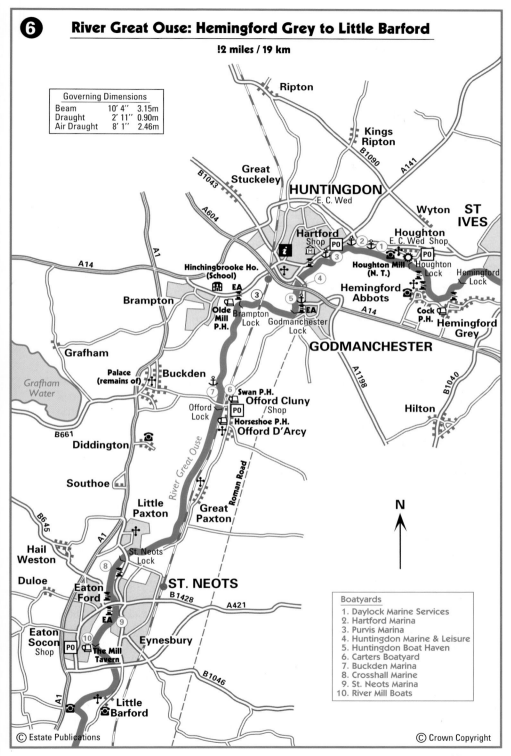

!2 miles / 19 km

Governing Dimensions		
Beam	10' 4"	3.15m
Draught	2' 11"	0.90m
Air Draught	8' 1"	2.46m

Ripton

Kings Ripton

B1090

A141

Great Stuckeley

B1043

A604

HUNTINGDON
E. C. Wed

Wyton

ST IVES

Hartford
Shop

Houghton
E. C. Wed Shop

A1

A14

Hinchingbrooke Ho. (School)

Houghton Mill (N. T.)

Houghton Lock

Hemingford Lock

Brampton

EA

Hemingford Abbots

A14

Cock P.H.

Hemingford Grey

Olde Mill P.H.

Brampton Lock

Godmanchester Lock

EA

GODMANCHESTER

A1198

Grafham

B1040

Grafham Water

Palace (remains of)

Buckden

Hilton

B661

Diddington

Offord Lock

Swan P.H.
Offord Cluny /Shop

PO

Horseshoe P.H.
Offord D'Arcy

Southoe

River Great Ouse

Roman Road

N
↑

Little Paxton

Great Paxton

B645

A1

Hail Weston

St. Neots Lock

Duloe

Eaton Ford

ST. NEOTS

B1428

A421

Eaton Socon
Shop

PO

The Mill Tavern

Eynesbury

B1046

A1

Little Barford

EA

Boatyards	
1.	Daylock Marine Services
2.	Hartford Marina
3.	Purvis Marina
4.	Huntingdon Marine & Leisure
5.	Huntingdon Boat Haven
6.	Carters Boatyard
7.	Buckden Marina
8.	Crosshall Marine
9.	St. Neots Marina
10.	River Mill Boats

© Estate Publications

© Crown Copyright

131

the river, but a 'landmark' of another kind was unearthed towards the end of Victoria's reign. It was a stone coffin from the Romano-Brit civilisation and was found in a field - just as these days we occasionally come across an old bath-tub now put to use as a drinking trough for cattle!

The procession of miniature communities continues with Houghton and Wyton, on the opposite side of the river from the Hemingfords. They are Siamese-joined on the bank and add more spires to the skyline. They each have their pride and joy: for Wyton it is the 13th century church and for Houghton it is the famous 17th century red-brick water-mill and the oldest timber-framed house around, dating back to 1480: it also boasts a gothic village pump.There has been a mill here since Domesday; the current 19th century four storey building is now owned by the National Trust and still produces flour for sale on-site. There are EA moorings on the island opposite Houghton Mill.

Before the near-conurbations of Godmanchester and Huntingdon take over the riverside, there is the hamlet of Hartford to be passed; and that is what most folk do, although it has its own modest attractions in the form of the Barley Mow and the King of the Belgians pubs. It is here that the well-used Hartford Marina is based and a little further on is the quite unpretentious Purvis Marina, run by Terry Kelly. Even if you don't need anything, just drop in (or drop out, as you might think) for a good chat. His personableness will reward you - as well as his singular sense of humour.

Godmanchester is linked (almost twinned) with Huntingdon by the 14th century bridge across the River Ouse; the original bridge having been destroyed by floods. The Huntingdon stone end is not the same as the Godmanchester bit. Legend has it the the City Fathers could not agree, and that they, just like the Channel Tunnel Backers, decided to start from each side. A 17th century causeway also linked the two. It was an important ford as far back as the Romans (a crossroad for Ermine Street and Via Devana), and the first fort was razed by Boudicca's rebellion, but later rebuilt as a service centre for both road and river traffic. It was granted a charter from King John in 1214AD, but it still seems more of a village than a town. The 18th century frontages of the Causeway and the famous Chinese Bridge are intriguing. It is worth noting that the river does tend to be quite narrow in this section.

Across the river, Huntingdon, is particularly famous as the birth-place of Oliver Cromwell (1599 -1658). In Market Hill you find the Town Hall (1745); the 15th century All Saints Church and the Falcon Inn, Cromwell's HQ during the Civil War. The Cromwells were all over the place: grandfather had the George Hotel, and that of course guaranteed their popularity and entry into whatever was on offer. Oliver was born in a house near Ermine Street, and the site has a plaque. He was christened in All Saints Church, wherein was buried his father. Hinchingbrooke House, to the west of the town, which is now a school, was the family home of the Cromwells. A Londoner by the name of Anthony Bartholomew turned the 12th century St John Hospital into a grammar school, two of the pupils being Oliver Cromwell and Samuel Pepys. The school is now a Cromwell Museum. After quarrelling with the City Fathers in 1631, Cromwell moved to St Neots.

For boating visitors, the charms of both towns completely outweigh any sorrowful memories that may linger for Roundheads or Royalists alike, and between them, they offer a tremendous choice in moorings and all boating facilities and services.

Moving out of Huntingdon and through Godmanchester Lock, where there are EA moorings, we next come to the nearby community of Brampton with its lock: a place of interest because of its pretty cottages and village green. Brampton's Old Mill features in the Domesday Book, but is now well and truly in this century's tourist industry as a pub and restaurant with its food served under old wooden beams by the old mill wheel. The pub in the village itself has a history: it changed its name from the New Inn to The Harrier - to pay respect to those airmen from RAF Brampton who had paid hard cash over the counters over the years. Further back in time, one John Pepys had a farmhouse near the church and his son, Samuel often stayed there while at Huntingdon Grammar School. He often returned: "most particularly during the Plague ... and is said to have hidden his monies in the garden - being afeared of a Dutch invasion ... " which does not say much for his confidence in his naval colleagues! It is also supposed that a pot of silver coins dug up in 1842 was part of this cache.

The historic village of Buckden is about 1 mile/1.6km away from the river and the eponymous marina. It is famous for the remains of the Lincoln Bishops' impressive palace. The 15th century gatehouse, and the tower remain; as did Catherine of Aragon for a while. The place was an important staging post, as witness the 16th century Lion and the 18th century George Hotels.

After Offord Lock comes more twinning: Offord Cluny and Offord D'Arcy, once famous as centres of lace making. The Cluny version has a 1704 red brick Manor House; an 1850 school with a plate to one Dr. Newcome, who gave monies for 'six poor children'; a 13th century church of All Saints; and a corn mill. D'Arcy competes with the tall spire of the retired mediaeval church of St Peter. Pubs and boating services are all to hand.

Still more pairing further on: the Greater and Lesser Paxtons. Great Paxton is the first, and its main characteristic is the thunder from the main railway line - once the famous LNER. The village has some attractive cottages; a 'minster' church from the beginning of the 11th century; and a splendid view from its own, Paxton Hill. Little Paxton has grown recently, but used to be a classic hamlet, supported and probably created by the 12th century church of St James and the over-lords of Paxton Hall - the mansion that was born again in 1738. The church of St James has a little fabric that goes back to the Normans; and in the churchyard there is an unlikely monument to one Papworth, architect to the King of Wurtemburg. The area is noted for its water-filled ex-gravel workings, Paxton Pits, round which folk walk for leisure.

No sooner are we past the Paxtons and St Neots Lock, than we reach the grouping of St Neots, Eaton Ford, Eynesbury and Eaton Socon; which between them offer all services. The first came about with the growth of a 10th century Benedictine Priory. Once again, a spire stands out, this time from the 15th century St Mary's Church; but in the event, no separation, be it historical, social or cultural is relevant (or even possible) since all parts grow into all other parts, and everything is connected to everything else. (However, there is a small stream that nominally divides the Eynesbury sheep from the Neots goats and it is known as Hen Brook).

The area, based originally on St Neots, was another important meeting and crossing place (the Great North Road like the LNER was truly self-seeking and self-fulfilling) and many of the roads that reached here go back to at least the 9th century. At Eaton Socon, an absolutely favourite watering hole is the Cross Keys - outwardly very lordly, inwardly with divided loyalties to the supporters of Cromwell and Charles. Socon was yet another of the river fords fortified by forts, this one known as Castle Hills - being a set of substantial, well-defended 12th century earthworks. Of the Benedictine Priory, which was founded about 1000AD, and which really established the community as more than a cross-roads, there is no sign.

Although there is no Nellie Dean, there is an old mill by the stream - together with a real Mill Race - and a 13th century Inn to go with it, still with many of the attributes of coaching days, such as well-used brickwork, exposed (low!) beams, gleaming woodwork and intimate alcoves. The church of St Mary the Virgin is an aggregation of

Perpendicular building, with friezes, buttresses and pinnacles finished off with a parapet that is not for the vertiginously challenged. The interior is in no way inferior to the lavish exterior, with its abundance of eclectic carvings. A switch from the spiritual to the spirituous takes us to the old Market Place Brewery and Malthouse.

A now fairly deserted landscape reveals itself as we progress towards the head of navigation at Bedford. Little Barford once had a poet Laureate, Nicholas Rowe, and it does have a riverside church with a touch of Norman, but is without facilities. Both Roxton and Tempsford together offer little to intrigue, charm or to detain other than an interesting stone bridge from 820AD, a funny little thatched chapel, a number of pubs and, of course, Roxton Lock

The next major halt comes at Great Barford with its lock, 17th century bridge with a challenging arch, and yet another spire with aspirations: that of the All Saints church tower. It is a classic riverside community with all its services together and within easy reach of the moorings - and the Anchor Inn is a special watering hole for many thirsty crews - book your seat well ahead! It is the last serious watering hole before we reach the end of the trail at Bedford; and all that tempts between is the tiny elongated riverside village of Willington above the lock: its entrance and exit being marked by a church and pub respectively. This is a pretty tree-lined area, and kingfishers and herons are not unknown - with the latter being now more approachable.

And so, after two more locks, Castle Mill Lock and Cardington Lock and Priory Marina, we reach journey's end: Bedford, a county town dating from the 10th century with a charter granted by Henry II in 1166.

First things first: prison is a quintessential feature of Bedford: John Howard, the campaigner for more humane prison conditions, was born here in 1726 (and now remembered by the Howard League for Prison Reform); and John Bunyan was born just outside the town in 1628. Nearly everyone knows he wrote his famous 'Pilgrim's Progress' while in the local prison; so, since it is impossible to escape the man, let us deal with him first.

Bunyan was born in November 1628 near nearby Elstow. His father was a tinker, to whom he was in apprenticeship for a time. Bunyan was christened in the village church (based on an 11th century Benedictine nunnery) where stained glass windows show scenes from The 'Pilgrim's Progress'. Later, Bunyan used to ring the bell, although later still he wished he had not practised such a vainglorious activity. The Moot Hall Museum is a 16th century timber and red-brick building, with a good tie-beam roof housing items from 17th century

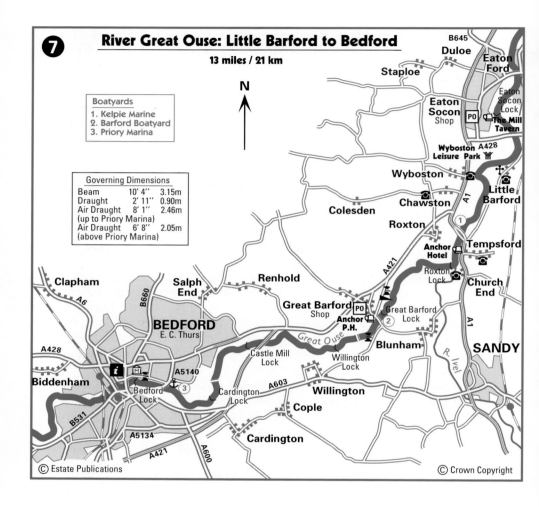

River Great Ouse: Little Barford to Bedford

7

13 miles / 21 km

N

Boatyards
1. Kelpie Marine
2. Barford Boatyard
3. Priory Marina

Governing Dimensions

Beam	10' 4''	3.15m
Draught	2' 11''	0.90m
Air Draught	8' 1''	2.46m
(up to Priory Marina)		
Air Draught	6' 8''	2.05m
(above Priory Marina)		

B645
Duloe
Eaton Ford
Staploe
Eaton Socon
Shop
Eaton Socon Lock
The Mill Tavern
A428
Wyboston Leisure Park
Wyboston
Little Barford
Chawston
Colesden
Roxton
Tempsford
Anchor Hotel
Roxton Lock
Church End
Clapham
Salph End
Renhold
Great Barford Shop
Anchor P.H.
Great Barford Lock
BEDFORD
E. C. Thurs
Castle Mill Lock
Willington Lock
Blunham
SANDY
A428
Biddenham
Bedford Lock
Cardington Lock
Willington
Cople
Great Ouse
R. Ivel
Cardington
A5140
A603
A5134
A421
A600
A6
B660
B531
A421

© Estate Publications

© Crown Copyright

English life and observances relevant to Bunyan.

From the age of 16 to 19, John Bunyan took up arms with the Parliamentary army. Shortly after, he married a dedicated Puritan and was apparently converted by this female; later taking instructions from the works of Martin Luther - by whom he thought his own condition was described. A little later, he was elevated to the status of a

Leader with a separatist group in Bedford. He became a popular neighbourhood preacher, often in conflict with the establishment of authoritarian clergy who felt he was improper and incompetent. After the Restoration, when Puritanism was no longer tolerated and services, other than coded C of E, banned, Bunyan continued to plough his own furrow - finally harrowing himself into Bedford county jail in 1660; and there he stayed for 12 years. He was permitted to read the bible and a book on martyrs and to make shoelaces to help eke out a pittance of a living for his family.

Bunyan was inspired by what he read, to write: and so came forth tracts and pamphlets and the biography, "Grace Abounding to the Chief of Sinners" which was published in 1666. Ten years later he was back in prison, and this brought forth his piece de resistance, 'Pilgrim's Progress', first published in 1678.

The Bunyan Museum is in Mill Street, where he had his first meeting place in 1672. The present 'Bunyan Meeting' was built in 1849, and has fantastic 'Pilgrim's Progress' bronze doors done by Frederick Thrupp in 1876. In the museum there are Bunyan's chair, his walking stick, his tankard, and nearly 200 versions of his Big Book. His first Bedford statue was erected in 1874: situate on St Peter's Green, it depicts parts of 'Pilgrim's Progress' on three bronze panels.

Back at the river, Bedford can show Spalding and Wisbech a thing or two when it comes to riparian development; the embankment being worthy of careful study. As is, indeed, the 14th-15th century church of St Paul, sitting splendidly as it does under yet another high spire. It was once Saxon and has undergone many changes - most occurring when a passion for Victorian over-ornamentation was all the rage. It is said that in the environs, John Bunyan was converted by one John Gifford, a drunkard turned priest; but I consider the marital version to be more likely.

Books have been written about Bedford, and enthusiasts may wish to turn to them; but boaters need to know that there are plenty of services and facilities for all boating, domestic and leisure needs. For example, there are, predictably, pubs and restaurants galore, as well as an art gallery, ten-pin bowling, a cinema complex and modern swimming pool - and all the Bunyan-related offices. These facilities are all within easy reach of the river: so too is the Corn Exchange which offers a variety of live entertainment. At Mill Meadow there is public mooring.

The river is navigable to Kempston Mill but many cruisers, once above Mill Meadow, are restricted by headroom. Actually, the Great Ouse rises 90 miles/144km above Bedford, but that is not navigable, and the present head of navigation is deemed to be Cardington Lock (just outside Bedford) or Bedford Lock in the town itself.

From here to the Wash it is a cruise of some 75 miles/120km with 22 locks. Much of it is flat; much of it is pretty; and you can count on true Fenland hospitality no matter where you throw your bowline or drop your land anchor. True, it is a little overcrowded, but by that very token, you are never far away from services, facilities and help. Verily I say, it is a river of variety, multiplicity and continuing charm, challenge and interest.

Environment Agency Moorings
Free to all river users, and most carry a 48 hour limit.

Denver
LH bank above Jenyns Arms.

Hilgay (River Wissey)
RH bank through second bridge in village.

Ten Mile Bank
Both banks above Hilgay bridge on Great Ouse. RH adjacent to Windmill Inn.

Brandon Creek
RH bank alongside the picnic area before the Ship PH

Brandon, (Little Ouse)
The lock landing stage at Brandon lock.

Littleport
LH bank between the Boathaven and the A 10 road bridge.

River Lark
LH bank about half a mile from junction with Great Ouse.

Prickwillow (River Lark)
LH bank between the road and railway bridges, in the village.

Queen Adelaide
RH bank immediately above road & rail bridges.

Ely
Two moorings, separated by the entrance to the Bridge Boatyard on LH bank between the first road and second railway bridges.

Little Thetford
LH bank below junction of Cam and Old West River.

Stretham (Old West)
LH bank 100 yards before the bridge prior to the Streatham Engine.

St Ives
In cut on RH bank adjacent to the Dolphin Hotel.

Houghton
On island forming LH bank of main river below Houghton lock. NB no access by land.

Godmanchester
Old lock walls adjacent to new lock.

Old Mills
On island forming LH bank of backwater

Environment Agency
For details of river levels, lock closures and stoppages call the Brampton Office Tel. 01480 414581

GOBA is the Great Ouse Boating Association Limited

The objects of GOBA are:-

To promote and encourage boating on the rivers Great Ouse, Cam, Lark, Little Ouse, Wissey and associated navigable waterways.

To forward the interests of all who use these waters for boating.

To promote the right use of these waterways and to provide a means for the discussion of common problems and all matters of interest to boat users.

To gather and disseminate information concerning these waterways.

To maintain liaison with all statutory bodies controlling these waterways.

To co-operate with other bodies, both local and national, having similar aims.

Here are some of the benefits which GOBA membership offers to those who boat on the River Great Ouse and associated waterways:-

GOBA aims to ensure that navigational interests are respected and maintained.

The primary concern of the controlling bodies used to be drainage and water supply. GOBA made sure that the legislation contained provision for the maintenance of navigation and that reasonable navigation charges were levied to support this.

GOBA raises with many authorities the needs and interests of boat owners which affect their pastime.

In order to do this GOBA needs to maintain its claim to speak for the vast majority of boaters on the Great Ouse and associated waterways. More members mean a stronger Association better able to represent their needs.

One of GOBA's most important tasks is to ensure that you have somewhere to moor when you need to.

GOBA provided landing stages at locks until the River Authority could take them oven GOBA rents stretches of bank for overnight moorings for members, and encourages the Environment Agency, Local Authorities, Marina Operators and Pub Owners to do likewise.

GOBA works continuously to see that existing services such as water points are maintained and that further necessary facilities are provided. We are pressing for sewage disposal arrangements so that these are provided economically and in sufficient numbers.

GOBA can be contacted as follows:
telephone: 01480 810244
e-mail: membership.goba@ndirect.co.uk
Christopher Grant
GOBA Membership, 32 Graveley Road, Offord D'Arcy,
Huntingdon, Cambridgeshire, PE18 9RB.

GOBA Moorings
'Right Hand' and 'Left Hand' refer to navigating downstream.

Priory Marina
Ask at reception: 24 hour free mooring to GOBA members

Great Barford
RH hank between the lock and the bridge

Offord
Adjacent to the landing stage on RH bank below lock

Mailers Meadow
LH bank between Buckden Marina and Brampton lock

Brampton
LH bank between Brampton Mill and railway bridge.

Pike & Eel', Overcote Ferry
LH bank immediately prior to entrance to Pike and Eel Marina. 200m in length.

Hemingford Meadow
RH bank between Sleeping Waters and Hemingford Grey.

Wicken Fen
LH bank at junction of Wicken Lode and Monks Lode (New River).

Lazy Otter (Old West)
LH bank for approx. 130 yards downstream from fence enclosing, P.H. moorings.

Grange Farm, Caravan Site, Whittington (River Wissey)
LH bank close to end of navigation. A short distance upstream from Stoke Ferry and immediately through the new road bridge. Water &

The Great Ouse

shower facilities available and mini-market, close by.

<u>Dimmocks Cote</u>
RH bank 170m before Dimmocks Cote Bridge.

<u>Isleham Marina</u>
LH bank below lock under the footbridge.

<u>Noble's Field</u>
LH bank between Hemingford Lock and St Ives.

<u>Aldreth Drain (Old West)</u>
LH bank 200m before High Bridge.

The use of GOBA moorings is free to members and hirers of craft operated by the Great Ouse Boatbuilders and Operators Association but only if the owners are members of GOBA. Please keep children and animals under proper control and do not light fires or leave rubbish. At Noble's Field mooring, St. Ives, it is part of our agreement not to use the mooring on regatta days, although you will normally be able to moor when racing is over.

Boatyards

Annesdale Marine, Riverside Boatyard, Ely	01353 665420
Barford Boat Yard, New Road, Great Barford	01234 870401
Bridge Boatyard, Bridge Boatyard,Ely	01353 663726
Buckden Marina, Mill Rd, Buckden	01480 810355
Carters Boatyard, Mill Road Buckden	01480 811503
Crosshall Marine, Crosshall Road, St Neots	01480 472763
Daylock Marine Services, Huntingdon Rd, Wyton	01480 455898
Daymond Services, Frojo Fleet Quay, Denver	01366 383618
C.D.Elbrow Marine	01223 63692
Fish & DuckMarina	01353 649580
Hartford Marina, Banks End, Huntingdon	01480 454677
Hermitage Marina, Earith, Huntingdon	01487 840994
Huntingdon Boat Haven, Godmanchester	01480 411977
Huntingdon Marine and Leisure, Huntingdon	01480 413517
Isleham Marina, Fenbank, Isleham	01638 780663
Kelpie Marine, A1, Roxton, Bedford	01234 870249
The Boathaven, Low Rd, St Ives	01480 494040
Littleport Boat Haven, Littleport, Ely	01353 861969
Loveys Marine, Waterside, Ely	01353 664622
Pike & Eel Marina	01480 463336
Priory Marina, Barkers Lane, Bedford	01234 351931
Purvis Marine, Hartford Road, Huntingdon	01480 453628
Quiet Waters Boat Haven, Earith	01487 842154
River Mill, School Lane, Eaton Socon	01480 473456
St Neots Marina, St Neots	01480 472411
Twenty Pence Marina,Wilburton, Ely	01954 251118
Westview Marina, Earith, Huntingdon	01487 841627

Public Launching Sites

Godmanchester	Ely
Huntingdon	Denver
St Ives	

The Great Ouse

Places of interest

Tales of the Old Gaol House, King's Lynn
Tel. 01553 763044
stories of local witches, murderers and highway men recreated in the original 18th-19th century cells: open daily Easter - end Oct 1000 - 1700; closed wed and thurs Nov - Easter

St George's Guildhall, 27 King St, King's Lynn (N.T.)
Tel. 01553 773578
largest surviving medieval guildhall in England now houses the Art Centre: open all year mon-fri 1000 - 1600; sat 1000-1300 & 1400 -1530

True's Yard Museum, North St, King's Lynn
Tel. 01553 770479
fascinating record of Lynn's fishing heritage: open daily 0930 - 1630

Prickwillow Drainage Engine Museum
Tel. 01353688360
1922 Mirrlees Buckerton & Day diesel engine still in running order: open daily Apr - Oct and winter weekends

Oliver Cromwell's House, Ely
Tel. 01353 662062
exhibition of Cromwell and 17th century domestic life: open Apr- Sept 1000 - 1730 ; Oct - Mar 1000 - 1700 mon - sat; sun 1215 - 1700

Stretham Old Engine
Tel. 01353 649210
9th century land drainage steam engine: open weekends Apr - Sept

Houghton Mill, Nr Huntingdon (N.T.)
Tel. 01480 301494
large timber-built water mill still operational: tel. for opening times

Ely Museum
Tel. 01353 666655
history of Ely from Ice Age to present day: open all year 1030 - 1630

Pubs on the Ouse

Jenyns Arms, Denver	01366 383366
Bluebell, Stoke Ferry	01366 500358
The Ship Inn, Brandon Creek	01353 676228
Cross Keys Hotel, Hilgay	01366 387777
Rose & Crown, Hilgay	01366 385414
Windmill, Ten Mile Bank	01366 386445
Bridge House Hotel, Brandon	01842 813137
Black Horse, Littleport	01353 860328
Judes Ferry House Inn	01638 712277
Cutter Inn, Ely	01353 662713
Fish & Duck, Popes Corner	01353 649580
Lazy Otter Inn, Stretham	01353 649780
Twenty Pence Inn	01954 252254
Riverview Inn, Earith	01487 841405
Crown, Earith	01487 841442
Pike & Eel Inn	01480 463336
Ferryboat Inn, Holywell	01480 463227
Oliver Cromwell, St Ives	01480 465601
Floods Tavern, St Ives	01480 467773
Dolphin Hotel, St Ives	01480 486966
Cock, Hemingford Grey	01480 463609
Axe & Compasses	01480 463605
Barley Mow, Hartford	01480 450557
King of the Belgians, Hartford	01480 452030
Old Mill, Brampton	01480 459758
The Swan, Offord Cluny	01480 810294
The Horseshoe, Offord D'Arcy	01480 810293
The Mill Tavern Restaurant, Eaton Socon	01480 219612
White Horse, Eaton Socon	01480 474453
Anchor Inn, Great Barford	01234 870364

Chandlers

Ely Boat Chandlers, 21 Waterside, Ely	01353 663095

Fishing on the Great Ouse its tributaries and the Middle Levels

River Lark

This miniature river rises from a source of numerous streams; and is, like all the local rivers, a favourite for roach and bream - with sighting now of dace and chub and perch. There is also trout fishing up from Barton Mills.

River Delph

This mini river has much well behaved roach, rudd and bream - with an outside chance for carp. Zander and pike are also among those present. NB: note the wildfowl reserve between the Delph and the Hundred Foot.

The Great Ouse

Downstream of Bedford is quite different from upstream, with roach in the predominance - but with stocked supplies of bream and tench.

Ely Ouse

This attractive stretch of river is very good for roach and bream - especially near the cathedral city itself. Predictably for a place that takes its name from Eel Isle, the creatures do abound.

Old West River

This quiet water is good for roach, bream and pike - with some zander also being present.

New Bedford (Hundred Foot) River

The waterway is fast, muddy and coloured and on the whole does not offer much sport - but the luckies among anglers get good bream and some zander.

Little Ouse

This little river has quite good showings of the typical Fenland classics, roach and bream, with some dace, perch, chub and pike.

Middle Level Drain

This is excellent fishing ground, with lots of pike and roach - but in particular has splendid opportunities for catching zander.

Old Bedford

This is very good in the summer season, with plenty of good roach and bream; while in winter the pike is supreme.

River Wissey

The river is famous for its trout - but also for its numbers of roach size of its chub. It is probably one of the best fisheries in the Fenlands, with its reaches sometimes packed with the greatest variety.

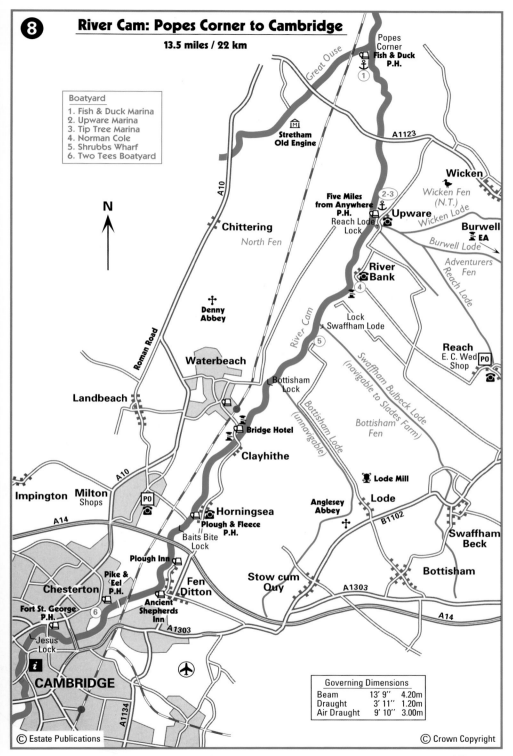

River Cam: Popes Corner to Cambridge

13.5 miles / 22 km

Boatyard
1. Fish & Duck Marina
2. Upware Marina
3. Tip Tree Marina
4. Norman Cole
5. Shrubbs Wharf
6. Two Tees Boatyard

Popes Corner
Fish & Duck P.H.

Great Ouse

Stretham Old Engine

A1123

Wicken

Wicken Fen (N.T.)

Chittering

North Fen

Five Miles from Anywhere P.H.

Reach Lode Lock

Upware

Burwell

EA

Wicken Lode

Burwell Lode

River Bank

Adventurers Fen

Reach Lode

Denny Abbey

River Cam

Lock Swaffham Lode

Reach
E. C. Wed
Shop

Waterbeach

Roman Road

A10

Swaffham Bulbeck Lode
(navigable to Slades Farm)

Bottisham Fen

Landbeach

Bottisham Lock

Bottisham Lode
(unnavigable)

Bridge Hotel

Clayhithe

Lode Mill

Impington

Milton
Shops

A10

Horningsea
Plough & Fleece P.H.

Baits Bite Lock

Anglesey Abbey

Lode

B1102

Swaffham Beck

A14

Plough Inn

Pike & Eel P.H.

Chesterton

Fort St. George P.H.

Fen Ditton

Ancient Shepherds Inn

A1303

Stow cum Quy

A1303

Bottisham

A14

Jesus Lock

CAMBRIDGE

A1134

Governing Dimensions		
Beam	13' 9''	4.20m
Draught	3' 11''	1.20m
Air Draught	9' 10''	3.00m

The River Cam
13.5 miles/22km

So, back to the parting of the ways: it is a case of plus ça change after Popes Corner and the Fish and Duck; for things are all different yet still feeling all the same. The first port of call is Upware with its eponymous marina and the quaintly (but no doubt perceptively) named Five Miles From Anywhere Public House.

At the Upware junction, you can take a load off your mind if you are looking for places to go that are different, for there is a splendid choice of Lodes through Reach Lode Lock: Burwell Lode, Reach Lode and the diminutive Wicken Lode. We are now in a location that could well attract the title 'Heart of Darkness' - except that place is in another continent - but we are well removed ... in every meaning of the phrase. This is another of those places for all those who have done the holes of the Lower Welland and the Witham Navigables and want more of them. An overview might suggest boredom, but in experience it is anything but and at the end of both Burwell and Reach Lodes there are plenty of modest attractions in the way of pubs and shops.

Burwell is the larger of the two villages, standing at the head of navigation, with a collection of pretty, ancient houses and a church purportedly inspired by Ely Cathedral. The churchyard has a sorry tale of an 18th century grudge burning: a puppeteer was in full flow in the barn theatre - behind 'closed doors' for secrecy. Fire flared up, and with the doors being locked, escape was well-nigh impossible and nearly 100 local folk were incinerated. Literati will want to know that William Heffer, the original of Heffer's Bookshop in Cambridge, was born in the village. The Cut was probably made in the 17th century to improve on the old Roman one.

Reach, the smaller village, is equally attractive; but like so many 'lost' ports, gives no indication of its notable commercial maritime past. Reach Lode truly reaches back in time: in fact, having been dug to the command of the Romans; and, probably in fiction just like an Ealing comedy, can claim to be an autonomous state as per its charter from King John. Denver Sluice put paid to most of its serious traffic many long years ago; but it was still not until the 1930's that the last and final ship sailed from the port with a cargo.

Very different, and very narrow and shallow, Wicken Lode was never navigable by any craft other than small shoal vessels designed to take peat from the village. If you can and if you will, Wicken Lode will take you into well-favoured protected country. The way in is through an old wooden bridge, and shoal craft of no more than 21'8"/6.6m LOA can reach the GOBA moorings and turning point. Best to take the dinghy first. This is the location of the nearby famous Wicken Fen National Nature Reserve. Set up in 1899, it is one of the oldest of the nature reserves. Run by the National Trust, it has more than 700 acres of fenland, most of it undrained, that runs the gamut from watery water wastes to thick thickets of woodland; most of it pullulating with flora, fauna and feathered flocks. It has an interesting relic in the form of a marsh-drainage wind-pump: coming from nearby Adventurers Fen, square, on a brick base and topped with a boat head, it makes for an intriguing sight. Cromwell's son Henry, the Governor General of Ireland, lived nearby and was buried in the village.

Now to cruise back on the main course of the Cam, which from here on tends to be both wider and, predictably, shallower - and, not so predictably, often tormented by summer's weed; but the way ahead is clear and plain: just a few steps and stops to Cambridge. The first of these comes at Bottisham Lock, closely followed by Waterbeach, a village well supplied with boating connections in the form of the Cambridge Motorboat and the Cam Sailing Clubs. The church has some 13th century works still standing; but it is the flat-as-water feature ashore that is most appealing: the classic village green. The Bridge Hotel is well-known for its good moorings and there are, as they say, 'some shops'. Across the river, squats the much smaller community of Clayhithe.

A little further upstream, Horningsea is a well-preserved proudly riparian community with a 13th century church; and very close upstream is the last lock, Baits Bite. Across the river, the under-privileged community of Milton struggles to keep itself rural (hardly pastoral though as it once was) between the thundering arteries of rail and road. The equally struggling brotherhood of Fen Ditton, with its Ancient Shepherds Inn, is the first and last to call itself countrified before the urbanity of Cambridge takes over unconditionally.

Jesus is not only famous in Cambridge for His college, but also for His Lock, just downstream of which are public moorings. In general, these are the head of navigation. It is well worth proceeding in one's dinghy, preferably rowing, through Jesus Lock, and exploring 'The Backs'. Punting on these waters is popular with both the eccentric exclusives and hoi polloi. For some sybarites it still seems appropriate to punt up to Granchester for breakfast after cavorting and carousing at the May Balls - no doubt touching the forelock in sycophantic style to that best-selling writing failure, Geoffrey Archer, who lives in the Old Vicarage where once ruled Rupert Brooke. Who haunts whom?

River Cam

Cambridge, settled as a ford by the Romans as Granta, grew to a market town in Saxon times. Legend has it that a group of students fled the Oxford Riots in 1209 and started up the rivalry. The first proper college, Peterhouse, was founded in 1284 after which the academic community quickly grew.

It was once noted for its eels, which managed (cleverly but stupidly) to navigate from the Gulf Stream right up the Fens. We haven't achieved that, but in the mini-odyssey from The Wash we have enjoyed such a variety of cruising experiences that it must take more than one season to exhaust them. The Cam is a miniature - but it takes an awful lot of moving to get to it - and it is all very well worth it.

Places of interest

Wicken Fen National Nature Reserve (N.T.)
Tel. 01353 720274
Britain's oldest nature reserve with a boardwalk nature trail, Visitor Centre and restored Fenman's Cottage: open dawn to dusk daily

Anglesey Abbey, Lode (N.T.)
Tel. 01223 811200
16th century house and gardens built on site of Augustinian priory: landscaped gardens and working watermill: tel. for opening times

Boatyards
Fish & Duck Marina	01353 649580
Upware Marina	01353 721930
Tip Tree Marina	01223 440065
Norman Cole Marine, Upware	01223 860528
Shrubbs Wharf, Lode Fen Lode	01223 811812
Two Tees Boatyard, 70 Water St, Chesterton	01223 365597

Chandlers
Roy's Leisure, 70 Water St, Chesterton	01223 365597

Pubs
Fish & Duck,Popes Corner	01353 649580
Five Miles From Anywhere	01353 721930
Bridge Hotel, Waterbeach	01223 860252
Plough & Fleece, Horningsea	01223 860795
Plough Inn, Fen Ditton	01223 293264
Ancient Shepherds Inn, Fen Ditton	01223 293280
Pike & Eel, Chesterton	01223 425521
Fort St. George, Cambridge	01223 354327

River Nene
91 miles/57 km

To approach the River Nene from the Wash, the first buoy to locate after Roaring Middle is the Cardinal Bar Flat. The second is the lit green No. 1, and, after that, almost all leisure craft will be able to reach the Cardinal wreck buoy (RAF No. 4) where there is usually at least 16'5"/5.0m. Just to the west of Outer Westmark Knock, to the north of the Cardinal Kerr, there is good and spacious holding ground. However, there is need for caution when tending to the south on a big spring tide: it can be tricky, even for those with local knowledge.

Even with no more than 3'3"/1.0m draught it is best to wait for the flood to get well under way before you set off if you want to be sure of not finding the bottom. Prudence recommends, here particularly, that it is better not to try to set off other than 2 hours before High Water at the mouth of the river. There is an unusual, very noticeable monitoring 'island station' just to the south of the anchorage. The locals go by a rule that says once there is water all round the wall, craft with 4'11"/1.5m draught can start for Wisbech with confidence; having tested out the theory myself with the aid of good binoculars, I have found it completely efficacious.

After the RAF No 4 beacon, the channel takes a dog-leg course marked by No.3 green, Lake south conical and Don Buoy red. However, 1$\frac{1}{2}$ hours either side of High Water, it is safe (weather permitting) to make a direct track from 'Lake' to RAF No.4. Please note that the buoyage in this area is subject to change in the near future - as at March 1999. The majority of beacons are starboard marks, except the last pair which mark the Training Wall, Big Tom and West End; the former being left to port and the latter to starboard, both by about a cable. Nearby is the classic 'Crab's Hole'.

From here, the mainly man-made channel is straight ahead, with the (now disused) lighthouses hoving quickly into view. They speak of the days when so many big ships came to Wisbech that it was emboldened to call itself the Capital of the Fens. One of the lighthouses was host to Peter Scott, the well-known painter and naturalist.

Next comes Sutton Bridge, now the main harbour office. The river below here comes under the jurisdiction of the Port of Sutton Bridge, while the authority for the stretch between Wisbech and Bevis Hall is the Port of Wisbech. This area is the last berthing possibility before the Town Quay at Wisbech. There is a staging by the West Old Light, and near the swing bridge there are the remains of an old dock. In the summer there is the pontoon facility of the Peterborough Yacht Club.

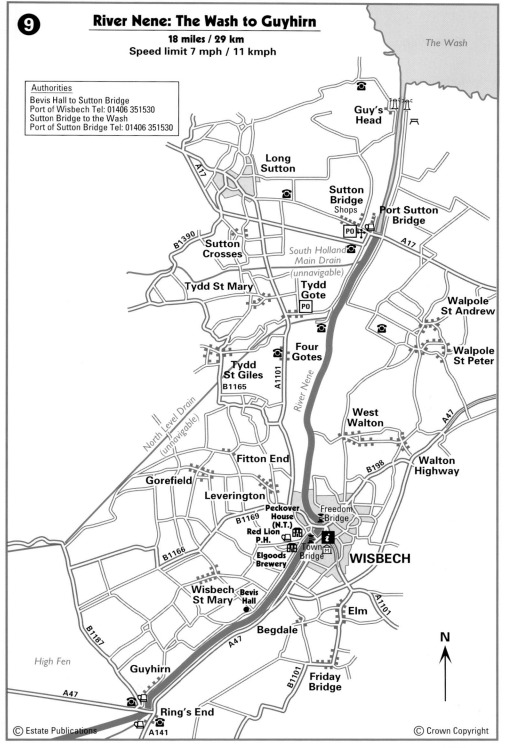

River Nene: The Wash to Guyhirn

9

18 miles / 29 km
Speed limit 7 mph / 11 kmph

Authorities
Bevis Hall to Sutton Bridge
Port of Wisbech Tel: 01406 351530
Sutton Bridge to the Wash
Port of Sutton Bridge Tel: 01406 351530

The Wash

Guy's Head

Long Sutton

Sutton Bridge
Shops

Port Sutton Bridge

A17

A17

Sutton Crosses

B1390

South Holland Main Drain
(unnavigable)

Tydd St Mary

Tydd Gote
PO

Walpole St Andrew

Four Gotes

Tydd St Giles
B1165

A1101

River Nene

Walpole St Peter

West Walton

A47

North Level Drain
(unnavigable)

Fitton End

Gorefield

Leverington

Peckover House (N.T.)

Red Lion P.H.

B1169

Elgoods Brewery

Freedom Bridge

Town Bridge

WISBECH

Walton Highway

B198

B1166

Wisbech St Mary

Bevis Hall

Elm

A1101

B1187

Begdale

A47

High Fen

Guyhirn

B1101

Friday Bridge

N

A47

Ring's End

A141

Moorings are still used by local fishermen and it is essential not to disrupt their routines: it is best to obtain prior permission. An over-tide stop is possible at all of these places by negotiation, should the need arise. However, that would be only for the skipper on his way out, awaiting his best departure time. It is not likely that any inward-bound skipper or crew would want to delay their arrival at the town quay.

Wisbech is undoubtedly a place of superb interest and character, and well worth a visit for domestics, food and drink. For those who have not visited the port for a year or two, and remember the difficulties of finding a decent berth, there is good news, for there are now floating alongside pontoons and facilities are being improved all the time. Efforts are more than afoot for moorings of up to 100 berths - plus first rate and exciting facilities. There are also pipeline plans for extra moorings at Sutton Bridge, and hopefully, south of Freedom Bridge and on Elgood's Bend. In addition, a specially detailed approach chart is intended. There is a strong run on the flood and ebb tides in Wisbech and these periods are best avoided.

For all but shallow-draught boats (less than 4'0"/1.2m), just below the bridge at Wisbech is considered to be the head of navigation. Skippers wishing to go further up river need to contact the keeper at the intriguingly named 'Dog-in-a-Doublet' lock well in advance, since there is often a shortage of water, thus preventing passage to Peterborough. True, much effort has been put into improving the accessibility into the inland waterways at this point, but loss of water and silting are factors with which the authorities (and boaters) still have to contend.

The old market town of Wisbech is remarkable in a number of ways. When the draining of the Fens took place in the 17th and 18th centuries, the farmland that was created brought great prosperity and even greater riches to the area; and this in turn brought increasing trade and commerce. The produce and products of the surrounding farmlands and artisans were dispatched via the port. Some of the results of the speedy wealth created thereby can still be seen today in the extraordinarily well-preserved and elegant houses and mansions. For example: Crescent and Museum Square both have very fine buildings, including the amazing Wisbech 'Castle' - a splendid example of Regency building. In addition, there are the two intriguingly named Brinks, 'North' and 'South'; presumably named because of their situation on opposing banks of the river. North Brink is said to be among the most famous and beautiful Georgian streets in England; and, in particular, situate there is Peckover House and its famous gardens, now administered by the National Trust. The walled garden is classic

Victorian, quiet and secret. The House was built in 1722, and bought by one Jonathan Peckover at the end of the century. He came from Fakenham and founded a local bank which was to become a part of Barclay's. The house is open to the public.

William Godwin was also a Wisbech man. He married Mary Wollstonecraft, and their daughter Mary, married Shelley. Mary Shelley is more remembered in the town than is her father - no doubt for her (in)famous Frankenstein book. The town was also the birthplace in 1838 of Octavia Hill, one of the founders of the National Trust and a worker for housing reform, and there is a museum to her memory in South Brink.

If Fosdyke truly offers the recherché essence of the Fens, then Wisbech must offer the eccentric. In this unusual township you will find the old and the new, the stylish and the plebeian, the rich and the poor, the generous and the greedy, and the licentious and the prude, side by side and almost hand in hand; for it is a place of captivating contradictions.

When proceeding to the calmer non-tidal waters above the intriguingly named Dog-in-a-Doublet lock, it is necessary first to navigate the fixed road bridges in Wisbech. The heights and states of the tide, your draught and air draught all enter in the complicated equation that must be worked out before you will know whether or not such a project is feasible. For best help you should apply to the local fishermen or the staff at Sutton Bridge. You will discover that you are likely to need to add two hours on those times listed for the mouth of the river for the lock to be in your favour.

The river is tidal for 28 miles/17.5km downstream of the Dog-in-a-Doublet Lock, which was built in 1937 to control the flow of water from the Great Ouse and its tributaries into the tidal channel to the sea. Registered craft can pass through the lock daily between 0730 and sunset by prior arrangement: tel. 01733 202219; VHF Ch 77: if a boat is coming up they will be on the water (Mobile: 07887 831883).

Between Peterborough and Northampton there are 38 locks and 66 fixed bridges: some of the lower structures have inverted gauge boards to assist boat owners to judge the amount of headroom available.

There are few signs of contemporary urban civilisation along this, the low road to Peterborough. The first well known name is that of the riverside community of Guyhirn, where the area shows itself to be unflatteringly flat, pretty well treeless and nearly featureless: all features which make up the classic feature of The Fens. The stretch is also a good introduction to what is the standard regime of waterways life in the Fens: straight-line cruising. In addition, most of the agriculture has

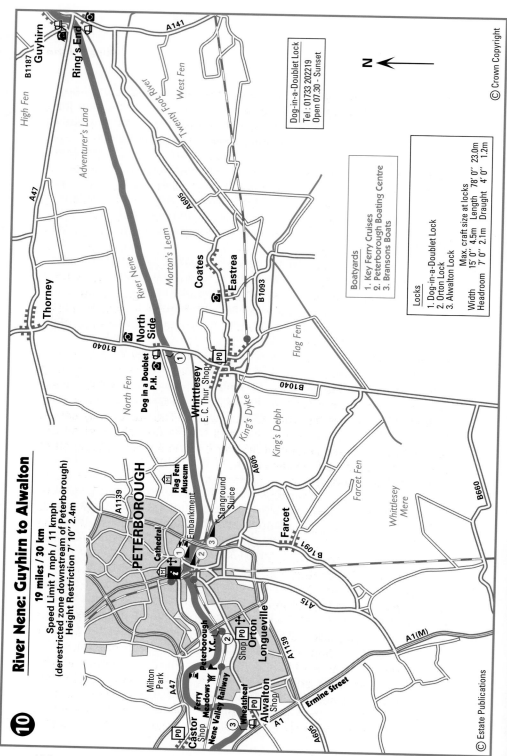

River Nene: Guyhirn to Alwalton

19 miles / 30 km

Speed Limit 7 mph / 11 kmph
(derestricted zone downstream of Peterborough)
Height Restriction 7' 10" 2.4m

Dog-in-a-Doublet Lock
Tel : 01733 202219
Open 07.30 - Sunset

Boatyards
1. Key Ferry Cruises
2. Peterborough Boating Centre
3. Bransons Boats

Locks
1. Dog-in-a-Doublet Lock
2. Orton Lock
3. Alwalton Lock

Max. craft size at locks
Width   15' 0" 4.5m   Length 78' 0" 23.0m
Headroom 7' 0" 2.1m   Draught   4' 0"   1.2m

© Crown Copyright

© Estate Publications

also succumbed to solid geometry. Only occasionally is there a waterway to be found wandering at its own sweet will. The villagers live below sea level, while the cruising fraternity lords it high above on water held back by massive banks. There is a small Puritan Chapel dating from 1660 (also somewhat ambiguously known as the Chapel of Ease) built with stone from the Thorney Abbey. Inside it is predictably bleak; and the date of its last service, 5th November 1960, is symbolic of the need to burn up the licence in the overwhelming advance of the Swinging 60's. From here, it is 8 miles/12.8km up to the lock with one of the most intriguing lock names in the country: The Dog-in a-Doublet. The nearby eponymous pub has a very good restaurant, much patronised by anglers as well as boaters. Downstream of Peterborough there is a derestricted zone where water-skiing is permitted. En route for Peterborough we pass the small community of Whittlesey, about which more is said on p.172 and the entrance to the Middle Levels (described on p.169) and the route to the Great Ouse via Stanground Sluice.

The city of Peterborough was originally known as Medeshamstede ('meadow homestead') around 600AD when there was the beginning of an abbey. After the Danes ravished the place around 870AD, there seemed no future, but God intervened in the form of St Aethelwold, ordering him, as was his wont, to build again. The saint finally settled on remaindered Medeshamstede and built a church. Just before 1000AD the battle-settlement (burh) took its name from its church of St Peter and became St Peter's Burh.

The first river crossing was built here in 1308 by Abbot Godfrey of Croyland. It was made of wood and survived a short-lived one-year-only tenure: it had cost £13. The second fared little better, lasting only eleven years more. Later, wooden bridges were superseded by the 1872 iron bridge. The present structure was erected in 1934. Peterborough has some special features: the East of England Ice Rink; the splendid 17th century Guildhall and the Queensgate shopping centre. In addition, Peterborough Cathedral is an outstanding achievement. The first monastery on the site was built in the 7th century. It became the Benedictine Abbey of St Peter (famous for the Anglo-Saxon Chronicle) and the present edifice, a brilliant example of Romanesque building, goes back to the 12th century. Henry VIII bestowed the status of cathedral in the mid 16th century. The Cathedral possessed one of the finest Norman interiors in England until it was vandalised by Parliamentary soldiers in the Civil War. One of the monuments they destroyed was the tomb of Catherine of Aragon, the first wife of Henry VIII, but her grave is still here - unlike that of Mary, Queen of Scots, who was buried here in 1587 but moved to Westminster Abbey in 1612 by her son James I. Luckily Cromwell's soldiers could not reach the remarkable painted wooden ceiling of 1220, bearing pictures of clerics, saints, and mythical beasts. There is fine 15th-century fan-vaulting at the east end of the chancel, and the massive arches of the 13th century West Front are awe-inspiring.

Peterborough offers a number of leisure attractions. Boaters have excellent access, via the Embankment into the city - and there is also access for launching canoes. There are basic facilities just downstream of the Key Theatre, where long and short term moorings are available.

As we approach Orton, the first lock after Peterborough, we pass the few remains of the fortified 14th century Longthorpe Tower: but only to be seen if you excavate the Thorpe Wood golf course for it has been long, long lost to the earth beneath. The village of Longthorpe itself, has a church dedicated to St Botolph - but nothing to rival Boston's. Peterborough Yacht Club's HQ come shortly just after the lock; with the Nene Valley Railway Station and Orton Mere to hand. The Ferry Meadows 500-acre country park, which forms a focal point in the much larger Nene Park, has meadows, lakes, the Lynch and Bluebell Woods and badger watches, as well as two first-class golf courses, fishing, watersports galore, bird-watching, cycling and a sailing centre. It was created by the extraction of 5 million tons of sand and gravel used in the making of roads and buildings in the 70's expansion of the city.

The village of Orton Longueville close by, with decent basic facilities is a pretty place with its notable Orton Hall and 13th century Holy Trinity Church. After a long haul round the 3 mile/4.8km bend, the next lock is Alwalton, with a small village that has the basics and moorings provided by the Peterborough Cruising Club. The old Roman settlement of Durobrivae is nearby: it produced some of the finest Roman pottery. Castor itself is built on the site of a 3rd century Roman villa.

The Nene Valley Railway runs a 15 mile/24km round trip through Nene Park, from Peterborough, past the NVR's HQ at Wansford Station, into the haunted Wansford tunnel and on to Yarwell Junction. On the opposite side of the A1 to Wansford stands the village of Stibbington, where there is a boatyard.

The next three locks are more or less equidistant at about 2 miles/3.2km. The first, Water Newton, has an attractive waterside village with little more than a telephone and post box; the next is

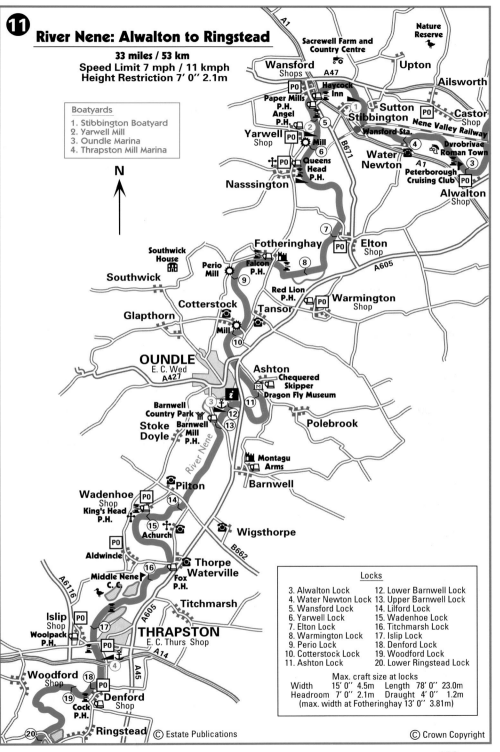

River Nene: Alwalton to Ringstead

11

33 miles / 53 km
Speed Limit 7 mph / 11 kmph
Height Restriction 7' 0'' 2.1m

Boatyards
1. Stibbington Boatyard
2. Yarwell Mill
3. Oundle Marina
4. Thrapston Mill Marina

N
↑

Nature Reserve

Sacrewell Farm and Country Centre

Wansford Shops
A47
Upton

Ailsworth

PO **Haycock Inn**

Paper Mills P.H.
Angel P.H.

Sutton
Stibbington
PO **Castor** Shop

Nene Valley Railway

Wansford Sta.

Yarwell PO
Shop
Mill

Dvrobrivae Roman Town

Water Newton
A1

Queens Head P.H.

Peterborough Cruising Club
PO

Nasssington

Alwalton Shop

Southwick House

Fotheringhay
PO **Elton** Shop

A605

Southwick

Perio Mill
Falcon P.H.

Cotterstock
Glapthorn
Mill

Tansor
Red Lion P.H.
PO **Warmington** Shop

OUNDLE
E. C. Wed
A427

Ashton
Chequered Skipper
Dragon Fly Museum

Barnwell Country Park
Barnwell Mill P.H.

Stoke Doyle

Polebrook

River Nene

Pilton

Montagu Arms

Barnwell

Wadenhoe PO
Shop
King's Head P.H.

Wigsthorpe

Achurch
PO
Aldwincle

B662

Thorpe Waterville
Fox P.H.

Middle Nene C. C.

Titchmarsh

A605

Islip PO
Shop
Woolpack P.H.

A6116

A14

THRAPSTON
E. C. Thurs Shop

Woodford Shop

A45

Denford Shop

Cock P.H.

Ringstead

© Estate Publications

Locks

3. Alwalton Lock	12. Lower Barnwell Lock
4. Water Newton Lock	13. Upper Barnwell Lock
5. Wansford Lock	14. Lilford Lock
6. Yarwell Lock	15. Wadenhoe Lock
7. Elton Lock	16. Titchmarsh Lock
8. Warmington Lock	17. Islip Lock
9. Perio Lock	18. Denford Lock
10. Cotterstock Lock	19. Woodford Lock
11. Ashton Lock	20. Lower Ringstead Lock

Max. craft size at locks
Width 15' 0'' 4.5m   Length 78' 0'' 23.0m
Headroom 7' 0'' 2.1m   Draught 4' 0'' 1.2m
(max. width at Fotheringhay 13' 0'' 3.81m)

© Crown Copyright

159

Wansford, with good village facilities. It often takes upon itself the superior nomenclature of Wansford-In-England. It has a brilliantly eccentric high-arched bridge; an interestingly old St Mary's Church and the big well-known old coaching post, the Haycock Inn. There are those in the Haycock who will tell you all, and more than all, about the man Barnabee and his part in the peculiar naming of the place.

And then we have pretty, stony Yarwell village (and lock) where there are boating facilities available at the mill with Nassington village next and very close. There are good moorings and facilities within easy reach of both. Another 3 miles/4.8km brings Elton and another two to Warmington. They are both miniature experiences, and are perhaps most significant since they lead us up to the (in)famous bridge at the (in)famous village of Fotheringhay, which has a magnificent church and famous lantern tower. The infamy is to be found unearthed by the remains of the motte and bailey, all that is left of the great Fotheringhay Castle where Mary Queen of Scots was improsoned in 1586 and beheaded on 8 February 1587, at the age of 45. It is said that Scots Thistles, said to have been planted by Mary, still flower each year - but no-one claims that they bleed.

Mary was held here for twenty years. After much so-called heart searching, she was tried and convicted of treason. At the castle, the first executioner to try his luck failed to do more than make a scratch. The second succeeded and it is said that when the head fell it changed, in Hammer Horror style from that of a beautiful queen to that of an old wizened hag. Afterwards, her clothes were burned and her heart cut out and secreted by the sheriff.

The famous Perio Mill and gravel pits lie in the loop of the river just before the next port of call: Cotterstock, a village that is quiet these days, but was once a busy Roman settlement; where, in fact, the Romans themselves may even have built the first mill here ... on the site of the present one. John Dryden stayed here once, and was fed on 'venison and marrow pudding' because of his ailing health. By the next lock at Ashton there is the intriguingly named pub, the Chequered Skipper and the National Dragonfly Museum is housed at Ashton Mill. Ashton is the host to some oddities: the village itself is believed to be wholly owned by the Rothschild family; the pub is believed to be named after a butterfly and the annual World Conker Championship is held there!

And now for the Barnwells and Oundle, where there are plenty of places to moor and plenty of things to do. Oundle is blessed with possessing its namesake marina, and indeed thrice blessed since it is home to the famous public school, founded in 1556 by a London grocer. Perhaps the school's most famous head was Frederick Sanderson who ruled (without a rod to spare or spoil the child) from 1892 to 1922. He believed that never a bad boy was born: all that was needed was something to fire a boy's imagination and he would automatically be won over to the joys of academe.

There are some fine buildings in the town, some built from the remains of Fotheringhay Castle. The Talbot Hotel's staircase is the one (it is said) that Mary walked down all in black. More cheerful is the news for anglers, for in season, the waterway is full of tench and carp; with the mouth of the canal being favourite. For boaters, the happy homes are with Oundle Cruising Club downstream of the road and, of course, the marina.

The good-walk-away village of Barnwell on the opposite bank has few facilities. Barnwell Castle and Manor were once in the glorious hands of the Duke and Duchess of Gloucester, who seemed to live there happily in consort with the ghost of a monk who supposedly brandishes his whip at all commoners - but in the presence of royalty turns it upon himself. The Castle was probably built in 1266.

Lilford Lock and Pilton are a very small community indeed, with the church house, the watch house and the manor house making an attractive trio for any boater with an easel to hand and a paintbrush in his hand, his hand, his hand.... and the same may be said of the village of Wadenhoe, where the King's Head will slake your thirst in a pretty rural stone-made community where supping the ale offers one of the finest riverside settings and affords glorious views. The Church of St Michael & All Angels has a Norman tower and a team of campanologists who are not entirely mad but are mad keen to make sure you know of their bells and their skills. The village is said to have its roots in the Iron Age; and its name is supposed to hail from the Saxon for 'Wada's spur of land'.

Thorpe Waterville comes next, with the remains of yet another Norman castle - but with few facilities except a pub. (The small man-made island you pass on the right bank on the way upstream is a good spot for fishing.) Further away, on the other side of the river is Aldwincle, with equally few services, but proudly boasting as the birth-place of John Dryden. He came into the world in 1631 in the rectory and went out in 1670 as Royal Historiographer and Poet Laureate, the first poet officially to hold the title. In 1681 he wrote his first and probably his greatest political satire, 'Absalom and Achitophel'. The village is not quite dry, for the PO has a licence; but there is no pub.

The next lock is Titchmarsh, where there is a weir, and a mill for the HQ of the Middle Nene Cruising Club. The most appealing features in the neighbourhood are the waterway known somewhat romantically as Thrapston Lagoon and the nearby Nature Reserve. The former, at 210 acres, is one of the biggest gravel pits in the country. The latter has 50 acres of flooded gravel pits, meadows and woodland and is famous for its heronry and for having well over a hundred breeds of birds coming in and out of its territory.

After Islip Lock, and its tiny village (with tiny facilities) and Woolpack pub comes the larger village of Thrapston with larger everythings; once upon a time having the mixed blessing of two railway stations. They are separated by the river and joined by a big mediaeval stone bridge. Of mediaeval origin, five arches were rebuilt following a devastating flood in 1795. The big Mill was still grinding corn until 1960. At Islip, the cognoscenti say the river changes it name from Neen to Nenn - and never the twain shall meet ... so watch your step, or your wash as the case may be.

After the out-of-town Thrapston Marina, we move on to Denford Lock and hamlet with its fine riverside church: the 13th century Holy Trinity with much warm stained glass. And then on to the larger Woodford village and lock. Here are pubs, stores, a village green and another church (St Mary) overlooking the water. This village also goes back to Saxon times. There is a legend here of another secreted heart found in the nave of the Virgin's church: the masons who were restoring stone work found one fully mummified. Stories abound as to its history - and if you have the inclination, you can make up your own based on the real thing - for it is now behind glass in the very spot where it was found.

Then, in quick succession, come the Upper and Lower Ringstead locks, where there are weirs, bridges and moorings in the vicinity. Ringstead village, which is not all that very close by to the east, goes back to Saxon times, and has one of two famous mills still standing: the Willy Watt Mill. Great Addington, with its Hare and Hounds pub, is about the same distance to the west. Still on the same patch (before we reach the greater commerce of Irthlingborough) there is another Addington to the south of the Great; it is Little Addington, with the Bell pub and phone by the church.

Irthlingborough itself, has two eye-catching features: the 14th century ten-arched bridge; and the lantern tower of St Peter's Church. Inside the church there is a lot to see, but the 'must' on the trip is the view from the top of the tower, where on a clear day you can easily spy the twinned settlement across the river: Higham Ferrers. The small town has good facilities and an important market place. It has an intriguing Bede House, going back to early 15th century, when it played host to

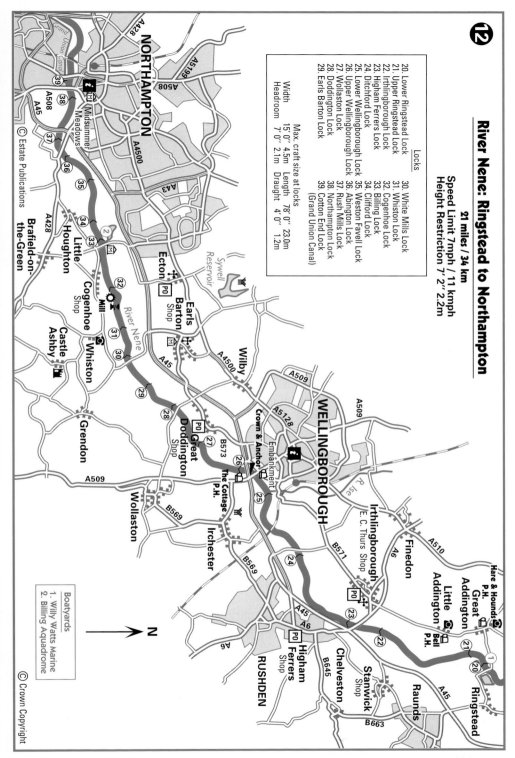

River Nene: Ringstead to Northampton

21 miles / 34 km

Speed Limit 7mph / 11 kmph
Height Restriction 7' 2" 2.2m

Locks

20. Lower Ringstead Lock
21. Upper Ringstead Lock
22. Irthlingborough Lock
23. Higham Ferrers Lock
24. Ditchford Lock
25. Lower Wellingborough Lock
26. Upper Wellingborough Lock
27. Wollaston Lock
28. Doddington Lock
29. Earls Barton Lock
30. White Mills Lock
31. Whiston Lock
32. Cogenhoe Lock
33. Billing Lock
34. Clifford Lock
35. Weston Favell Lock
36. Abington Lock
37. Rush Mills Lock
38. Northampton Lock
39. Cotton End Lock
    (Grand Union Canal)

	Max. craft size at locks		
Width	15' 0"	4.5m	
Length	78' 0"	23.0m	
Draught	4' 0"	1.2m	
Headroom	7' 0"	2.1m	

© Estate Publications

Boatyards
1. Willy Watts Marine
2. Billing Aquadrome

N

© Crown Copyright

163

River Nene

"12 poor old men" (whatever they were) and "a female attendant" (whatever she was). All in all it sounds like something from a mediaeval Beckett (Sam not Tom). Not only is there good shopping hereabouts, but also first rate bird-watching in the sanctuaries.

All of which is good stuff, since the prophet of all this sort of rural shenanigans, HE(MAN) BATES, spent much of his childhood on a farm near Higham Ferrers. At 16, he was a junior reporter on the Northampton Chronicle & Echo. Later he wrote in spare hours, and had his first novel rejected nine times. Like Thomas Hardy, he used local locales, with pseudonyms: e.g., 'Nenweald' was perhaps Irchester; 'Evensford', Rushden; 'Nenborough', Wellingborough) - and Northampton and Addington as such, actually get honourable mentions.

Moving on, by Ditchford Lock, there has been a bridge for over 700 years, and the Domesday Book speaks of a mill. Today, it is known among county anglers as being an excellent spot for sport.

The confluence of the river Ise with the Nene has made Irchester and its crossings one of the most important stages on the river's course - which it was for centuries. Relics go back not only to the old Roman town, but also to the Iron Age. As for more recent achievements, the magnificent Wellingborough viaduct carries trains from all round the area to London. The locks at Irchester are the twinned Lower and Upper Wellingboroughs.

When we come to Wellingborough itself, we move into non-rural, non-riparian and therefore, foreign territory, as the 'other' world takes over. Unlike Wisbech, Wellingborough's town centre is full well removed from the river; but like that other Nene capital, it has its elegant grandeurs, in this case The Walks. The famous school goes back to Richard II and still has bits of its fabrics remaining. A great fan of the mad peasant poet Clare was born here: John Askham was the poor son of a poor cobbler born in 1825. He published five volumes of verse in all, and got Queen's monies to the tune of £50. His obsession with his master took him to name his home after him (Clare Cottage) where he died in 1894, a pretty old and broken 69.

Wellingborough, like Bath, had its wells and springs. Red and White Wells were so called because the red had iron - good for the red corpuscles and the White Well no doubt good for the other. (Though it is doubtful whether Bernard Shaw would have had any of this - as he exposed this and 'stimulating the phagocytes' in his 'Doctor's Dilemma'.) Later, a brewery tried to exploit the idea, but no-one made any serious money out of the project - and it died a quiet death.

Wollaston and Doddington Locks share what Great Doddington has to offer, which is not much more than a shop, PO, a pub, a church and a manor house: there is a pleasant path to the village. Thomas A Becket is supposed to have tried to gain refuge at Hardwater Mill after fleeing Northampton. The nuns of the local abbey are said to have tried to save the meddling priest before he failed to save himself.

Hardly any distance upriver, it must be admitted that Earls Barton is a larger and more appealing prospect, with a most promising church (although it must also be agreed that there is a plenitude of such around here). Its Saxon architecture was a watch tower and battle mark well before the Norman Conquest. It was originally called Barton, but just like most of Jane Austen's upstart relatives, it was not happy to leave well alone and pompous additions had to be acquired. In this case it was Earls, taken on, in the 12th century, no doubt to appease an irate Earl of Huntingdon, or as a sycophantic gesture simple. It is perhaps less of a walk to Earls Barton from White Mills Lock, than it is from the eponymous neighbour. Moving up, it is probably better to pass straight through Whiston Lock, missing out on the village and proceeding directly to Cogenhoe (mouthed by those who know as Cuck'no). The place first suffered its embarrassing cognomen at the hands of its Lordship of the Manor, Nicholas de Cogenhoe.

Ecton is a pretty place on the other side of the river, famous for the visit Benjamin Franklin made to the grave of his uncle - and for little else. It has few ministrations to offer the boater. Then we come to the Billing complex: the Billing and Clifford Hill Locks, Aquadrome and pubs and leisure all around: all a good reminder that the heavy business and high life of all Northampton is now very close. Just three locks to go: Weston Favell; Abington; and Rush Mills. The northern and western feeding arms of the river come together here, by the South Bridge, near the Northampton Branch of the Grand Union Canal which is entered at Cotton End Lock. For those seekers out of the truth, the real thing, the indubitable head of Nene navigation is just up the northern course, at West Bridge.

The Northampton Branch of the Grand Union Canal extends 4 miles/6.4km before joining the main Grand Union Canal at Gayton Junction: the restricting dimensions on this stretch are 70'0"/21.4m x 7'0"/2.1m with air draught of 7'0"/2.1m.

Northampton is famous world-wide for its supremacy in the foot world for its shoes and boots (ironically, but not for its football - where the word infamous is often heard!) and totem to that claim is the town's Central Museum and Art Gallery, with the most comprehensive and definitive exhibition of footwear - as well as the machinery - in the world. Favourite exhibits on show are Queen Victoria's wedding shoes; the shoes of Nijinsky and Fonteyn; and one for an elephant. It is, therefore, quite wrong to issue the charge that it is nothing but a load of old cobblers.

A Little History

Little or Large, it goes way back: excavations have established that folk have been around here for around 5,500 years and some exposed earthworks showed sites for Neolithic rituals. Archaeologists suggest the regime was in operation from about 3500BC, falling out of fashion about 2000BC. There is a written record from 913AD of fighting men from 'Hamtun' marching out to attack marauders. As a Saxon town, it was sacked by the Danes but fully reinstated by the Normans who built a vast castle (on the site of the present railway station) and it had a vast mediaeval market square to go with it . Legend has it that in 1213, King John bought a pair of boots here for ninepence, perhaps setting in motion the regime whereby every regiment in the English army since Cromwell has been shod by goods from Northampton. (The Roundheads ordered 4,600 pairs of boots and shoes in 1642 for tramping through Ireland, and the industry never looked back; disproving the concept that an army marches on its stomach!).

Wars and rumours of wars were not unknown to the city. In 1264 an army of dissident knights joined forces here, to be defeated by Henry III. In the event, the knights got off lightly, but the town was raped and pillaged; and in 1460 came the Battle of Northampton, when Earls Warwick and March took Henry VI prisoner in battle; and right at the beginning of the Civil War, the town was attacked by (that foreigner) Rupert and his 2,000 strong army. He got nowhere; anti-royalism being very strong - strange for a place with Althorp so near and dear to its heart.

While the Plague actually and exactly decimated many towns, Northampton escaped such a fate; although half the inhabitants succumbed in 1349 - and nearly a sixth again in 1638. Nor was The Plague the town's only marauding enemy: fire also was a continuing hazard. The first terrible conflagration was in 1516, but the worst was the great fire of 1675, which engulfed almost all of the town - but the townsfolk rallied to their own defence, rebuilding the Norman tower shortly after. At one time the denizens could lay claim to living in the third largest town in the country.

Today Northampton still thrives: John Clare was pent up for his last twenty years in the local lunatic asylum - it is said his ghost still walks. These days his haunts and hauntings can be different: for ever since 1972 he has been able to indulge his passion for drunk writing by visiting the Carlsberg Brewery which has brought great employment (of every kind) to the town.

This may not be an absolutely true picture of the Nene and its territory, but I like to think it can stand in tribute to the river, its ambience, its history, its culture and its people - past and present.

My Early Home. John Clare: 13th July 1793 - 20th May 1864

Here sparrows build upon the trees,
And stockdove hides her nest;
The leaves are winnowed by the breeze
Into a calmer rest:
The blackcap's song was very sweet,
That used the rose to kiss ;
It made the Paradise complete:
My early home was this.

Boatyards and Facilities

Bransons Boats, Stanground Sluice	01733 322811
Peterborough Boating Centre	01733 566688
Peterborough Embankment	01733 317386
King Ferry Cruisers	01933 680743
Stibbington Boatyard	01780 783144
Yarwell Mill	01780 782247
Oundle Marina	01832 272672
Thrapston Mill Marina	01832 732850
Willy Watt Marine	01933 622038
Wellingborough Embankment	01933 229777
Billing Aquadrome	01604 408181
Midsummer Meadows, Northampton	01604 233500

Places of interest

Peckover House, Wisbech (N.T.)
Tel. 01945 583463
18th century merchant's house and Victorian garden: open end Mar - Nov, wed, sat, sun 1230 - 1700: gardens only mon & tue 1230 - 1700

Elgoods Brewery, North Brink, Wisbech
Tel.01945 583160
independent working brewery : open May - 10 Oct., wed - sun & bank hols. 1300 - 1700; brewery tours wed - fri at 1430

Wisbech and Fenland Museum, Wisbech

Tel. 01945 583817

local history: open Jan - 27 Mar, tue - sat 1000 - 1600; Apr - Sept, tue - sat 100 - 1700; Oct - end Dec, tue to sat 1000 - 1600

Octavia Hill Birthplace Museum, Wisbech

Tel.01945 476358

museum commemorating the life and work of the social reformer and co-founder of the National Trust: open 3 mar - end Oct wed - sun & bank hols.1400 - 1730

Railworld, Oundle Rd, Peterborough

Tel.01733 344240

train exhibitions, mainly modern: open 1100 - 1600 mon - fri and at weekends from Mar to end Oct

Nene Valley Railway, Stibbington

Tel. 01780 784444

runs for 7.5 miles from Peterborough to Wansford with over 28 steam and diesel locomotives: open daily 0930 - 1630

Sacrewell Farm and Country Centre, Thornhaugh

Tel. 01780 782254

500 acre farm with working watermill, farm displays and nature trails: open daily summer 0930 - 1800; winter 0900 - 1700

River Nene Fishing

The source of the river is out of our scope, being well to the west of Northampton. Because the river is so abundantly and efficiently locked, there is seldom anything like a swift flow. The consequence of this for the man after roach and bream is an almost constantly optimistic proposition; with the former being very forthcoming during the summer between Oundle and Orton. Upstream of Northampton, chancing for chub and dicing for dace always puts the odds with the angler. Most recent news is that barbel are being fed back.

Near Ringstead, in the gravel pit known as Ringstead Shallows, is a site well known as the home of the one-time biggest carp in the UK.

The Middle Levels

Between Peterborough in the west and Ely in the east, lie the Middle Levels, a network of (barely) navigable waterways which forms an intriguing and quite backward-looking link between the Rivers Nene and Great Ouse. Falling under the jurisdiction of the Middle Level Commissioners, from whom further information can be obtained, they form a fascinating area to explore, as well as providing a link from the Great Ouse to the inland waterway system via the River Nene from Peterborough to Northampton and thence to the Grand Union Canal via the Northampton Branch.

Because the primary purpose of many of the Middle Level waterways is drainage, it is essential to get up-to-date information before embarking on a passage. Some of the smaller drains and rivers, such as the Forty Foot are available only at certain times: please see page 176 for further details.

For those who wish to move on without exploring, the closest approach to a direct route is from Peterborough through Stanground Sluice, and along Kings Dyke, Whittlesey Dyke and the Old River Nene to March, then via Well Creek through Outwell and out through Salters Lode Lock onto the tidal river at Denver, a trip of just under 30 miles/48km. You can then travel along the New Bedford River to Earith or pass through Denver Sluice to go up the Great Ouse to Ely. (For details of Denver Sluice, please see p.115).

In the slang of Scunthorpe (where I was born) a tenfoot was an alley with that exact measurement - often between the back-gardens of terraced houses. So; in the Middle Levels, many of the channels are known by their original lengths: for example, 'Hundred Foot Drain'; 'Forty Foot' (or Vermuyden's Drain). The Dutchman probably did much better than he knew; and he certainly did up the Thames, where he finally settled and made a fortune. While the original and principal purpose of the drains was drainage, from their very inception they were exploited for their transport potential. The idea was formalised in 1754 by a Parliamentary Act which established the right to navigation, and field crops (especially beet), fuel and building materials were being ferried hither and yon; but for decades now commercial traffic has gone and it is only small leisure craft that use the waterways.

Kings Dyke and Whittlesey Dyke

The first station out of Peterborough is Stanground Sluice. It is necessary to notify the lock-keeper (Tel.01733 566413) 24 hours in advance of a required locking. There can be a dangerous undertow - so do not

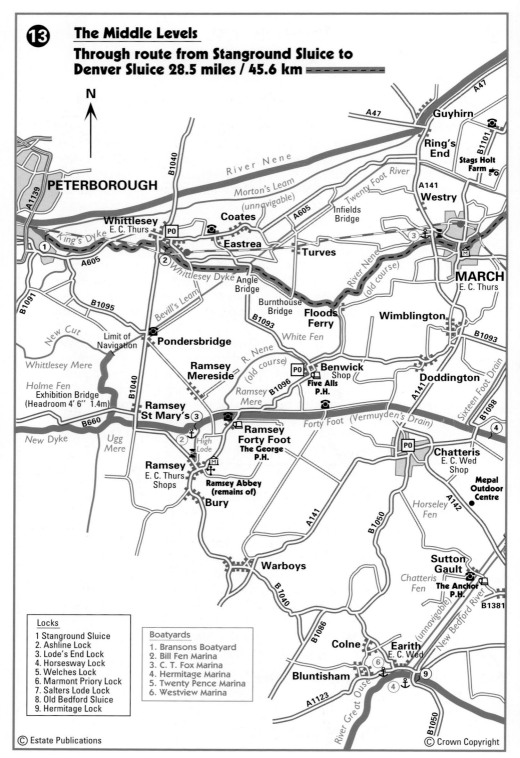

The Middle Levels

Through route from Stanground Sluice to Denver Sluice 28.5 miles / 45.6 km - - - - - - -

N

PETERBOROUGH

River Nene

Morton's Leam (unnavigable)

A47

Guyhirn

Ring's End

Stags Holt Farm

Westry

A141

Whittlesey E. C. Thurs

King's Dyke

Coates

Eastrea

Whittlesey Dyke

Angle Bridge

Infields Bridge

A605

Turves

River Nene (old course)

MARCH E. C. Thurs

Bevill's Leam

Burnthouse Bridge

B1093

Floods Ferry

White Fen

R. Nene (old course)

Wimblington

B1093

Limit of Navigation

Pondersbridge

Ramsey Mereside

Ramsey Mere

B1096

Benwick Shop

Five Alls P.H.

Doddington

A141

Sixteen Foot Drain

B1098

New Cut

Whittlesey Mere

Holme Fen
Exhibition Bridge
(Headroom 4' 6" 1.4m)

B1040

Ramsey 'St Mary's'

Ramsey Forty Foot
The George P.H.

Forty Foot (Vermuyden's Drain)

PO

Chatteris E. C. Wed Shop

Mepal Outdoor Centre

A142

New Dyke

B660

Ugg Mere

High Lode

Ramsey E. C. Thurs Shops

Ramsey Abbey (remains of)

Bury

A141

Horseley Fen

B1050

Warboys

B1040

Chatteris Fen

Sutton Gault

The Anchor P.H.

B1381

(unnavigable) New Bedford River

B1086

Colne

Earith E. C. Wed

Bluntisham

A1123

River Great Ouse

B1050

Locks
1 Stanground Sluice
2 Ashline Lock
3 Lode's End Lock
4 Horsesway Lock
5 Welches Lock
6 Marmont Priory Lock
7 Salters Lode Lock
8 Old Bedford Sluice
9 Hermitage Lock

Boatyards
1. Bransons Boatyard
2. Bill Fen Marina
3. C. T. Fox Marina
4. Hermitage Marina
5. Twenty Pence Marina
6. Westview Marina

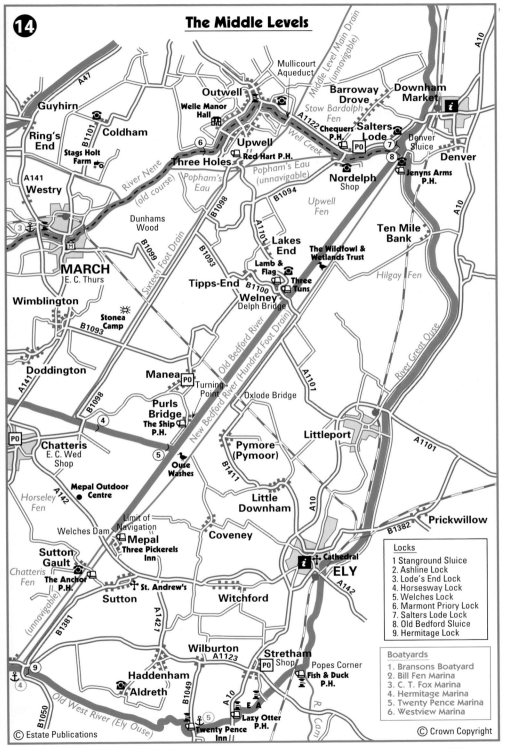

The Middle Levels

14

Locks
1 Stanground Sluice
2 Ashline Lock
3 Lode's End Lock
4 Horsesway Lock
5 Welches Lock
6 Marmont Priory Lock
7 Salters Lode Lock
8 Old Bedford Sluice
9 Hermitage Lock

Boatyards
1. Bransons Boatyard
2. Bill Fen Marina
3. C. T. Fox Marina
4. Hermitage Marina
5. Twenty Pence Marina
6. Westview Marina

© Estate Publications

© Crown Copyright

enter the lock before the lock-keeper has given his go-ahead, and the lock can be a bit brutal in its working - so be cautious. Restricting dimensions are: LOA: 49'0"/15m; Beam 11' 6"/3.5m; with a cill depth of 2'3"/0.7m. In favourable conditions the lock-keeper may possibly be able to 'flash' you through even if you are a little deeper. Stanground Creek is also known as Broadwater or Back River.

On Kings Dyke there are 8 bridges with a minimum headroom of approx. 7'0"/2.1m. There are shoals and shallows on Whittlesey Dyke where there is also a minimum headroom of approx. 7'0"/2.1m, the lowest bridge being Burnthouse Bridge. At Whittlesey Briggate, there is a notoriously sharp corner and the width between the walls narrows to no more than 14'0"/4.3m. The speed limit here is 4 mph.

Ashline Lock, just outside Whittlesey, is unattended and requires an Ouse Key. There is a winding hole for craft up to 70'0"/21.0m and a landing stage. Care is required when near the old upstream weir. Near Ashline Lock is the leisure centre of Manor Fields with very useful moorings, sited on what were the outskirts of mediaeval Whittlesey. Whittlesey itself is a small town that does not flaunt its waterway - most of the time hiding it behind walls. The spiritual centre is the 17th century Butter Cross; and the spirituous incongruity is the pub called 'B', its title going back to the days when there were so many pubs that names were foregone in favour of initials. One of these survives in Church Street. Wisbech real ale is readily available.

Dating back well before the Butter Cross is the January Straw Bear festival: a specially elected man, attired in apparel of straw, cavorts in the streets - dancing to the tunes of an assembly of Morris Men and dancers. This kind of Festival (bringing to a conclusion the Fool King's reign for a year) was still practised at the beginning of the century in the more remote parts of the country - including the ritual slaughter of the poor fellow. His blood and his progeny (for the King's Oats were wildly sown) were intended to guarantee fertile folk and fields - as well as bountiful crops. It is a hangover from pagan times.

The church is of interest because of its splendid spire and 15th century tower. Whittlesey Museum in the Town Hall, Market Street, has a large collection of local photographs and an even larger one of the tools of brickmaking, along with the Sir Harry Smith exhibition of 'A Brickmaker's Living Room' - all very appropriate when one considers that all around are the creators of a substantially large part of the material which makes up London; for here are England's biggest brick-works, with sky-raking 'shafts' (chimneys) and vertical-sided pits deep down into the gault clay. It is from here and from Fletton near Peterborough that the cheap red moulded bricks that make up so much of modern England come in such prodigious quantities.

To the south, Whittlesey Mere, was once the biggest of the open waters of Fenland. Big sailing vessels once sailed its waters: one of them which had sunk with a cargo of stone was discovered when the Mere was drained in 1850 - an act which extinguished the last of the great copper butterflies of this country. The draining was accomplished by the powerful new Appold Pump which had been on display at the Great Exhibition at Crystal Palace the same year. The pump, with a diameter of 4'11"/1.5m and driven by a twin-cylinder steam engine, discharged the waters of the mere at the rate of 1,652 gallons a minute from a new sluice erected at Johnson's Point, from where it was conveyed to the Bevills Leam drain. The receding waters of the shrinking mere revealed hundreds of tons of fish, most of which were left to rot. Among the dying masses of roach, bream, tench, perch and eels was a huge pike said to weigh 52lb, and which measured 55"/1.4m long. It is accepted by many authorities as the biggest pike ever recorded in England. The same fish - or another of similar size - had been seen two years earlier by a young naturalist searching the shallow pools around the mere's reeded edges for the nest of a rare savi's warbler. He was astonished to see the huge pike grab a fully grown swan by the neck, drag it beneath the surface and, apparently, devour it! Also uncovered after the draining were skulls of wild boar and wolves, while deep beneath the peat was found the fossilised skeleton of a killer whale that had roamed this area hundreds of thousands of years earlier when it was beneath sea level. Out in the centre of the mere bed, and dating from more recent times, was a one-piece boat, cut from the trunk of an oak tree and measuring 27'0" /8.2m long by over 3'0"/0.9m wide. Nearby were discovered the silver 'Ramsey Abbey Censer' and 'Incense Boat' dating from c.1325 and identified as coming from Ramsey Abbey: they were probably lost out on the mere during a great storm as the monks attempted to flee from Viking raiders.

Holme Fen nature reserve, with its birch woodland and flooded pits formed by peat extraction, stands on the south-western edge of Whittlesey Mere. Once covering 2,000 acres of low-lying fenland, the mere was one of the largest freshwater lakes in southern Britain. In 1848, three years before it was completely drained, a timber post was driven through the soil into the underlying clay to measure the rate of peat shrinkage. In 1851 the post was replaced by a cast iron pillar, reputedly from the Great Exhibition at Crystal Palace. Originally level with the surface of the peat, the top of the post is now more than 12'0"/3.6m above the ground. A second post, erected in 1957, shows the drop in ground level at various dates. Since the land around Holme Fen is 9'0"/2.7m below sea-level, it is also the lowest- lying area in Britain.

A little to the north of Whittlesey, we come across the unnavigable Morton's Leam (or Leap), dug, in an almost exact easterly direction, to the orders of one Bishop Morton, who as the Abbot of Ely in 1480 had financial ambitions well beyond the benefits of his See. His scheme chopped out a huge piece of the River Nene from Peterborough to Wisbech. His idea was sound, but the work was imperfect and eventually another Cut had to be made - that of the present course of The Nene. While, almost back on track again, just up the Twenty Foot River is the small village of Coates with its large grassy green and small yellowy church. A little further along, past Turves, is Infields Bridge with a minimum headroom of 5'11"/1.8m.

By Angle Bridge, Whittlesey Dyke crosses the Twenty Foot River to the north and Bevill's Leam to the south. Off the main drag, Bevill's Leam is just navigable - but only as far as the pumping station.

Old River Nene

In spite of the array of drains and the plethora of the straight lines of the man-made dykes, it is really pleasing to be able to see the Old River Nene still running its own course, wandering freely through the flat lands from Ramsey St Mary's and Lodes End Lock to Denver - not forgetting the entertainingly named Ugg Mere. The new works all started with Bishop Morton towards the end of the 15th century, and further inroads were made around the beginning of the 17th century. The diminutive Well Creek, which was once the outfall of the old course of the Nene, at no more than 2560 rods in length (18 miles/29km), played a vital part in the Ways of the Romans and also in the carriage of Barnack stone. This specially valued stone, which crept into every corner of the lowlands, and was of particular use in the construction of Ely Cathedral, was shipped along this route.

Moving down from Whittlesey Dyke into the Old River Nene and towards Ramsey and all its offshoots, we encounter Benwick with a strangely named pub: The Five Alls. The argument goes like this: lawyer; "I Plead for All"; parson; "I Pray for All"; soldier: "I Fight for All'; Queen Victoria; "I Rule All"; Fenman with hand to plough: "I PAY FOR ALL".

The village itself is suffering from the sinking feet that come with the settling of peat - and the buildings are consequently deteriorating. Houses with their front rooms built on the gravel of a dried-up river, and their back rooms on the changeful peat, soon move out of the vertical - to vie with Pisa. Nearby, is the small village of

Doddington, which, in its heyday, was the site of one of the palaces of the Bishops of Ely. At a slightly lowlier level, one of their rectors, one Christopher Tye, is renowned for penning the tune for 'While Shepherds Watch their Flocks by Night'. Legend has it that he dared to comment on Queen Elizabeth I's poor hearing and tastes in music; a most unlikely tale, but the legend, like anon, is blamed for much!

Down to High Lode, and more of the Old River Nene we encounter a host of places, not faraway, but certainly with strange-sounding names: for example, near Ugg Mere is Nightingales Corner; then come just too many Fens and too many Meres (too many to visit for sure and perhaps too many to count even); but to polish all off are the Ramseys, with a list reading rather like the bible with its so-and-so begat so-and-so, and so-and-so begat so-and-so; for these are the names of the Ramseys: Mere - Mereside - Forty Foot - Ramsey St Mary's ... and, of course, not forgetting the firstborn: Ramsey Simple.

Ramsey is a market town based on the ruins of Abbot Ailwin's Abbey, which he set up in 969AD. His Benedictine Abbey flourished, and in the 12th and 13th centuries his was among the Top Ten - although Ramsey was not mentioned in the Big Book of 1086. Indeed, the wealth of the establishment there contended with that of Ely and Peterborough. All this came tumbling down with the Dissolution. The stonework of the Abbey itself was dismantled, and re-used to erect important buildings elsewhere, such as Caius, Kings and Trinity Colleges at Cambridge; the Abbey's lands went to Sir Richard Williams, Oliver Cromwell's Great Grandpa, with some of the gatehouse going to Hinchingbrooke House, west of Peterborough; but later, Ramsey Abbey was the family home.

There were other disasters: the Great Plague in 1666 removed nearly 500 souls, when the infection was transferred to the town by a bale of cloth, brought from London and intended for a coat for Sir William Cromwell; while fires in 1636 and 1731 did serious disservice to both town and townsfolk. For more recent times, the Ramsey Rural Museum speaks of the local craftsmen's former importance and status. The church of St Thomas A' Becket is not to be missed: it has fine 12th and 13th century detail. A Purbeck Marble effigy of the sainted Ailwin may also be seen. There is also a working duck-pond - and legend has it that the deeds of Matthew Hopkins, the Witchfinder General, reached this far.

There are some navigational points to be heeded in the area: Lodes End Lock is unattended, and an Ouse key is needed - and much elbow grease. Do not overlook the fact that craft of more than

25'0"/7.5m LOA will not be able to turn at Ramsey; nor the fact that Exhibition Bridge with a minimum headroom of 4'6"/1.4m is one of the lowest on the Levels, with its height varying eccentrically from one side to the other. On the plus side, pleasant moorings are to be found by the mill and Bill Fen Marina with many facilities is also nearby.

Forty Foot (Vermuyden's Drain)

Moving on and easterly round Ramsey Mere and into the Forty Foot (Vermuyden's) Drain takes us past the junction with the Sixteen Foot Drain and on to first, Horseway Lock (where an Ouse key is required), and second to Welches Dam Lock. These locks can only be used for access to the Old Bedford River at specified weekends: contact the Environment Agency (Tel. 01353 666660) for further details. At other times, it is necessary to return to Denver and come down the New Bedford (Hundred Foot Drain) to get to Earith. We'll travel that stretch at p.179.

Old River Nene

Now, we tackle the Inner Circle of the Old River Nene, with the Twenty Foot to the west and the Old Nene to the east. There is only one major watering point whichever way you tackle it, and that is what was once a small Tudor port, perched on an island surrounded by marshes, namely the community of March. Earlier this century, it was also a mini-Crewe, linking Ely, Peterborough, Wisbech, St Ives and Spalding. In the year 1921, 25% of Marchmen were working on the railway hereabouts.

The town has excellent markets on wednesdays and saturdays. It has some very pretty Georgian houses, and the riverfront is especially attractive. Do search out the King George V memorial fountain cast in iron in 1911 to commemorate the coronation; and the church in Church Street, where the ornamentation and embellishment pay tribute to the town's past opulence; as does the famous church of St Wendreda in Church Street: its spectacular late 15th century dou-ble -hammer beam angel roof with hanging carved angels sprouting outspread wings (and only one devil) telling of the town's mediaeval prosperity ... while the exterior equally speaks also of serious cash investment. It is believed that the church inspired the background for Dorothy L Savers novel 'The Nine Taylors'; and this may well be true, since John Betjeman said it was 'worth cycling 40 miles in a head wind' to see.

March Museum, Stags Holt Farm & Stud, Dunhams Wood with its trees and trains and Stonea Camp, site of the lowest hillfort in Britain

The traffic may thunder by a mile away, but little Lincolnshire Saxilby
is seldom anything but peaceful.

The towers of Hugh of Lincoln oversee or overlook all those in Brayford Pool . . .

. . . while the city's Glory Hole is one of the joys/challenges of the Witham.

Ely Cathedral: once a beacon for pilots, it still shines
like a good deed in a naughty world.

The lock at Bardney: a good old push'n'pull affair that offers
sports club exercise at bargain basement prices.

Visitors at one of Lincoln's refurbished bridges . . .

. . . are of a different brood and breed
from those who navigate both old and new at Tatershall.

Reaching for the skies part one: a grey day for the church of St Botolph, alias Boston Stump.

Reaching for the skies part two: sundowning in Torksey Cut.

It's all in the Wash - which can be all things to all men.

And one must travel far and wide to find a finer place than King's Lynn
- steeped as it is in maritime history.

Close to (approx. 250 yards): Middle Level, 16 foot, Popham's Eau

are all within easy reach. Of immediate interest to boaters are the overnight moorings by the park and the associated indoor swimming pool. There is a sanitation station on the Old Quay, adjacent to the Town Bridge. On the outskirts of the town is Fox's Marina, with many facilities and boats available for hire.

The river up to March is wide, but narrows when running through the town, to widen once again: there is plenty of headroom. Further along the river Popham's Eau branches off just south of Upwell. This name is a real oldie. At first glance, it appears to derive from Norman/French, but it is much more likely that it came from Anglo-Saxon - and perhaps has connections with Geoffrey Chaucer. Those in this immediate area who are supposedly in the know pronounce that the word is pronounced 'ee' and not 'oh' as in Anglicised French. However, they are not the only authorities, and those from nearer Boston have another version, and that is 'ew' (NB: not yew nor ewe, but just 'ew'; or as Hugh without the 'H'). It is navigable only as far as Three Holes Bridge where the Red Hart pub may be found.

Between Popham's Eau and Marmont Priory Lock (92'0"/28.0m x 12'0"/3.7m), which requires an Ouse key for operation if unattended (Tel. 01945 773959) it is relatively shallow. When we get to the twinned villages of Upwell and Outwell, we see that in reality they merge into one long experience of ribbon rather than two strings. Low bridges, overhanging trees and waterside pubs are some of the charms leading to the Outwell Basin, where there are moorings in what was originally part of the 18th century Wisbech Canal. Although they cannot claim to be Biggest Village in the world, they can certainly vie for Longest Lane. There used to be a packet service to Wisbech: two (very old) pence per person per trip.

For centuries, those who live here have been dependant upon the waterways for their livelihood - if not indeed very existence from time to time.

Still near to Popham's Eau is Nordelph; a pretty spot with a mooring near the post office and shops. Well Creek passes through all of these places before arriving at Mullicourt Aqueduct which carries it over the Main Drain and thence to Salters Lode and its lock. It is possible to lock through to the tidal river for limited periods each side of high tide by arrangement (Tel. 01366 382292). Restricting dimensions are length 62'0"/19.0m and width 12'6"/3.8m.

Just to the south on the Old Bedford River, is Welney, close by Delph Bridge. The church is not prominent, but the Three Tuns and Lamb and Flag pubs make up for any deficiency. Passage through Old Bedford Sluice is made by arrangement with the lock keeper at

Salters Lode, but is not always possible due to insufficient water.

Of serious interest to nature lovers is the Wildfowl and Wetlands Trust at Welney, being a strip of land between the Old and New Bedford Rivers designated a 'Wetland of International Importance'. Such unusual birds as the ruff, the black-tailed godwit and the black tern are commonly in residence. The Wetland is an important resting stage on the migration route and wigeon have been seen in great numbers; as have bewick's swans; gadwall; goldeneye; gulls; lapwing; little plover; pintail; pochard; raptors; ringed plover; scaup; smew; teal; and tufted duck. Hides and accommodation are available.

The New Bedford River

So, it is back to Denver to go back down the New Bedford (Hundred Foot Drain) in order to reach the tiny communities of Mepal and Sutton. For details of passage through Denver Sluice please see p. 115. This navigation is the straight 20 mile/32km course cut by Vermuyden in 1650, and, for the cognoscenti, it is a brilliant short cut between Earith and Denver, but please note that hire craft are not permitted. The surrounding area is on the bleak and featureless side, with the bridges and sluices being the only markers.

Depth is very much affected by rainfall and what fresh is held back or released. It can vary from the minimum, when even floating becomes impossible, to the maximum when it becomes impossible to pass under any of the bridges! Normal summer air draughts are:

Bridge	Headroom	
Earith	11'10"	3.6m
Sutton Gault	9' 6"	2.9m
Mepal	10' 9"	2.7m
Oxlode Railway Bridge	8' 9"	2.7m
Welney(Delph Bridge)	7'10"	2.4m

At Denver, tides flood for 3 hours on springs and 3½ hours on neaps. The time to leave Denver for Earith is about -1hr HW King's Lynn, and this should find good water even through the shoal area by Oxlode railway bridge. At Earith, spring tides flood for 2 hours and ebb for 10½ hours: the best time to leave Earith for Denver is about HW King's Lynn.

Mepal is the smaller of the two communities and has been known for years because of its Three Pickerels Inn. It is a truly isolated spot by a bridge that goes nowhere; but if you're not pickled or soused, you can walk the footpath to the village church.

Middle Levels

Sutton is a different kettle of fish - and no red herring neither. When on passage from Earith to Denver, it is best to enter at high water to get what advantage there may be from the tide and a decent drop of water underneath. Sutton has the benefit of the famous tower of St Andrew's Church, which is visible for miles; as is Ely Cathedral which is supposed to have inspired its construction. Indeed, many a traveller has mistaken it for the Cathedral. In particular to be noted is the 14th century double octagonal lantern (one perched atop the lower which itself is perched atop the square) which definitely tried to outshine Ely. Gargoyles, vaulted workings, bosses and the arms of the well-heeled Bishops of Ely, Barnet and Arundel are there to astound those who have the time and energy to study them carefully. Although only a small community, it has found fame and favour because of its much refurbished church: a relic of the terrible wealth of the godly of those days.

Sutton Gault is well worth a special visit if only for the joys of the river-side pub, the Anchor. It is an old eating house of a high order, with log fires in the winter, but needing folk to lower their tackle when venturing through the entry.

Old West River

Before Bedford's Flying Dutchman's developments were put into action, the old channel of the River Great Ouse was quite different from what it has been in recent decades. In the past, when in spate, the flood waters would rush up the old Aldreth River and inundate the Cam near Stretham. Today, this section is known as the Old West River, since it used to flow in a westerly direction. The Cam and Ouse were made to run together in an entirely new channel between Littleport and Stowbridge and, predictably, the primary course of the river began to silt up and stultify; until, with the creation of the Old Bedford River in 1631 and the New Bedford River (Hundred Foot Drain) in 1651 it finally went the way of the dinosaurs.

The Old West River has three important places for boaters' calling cards: at one end, Popes Corner, with the Fish and Duck; at the other Hermitage Marina by Hermitage Lock; and Twenty Pence Marina falling for the middle-for-diddle position. The Old West River has no natural flow, carrying only water from pumping stations; so predictably it is not best suited for cruising, being not only narrow but also tending to shoal at the bank-sides. It is important to keep the centre of the water course; to cruise at a modest speed, causing no wash; and not to pass another craft under a bridge. A central course is essential, and since some bridges are blind, dead slow ahead is essential.

This waterway is covered in the Great Ouse chapter on p.105.

Boatyards

Bill Fen Marina, Ramsey	01487 813621
Fox's Marina, March	01354 652770

Addresses

Middle Level Commissioners,	01354 653232
Middle Level Offices,	
Dartford Road, March	

There is no licence or toll for entering the Middle Levels, but all craft must register on entering at Stanground Sluice or Salters Lode lock. Keys for access to March sanitation station and the Security Compound at Lodes End Lock can be purchased at Stanground Lock, Salters Lode Lock, Fox's Marina or at the Middle Level Offices in March.

Denver Sluice	01355 382340
Salters Lode Lock	01366 382292
Stanground Sluice	01733 566413
Environment Agency, Ely	01353 666660
(for information on Welches Dam & Horseway Locks)	

Places of interest

The Wildfowl & Wetlands Trust, Welney

Tel.01353 860711
famous nature reserve: open daily 1000 - 1700

Whittlesey Museum

Tel. 01733 840986
exhibits of local history including Sir Harry Smith exhibition of local brick-making: open all year fri & sun 1430 - 1630 and sat 1000 - 1200

Ramsey Rural Museum

Tel. 01487 815715
collection of local farm implements and Victorian home life: open Apr Sept, thu & sun 1400 - 1700: tel. to confirm times

Stags Holt Farm

Tel.01354 652406
heavy horse centre: tel. for opening times

March Museum

Te. 01354 655300
collection of artefacts, agricultural tools and local photographs: open all year, tel. for times

The River Welland to Spalding .....and The River Glen
35 miles/56km   12miles/19km

Approaches

The regime for entering Welland Cut is the same as that for the Witham (see p.194); however, it is, if anything, better to leave it later, since there are some bits of the river bed that are not only uneven but also too 'near' (as Jane Austen would have it) or too 'close' (if you prefer), for the comfort of a little ship's bottom. The flood tide generally shifts at a fair rate of knots on its way up to Fosdyke Bridge, and Spring Tides can really sprint at an horrendous pace. Moreover, it is unsound and potentially unsafe to have your bows stuck fast on the mud with a spring flood up your stern. It is prudent, therefore to consider access to be no better than HW +/- 2hrs for entering from The Wash. The manifest signposts for the Welland Cut are the Tabs Head, which is left to starboard and Welland beacons.

The first stretch, The Cut, lies between sandbanks known as Herring and Scalp. We all know about Herrings, Herringbone and Salty Dogs; but the derivation of the other bank's name could be of interest. For example, Scalping, means the cutting and the tearing of the headskin of an enemy - either alive or dead (and the rhyming of headskin with redskin cannot just be coincidence!). The severed scalp was believed to bestow on the victor the power of the victim and frequently served as a trophy. Less esoterically, and certainly more probably, the name derives from a 'bare rock projecting above water level'. No matter; 'Beware' is the watchword.

Right up to Cut End and the River Welland itself, the buoyage is standard and well lit; and the Welland Cut channel is straight, well-trained by walls and marked by beacons that stand high enough on the banks. The beacons are lit, and most of them have radar reflectors.

In general, Fosdyke Bridge is the head of navigation for visitors, and definitely so for fully-masted vessels. So; if you cannot pass under the bridge, turn really well before it so that you have plenty of time to stem the tide, which can get up to 5+ knots. It is a good idea is to start turning just before you reach the moorings on the starboard (north) hand. This turn should be made to the south and it is essential to have plenty of power and preferably some in reserve. Mooring is problematic both below and above the bridge. Whatever your intentions, a prior visit or telephone call should be made to the Port of Fosdyke Ltd.

Between Spalding and the Wash, maximum draught is 8'0"/2.4m on the biggest tides; but from Spalding to Deeping St James the river

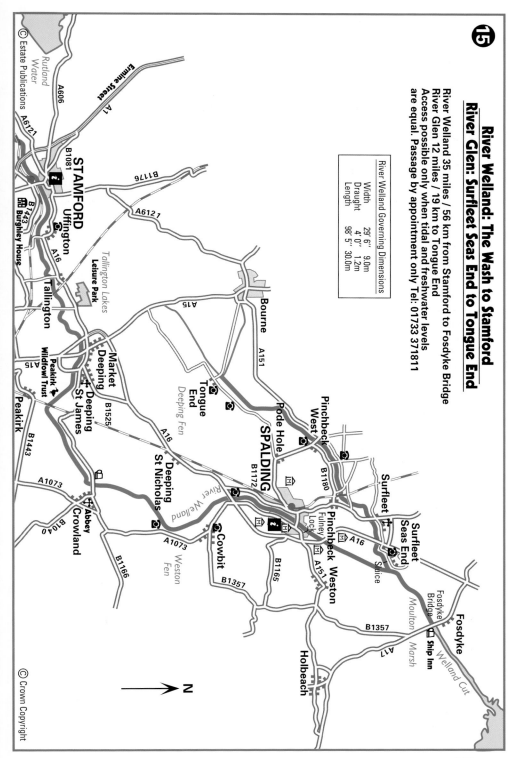

River Welland: The Wash to Stamford
River Glen: Surfleet Seas End to Tongue End

River Welland 35 miles / 56 km from Stamford to Fosdyke Bridge
River Glen 12 miles / 19 km to Tongue End
Access possible only when tidal and freshwater levels
are equal. Passage by appointment only Tel: 01733 371811

River Welland Governing Dimensions		
Width	29' 6"	9.0m
Draught	4' 0"	1.2m
Length	98' 5"	30.0m

Ermine Street

Rutland Water

© Estate Publications

A606

A6121

A1

B1081

STAMFORD

B1176

i

B1443

Uffington

Burghley House

A6121

A16

Tallington

Tallington Lakes
Leisure Park

Bourne

A15

A151

Peakirk
Wildfowl Trust

Market
Deeping

Deeping
St James

A15

Peakirk

B1525

Tongue
End

Deeping Fen

Pode Hole

Pinchbeck
West

SPALDING

B1172

B1180

Surfleet

A16

B1443

Deeping
St Nicholas

A16

River Welland

i

Fulney
Lock

Pinchbeck
West

Weston

Surfleet
Seas End

Sluice

Fosdyke
Bridge

A1073

Abbey
Crowland

Cowbit

Weston
Fen

A1073

B1165

A151

Moulton Marsh

Welland Cut

Fosdyke

Ship Inn

B1040

B1166

B1357

B1357

A17

Holbeach

N

© Crown Copyright

183

becomes much more modest with a maximum depth of 3'11"/1.2m. A strong tide affects the river from the Wash to Fulney Lock, a mile downstream of Spalding Bridge, and occasionally there is the possibility of a small bore. Although locals still refer to it as a 'tidal wave', there is no way in which it can contend with that on the River Trent.

Up the Welland Cut, the channel runs through low-lying marshlands where, shortly after entering and on the starboard hand, there are one or two 'last ditches'. While these miniature courses can hardly be called channels, nevertheless, those with a mind to really getting away from it all can navigate at springs - and find for themselves the joys of one of the classic Better 'Oles. This pleasant, wildlife anchorage just in the back of beyond Boston offers real sanctuary, provided that you are fully self-supporting, physically and psychologically, or that you enjoy regularly tripping the light fantastic in the dinghy. The only risk is that you will become so Lotus Eater-like that you will get neaped.

During an autumnal sundown, but without a sundowner, from water level, you may perceive the domain as one that is overwhelming and near to being damned, dominated as it is by the by the looming silhouette of Fosdyke Bridge. Succour, sustenance and spirituous liquors of all kinds are happily to hand at the close-by Ship Inn - where sun-downing can soon achieve the drowning of sorrows ... real or imagined. Inside, you, the unexpected visitor, will always receive a warm salutation, since every local in there will be more than impressed that you had actually heard of Fosdyke and even more stirred by the fact that you managed to get there!

Alternative entertainment is to be found in the area of the bridge: it presents itself in the form of searching out one of the members of the Lineham family, who have been in the area for centuries - and are said, by some hardy souls, to have been responsible for the demise of many a centurion who knew neither his place nor his onions (or indeed, his cauliflowers for that matter, for this is a superb belt for them) and had invested his time and effort in sowing wild oats when he should have been turning to his muttons. Wherever you find a Lineham you are bound to get a good chat, hilarious tales, generous assistance in all things and as much advice as you can take. Whatever time and effort you have expended on actually getting there in the first place and finding a berth in the second, you are sure to feel yourself well rewarded.

If you can get under the bridge, you will find there are some private moorings on the starboard-hand; and here it obtains even more that no-one arrives by chance. But those who are there before you, with their own well-preserved territorial pride in the few moorings that are available, will verily show you that they spring from first-rate yeoman stock - and see to it that you are looked after like a gentleman.

However, on the downstream side of the bridge, the quayside at Fosdyke (on the starboard hand going upstream and only just below the bridge) is a bitter place to berth. Not only is there the usual dramatic rise and fall of a Wash tide with its associated fast flood; but there is also the complication of strong back eddies created by the arched masonry. Fosdyke Bridge, the virtual head of navigation for all but modest craft, is a very substantial affair that will see off any assailant; and for sure it is best to make no familiar acquaintance with it - and certainly not to aspire to a close encounter. I say again: power is essential, in order to turn easily and hold your own against the flood tide; and plenty in reserve will help you do it without stress.

The Port of Fosdyke Ltd. is a small commercial quay with no official or even unofficial facilities for yachts. Getting a line to that high jetty can be a fraught job, especially if there is no one ashore to help. With prior permission, you may be able to lie alongside a big ship: also a problematic exercise. But, Fosdyke is extremely 'special', if only for being one of the few remaining 'open' ports left in the UK.

This isolated part of the countryside possesses little in the way of clichés or plastic Brummagem, and for that reason alone it is may be worth a somewhat troublesome trip; by dinghy or public transport. There is a well-stocked shop; the beer is of Bateman's best; and the company is even better. In the wise locals you will find friendly advisers who are expert on the ways and wiles of the Wash. If you keep your ears and eyes open while you stay for a while at Fosdyke Bridge, you cannot fail to be impressed for there will be much to read, mark, learn and inwardly digest.

From Fosdyke, neither Spalding nor Boston is actually far away; and the complexities of reaching them are, for once, not so serious as they often are when moving through the channels and waters of The Wash from place A to place B. For once it is actually possible to progress from one port to another on one tide without having to anchor off in The Wash. To reach Boston from Fosdyke, all that is needed is the simple manoeuvre of turning north at Tabs Head corner.

Although agriculture rules, many of the indigens have a really hard time. Some of them do no more than scratch a living from meagre smallholdings - rather like the Poor Whites in the Deep South. I still recall with warmth, that on one of my many weather-bound stopovers at Fosdyke, I found myself dejectedly looking at a small patch of quality cauliflowers. It was hardly any time at all before I was encouraged out of my miserable pondering, by the grower; proudly carrying a sack filled with four gorgeous exhibits. The phrase 'Beware of Yellow-bellies Bearing Gifts' was entirely inappropriate, insulting even, for the man would permit no money to change hands. I managed, however, to put the matter to rights later in the day at the pub. Fosdyke is an unique experience; best appreciated by those with a penchant for the recherché. Some of the locals have ancestors who were there before the Romans.

Spalding to Stamford

Spalding, 7 miles/11.5km above Fosdyke Bridge, has a population of nearly 20,000 and is the administrative centre of South Holland. Found midway between Boston and Peterborough, with good road and rail links, it is an important agricultural town - and, in particular, an important centre of the flower industry that is vital to the locality: for example, the Bulb Auction that is known internationally and is a centre much patronised by the Dutch.

Years ago, it was a thriving seaport, in spite of being situate deep in the heart of agricultural acres well removed from the sea. Some of the merchants' magnificent mansions still stand totem and token to the commercial drive and success of the local Fenland businessmen and entrepreneurs. In Spalding itself, the waters are above a lock (Fulney Lock), so there is not a sign nor a portent of the ferocity of the Wash Waters at the river mouth or the Tide Rip at Fosdyke. In fact, craft drawing as much as 3'3"/1.0m can negotiate the upper reaches just outside the town - that is, of course, on good tides and after arranging a passage through the lock. However, it is sad that these days there is little to attract the boating fraternity, although the town has much to offer in the way of botanical features and strong vegetables.

Historically, Spalding was a place of real consequence by the time the Normans came; but unfortunately there is even less evidence of its splendid castle than there is of its sea-faring past. In 1051AD, the Benedictines founded a monastery which played host to 30 monks and was to become one of the richest religious houses in the whole of Lincolnshire at large (and quite some largesse it was, at one time consisting of Lindsey, Spalding and Parts of Holland). After the priors went, the mariners came, and the town grew into a large trading port, exporting corn and importing coal and wood. In the 16th century it was described by James Camden, the historian, as a 'most handsome town'. Much of this accolade must have derived, as it still does derive, from the host of pleasing brick buildings that proudly stand in this old town that is unexpectedly bisected by the Welland in a style that is so recognisably Dutch that it must have originated with the Hollandaise saucy traders.

The claim to being a 'most handsome town' is justified by its possession of its Ancient Gentlemen's Society, founded by Maurice Johnson of Ayscoughfee Hall in 1709. The Society began with a few local gents getting together to talk over (amongst gossip, scandal and shaky business deeds) local antiquities - and, oh joy of joys, to read the recently established Tatler. Among its members were to be counted Sir Isaac Newton and Alfred Lord Tennyson; and its museum is next the oldest in the country - giving way only to the Ashmolean.

Medieval Ayscoughfee Hall is one of Spalding's oldest buildings, having been built by Richard Alwyn in the 1430's. It still has a lot of its first fabric in situ; and you can still see originals: a superb bay window, a brick-vaulted cellar and an absolutely splendid timber framed roof. After 300 years, the classic ceiling, very unusually plastered, was finished above a refurbished hall; and the library, panelled out in the 18th century is in excellent condition. In the mid 19th century, William Todd is credited with having rebuilt the façade, with the lone screen and crenellated, gabled bay windows.

Many generations of the Johnson family lived there in the hall: the Spalding Gentlemen's Society, was founded by Maurice, the second of the line, in 1709. But times move on and fashions change: since 1983 Ayscoughfee Hall has been a conscript in the South Holland District Council's Museum Service - not in the ranks, surely, but not as C.O. either.

Only a little further south, and not far from The Welland, en route for one or other of the many Deepings in the area, is the small town of Crowland, found and founded around its 8th century Croyland Abbey. It was built to honour the island in the Fen where the quaintly named St Guthlac had fabricated for himself an habitable hermitage noted for its isolated whereabouts. When boating on the Welland (one of his favourite forms of transportation) the saint was obliged to alight from his craft more than a mile from Crowland - but fortunately for him, being saintly in all things, he was a natural nature-loving-soul ... both on land and water. In Crowland itself, there is an intriguing 14th century triangular stone bridge, with 3 inter-linked arches that formerly crossed the three feeding streams of the Welland.

Until late in the 19th century, the river was navigable to Stamford, by grace and favour of a series of locks, the upper numbers of which have long been derelict.

Nearby Deeping St James is a large village with a derelict lock. Carted boats can progress up the river to the veritably charming 'village' of

River Welland

Market Deeping. It is in fact a small town with a remarkably wide street of many pretty stone houses. Its famed (partly) 12th century church of the previously mentioned St Guthlac is found vying for visitors with the old mill and its disused lock. Just to the south of Deeping St James and the drainage channel known as the Maxey Cut are some sections of the Roman Car Dyke that used to run through a large osier bed (a willow swamp). The dyke was built to connect Peterborough with Lincoln.

Not far away, on the way to Helpston, there is more religiosity, for the tiny community of Peakirk has a church uniquely dedicated to St Guthlac's sister, one St Pega, who was here in the 8th century. However, the most well-known attribute of the locality is the 20 acres of the Wildfowl Trust, part of the heritage of Sir Peter Scott - he of the Wetlands Trust and the guardian lighthouses, where he sometimes lived, at the entrance to the River Nene. Among its near 1,000 birds are many kinds of ducks, geese, swans, and flamingoes ... and oddities like hawaiian and andean geese, chilean flamingoes, and trumpeter swans. Surprisingly, some are very tame.

There is more fame to be rehearsed in nearby Helpston, in the birthplace of the famous (or infamous) genius (or madman) writer (or scribbler) the 'Northamptonshire Peasant Poet' himself, John Clare. He was born in 1793, in a none too 'des-res', to a farm-labouring father (a lover of fine and fancy words) and (ergo surprisingly) an illiterate mother. In plain words, his home was an hovel - as were many of his co-workers' - with resultant rampant infant mortality. Close to home, Clare's twin sister died shortly after being born. The thatched cottage still stands next the Blue Bell Inn - where Clare worked betimes as a potman. This would have been a job much more to his liking (taste) than those he had to endure at local estates such as Woodcroft Castle, where he was turn and turn about, ploughboy, reaper, thresher, gardener and lime-burner. Since he was a Clare of small brain and even less education, he had no choice. In those days, 'O' levels in carpentry were unknown, so Clare turned all of his limited early-learning skills towards nature - to flora and fauna as well as the euphemistic 'Birds and Bees'. Indeed, this John contained within his weak and slender frame many an unexpected potential: Jack the Lad; Jack o' the Lanthorn; and, perhaps inevitably, Jack of all Trades. And from this latter, sprang the most unlikely achievement: he taught himself to read and write; started versifying the minute he hit his teens; and immediately fell for the Scots poet James Thomson and his piece, 'The Seasons'. He also became an under-gardener under the Marquis of Exeter, where he first took up serious drinking. Not long after, he also fell for Mary Joyce, a local farmer's daughter. Thomson's writing was beyond his reach, Mary was not only well below the age of consent but equally well Above His Station; so the deeply frustrated lad turned his back on it all: turned away from home; turned in circles in his head; and finally turned to such strong liquors that he hardly knew where he had travelled - or how he had survived.

Returning to Helpston he also returned to casual work and writing verses. In 1817 he got a real job in a lime kiln, and more old habits returned: he was once more in love - this time with Martha Turner. Although not seriously above his station her parents objected - and not without cause, for his reputation was well noised abroad. He had been with his employer only a short time when he was sacked for wasting his time 'scribbling' and went on the parish for relief. After two years of unfruitful fragments, John Clare was close to terminal despair when one of the people to whom he had applied for succour came to his aid. And so it was that, in 1819, one Mr Drury, a Stamford shop-keeper with an addiction to books, came across a halfsheet of dirty foolscap paper, on which was penned 'The Setting Sun' with a letter attached from the author. This beneficent bibliophile not only found a publisher for Clare but also gave him money. 'Poems, Descriptive of Rural Life and Scenery', by John Clare, a Northamptonshire Peasant, was published in 1820 to immediate acclaim. Clare now put his fingers up to Martha (Patty) Turner's parents and married her. The first child was born one month later. A year later another book of verse came out, 'The Village Minstrel and Other Poems'. It met with less success, but this did not stop Clare from living the life of a poet - turning to drink; churning out verse; and fathering children willy-nilly. He also moved 'house' to Northborough a few miles away where his wife is buried. It was not long before he was forced to try his hand at real work again, but unhappily for his family, he was doomed to live most of his life in poverty - failing disastrously in most of his enterprises.

His 'Shepherd's Calendar' came out in 1827 and he literally trekked round the country trying to flog copies - but to an avail. In spite of his unstable state and failure in most of his ventures, Lord Fitzwilliam of Milton Park gave Clare, in 1832, a new cottage near Helpston. Three years later, more verse was published, 'The Rural Muse', but Clare was going downhill in every way. Although this got a better press, by June 1837 it was clear that Clare needed care. He was admitted into an asylum, Fairmead House in Epping Forest, where one Dr Allen seemed to handle him with some skill and kindliness. But Clare was not to succumb to such incarceration at this first attempt: in July 1841 he escaped, running off to find Mary Joyce, whom he believed to be his wife. (Mary Joyce had died unmarried in 1838.) He did join his proper wife, but it was (predictably) a calamity, and after five months of Clare's mental confusion and emotional chaos, she had him committed to Northampton General Lunatic Asylum.

John Clare died on 20 May 1864. His body was taken to Helpston churchyard and a memorial set up at the cross-roads. Such a site must be most apposite for one who was famous in his heyday as a curiosity, and who wrote of himself: 'A peasant in his daily cares, a poet in his joy'; and also 'I am: yet what I am none cares, or knows.'

Back in the land of the living, if not absolutely the sane, we reach the village of Barnack. It was the site of one of the most famous limestone quarries in the area, having supplied much stone not only for Ely and Peterborough Cathedrals but also some colleges in Cambridge. The village is composed of drystone walls, many pretty cottages and barns, and two old pubs. There is a nature reserve which is one of only two sites in the country where may be seen the bell-shaped pasque flower. Two other facts intrigue: Charles Kingsley, of Water Babies fame, came here as a five year old with his clergyman father, to the rectory now known as Kingsley House. Second: one pub is called The Fox - very neat when we know that much Barnack stone was used to build Burghley House. Fox, but why? Read on!

Burghley House is famous as one of England's most splendid Elizabethan houses. It was built by William Cecil, who was the first Lord Burghley, towards the end of the 16th century. Elizabeth I used nicknames for all her advisers, she had 'Eyes', 'Ears', 'Nose' and Cecil, undoubtedly he favourite counsellor, was her 'Fox'.

Little of the outside of the mansion has changed, but most of the inside and its innards are from a much later period. There is a bedroom for the Queen, and there is also a Heaven room and Hell staircase - both decorated with 17th century wall paintings by Antonio Verrio. There are Grinling Gibbons' woodcarvings from roughly the same time, and among the many paintings are Holbeins and Van Dycks. Burghley, once described as more like a town than a house, is perhaps best known for the Burghley Horse Trials (which are held in the park every September).

Stamford straddles The Welland at a point in touch with Lincolnshire, Leicestershire, Northamptonshire and Cambridgeshire. It is a market town that started life as a basic settlement at an important ford. Many ancient routes converged here, including the well-known Ermine Street. During the 10th century it was one of the Big Five of the Dane-law. The others, now all grown high and mighty, were Leicester, Derby, Lincoln and Nottingham. Limestone crops up again in Stamford, its biggest monument being Lord Burghley's 1597 Hospital.

The River Glen
12 miles/19km

To complete the picture of the Welland, we note that the miniature River Glen, right back towards The Wash, is actually of a similar disposition to its big brother, and is navigable from its junction at Surfleet Seas End, midway between Spalding and Fosdyke to Tongue End, about 12 miles/19km upstream. The only lock is a pair of tidal gates at the entrance, which can be passed by prior arrangement, when a level is made by either an incoming or an ebb tide. The best time to make an exploration is in spring, when the bulbs are in flower. The only villages en route are Surfleet, whose church spire leans 6'0"/2.8m from the vertical, and Pinchbeck, where there is a drainage engine museum. Upstream of Pinchbeck, the river is very shallow and only navigable by light craft and canoes.

River Welland Fishing

Fishing on the Welland divides itself into two regimes; splitting into more or less two areas and two types. Upstream of Market Deeping the river, while not the easiest of stretches of water to reach and fish, is renowned for large catches of chub and roach - especially in winter. Downstream, the river is much wider with regular banks and excellent access - an altogether more favourite location.

The Stamford area often has really good chub and roach - some coming out at more than 20 kilos. Summertime sees the secret angler come into his own (since matches are much less frequent) after the big stuff hiding in their territorial pools. The generally slow run is, of course, attractive and suitable for bream, roach and tench - all of which thrive, as do those omnipresent pestilential creepers, the eels. Bream in the area can be populous - but often will take only after dusk; and there are many good tales of pike landings. The majority of the Welland river in Spalding town itself is susceptible to free fishing.

Rivers Welland & Glen

Facilities

Port of Fosdyke Ltd.	01205 260240
Rivers Welland and Glen	01522 513100
Fulney Lock	01733 371811
Surfleet Sluice	01733 371811

Places of interest

Ayscoughfee Hall, Museum and Gardens
Tel. 01775 725468
medieval house with museum of local history: open all year except
winter weekends: the T.I.C. is also housed here

Burghley House, Stamford
Tel. 01780 752451
Elizabethan house open daily 1Apr - 4thOct, 1100 - 1630

Peakirk Wildfowl Trust
Tel. 01733 252271
20 acres of water gardens: open summer daily 0930 - 1730, winter
0930 to dusk

Gordon Boswell Romany Museum
Tel. 01775 710599
collection of Romany caravans and photographs: open Mar - Oct
1030-1700, closed mon and tues (open BH mons)

Spalding Bulb Museum, Pinchbeck
Tel. 01775 680490
open Apr - Oct daily (except 12th April) 1000 - 1630

Croyland Abbey, Crowland
Tel. 01733 210499
open all year 0900 - dusk

Pinchbeck Engine and Land Drainage Museum
Tel. 01775 725468
renovated working beam engine: open Apr - Oct, 1000 - 1600

Spalding Tropical Forest
Tel. 01775 710882
open all year daily summer 1000 - 1730, winter 1000 - 1600

Witham and Fossdyke
49miles/78km

Once upon a time, there was a full-blooded, full-bodied County of Lincolnshire. One of the largest and proudest of the shire counties, it had its ridings; and not the least of the Parts of Lincolnshire was the Part called Holland. One of its claims to fame was the historic port of Boston; indeed, although the Part known as Holland is now long gone, the port is still revered, and, is, even now, undergoing something of a revival. No City Father dreams today of emulating the famous Pilgrim Fathers, nor of wreaking havoc in revenge for the Boston Tea Party; and while not one of them aspires to approach the calibre of one of their merchant adventurer forebears, many seem intent on becoming, if not exactly adventurous merchants, then at least successful entrepreneurs.

But the essence of successful adventures does not prevail along the banks of the river that leads up to the Grand Sluice. Grand usually means impressive and magnificent. Occasionally it means just large — and in this latter context the mot is juste, but for any thought of the sluice being illustrious or imposing the word is anything but apposite. The same proviso obtains the above mentioned stretch of waterway, for it is an absolute disgrace — and no mantra-like reiteration of its deceptive designation — The Haven — can ever make it otherwise.

It may need more than just a little imagination to put the river and its frontage to rights; but it certainly wouldn't cost much in terms of finance, time or even effort; and it is a task that should be undertaken soon, for the banks and river bed are all foul for a considerable distance downstream from the Grand Sluice. Even if the town nabobs have little care for the needs of pleasure craft, they should at least respond with enthusiasm to a scheme that would pay for itself over and over again by the monies brought into the presently dead and downtrodden area by committed and well-heeled sightseers. Decent moorings would command a good price, and the riparian neighbours would get nothing but a good deal - in both aesthetics and cash.

However, as things are, the unprepossessing construction of the Grand Sluice stands as a suitable symbol for the singularly unbeautiful river that is the Witham below the lock. Boston has had a tidal flood sluice since 1766 — and it looks like it. Even the lock-keeper's land-locked basic concrete slab-like miniature office and his similar control room over the water do little to suggest that much has changed during the past 200 years. But of whatever vintage, the sluice and its mighty gates and doors controls the movements of all cruising men who wish

to pass from fresh to salt. It is indeed a classic watershed, insofar as 'The Shorter Oxford English Dictionary' offers the following choices:
  the line separating waters flowing into different rivers, basins, or seas;
  a narrow ridge between two drainage areas;
  a turning-point in affairs, a crucial time or occurrence;
  the slope down which the water flows from a watershed.

Indisputably, both vertical gates and horizontal doors are bona fide ridges, and they make an undeniable dividing line between the muddied sea-waters of the downside Haven and the altogether cleaner, clearer pond-like quality of that upper-class river, The Witham: one view is of rough and tumble waters in a mud and stone ravine; while the other is made up of not-inexpensive craft idling at their mooring, while their owners dream of waters far away or imbibe in the nearby Witham Tavern. Downstream is all gloom and threat, while upstream is a leafy glade filled with the British Waterways Board's rich promise of a cruising paradise - provided your craft doesn't exceed the restrictions of draught.

It is difficult to hypothesise a pair of waters with so many dissimilarities: indeed, it is not only an eye-opening revelation but also a guerdon (free, gratis and for nothing) to gain the contrasting experiences that come from perceiving the vistas, first from one side of the bridge, and then from the other. For the cynics who think this to be hyperbole; please try it for yourselves before reaching a censorious judgement.

No vessel drawing much more than 3'3"/1.0m is really well-suited to the weedy, shallow and frequently silted Witham and Fossdyke as it flogs its way up to Torksey. Anything more can make for an anxious trip. Things are better when approaching from seaward, although there are still considerable problems affecting the progress of any boat drawing more than 3'11"/1.2m if the skipper wishes to get to Boston early on the tide. However, they are surmountable, and the way in through the watery wastes of The Wash abounds with joys and challenges; so let us go out there and discover.

Once in the Wash, with the North Well astern, the next buoy to find is the well-known Roaring Middle. Not long ago, it was a rather strange-shaped, yellow float that looked rather more like a surfing banana than an important aid to navigation. Now, it is red and white, but its new colours have done nothing but elaborate the colourful scheme and it now stands more proudly and more conspicuous than ever before. From the Roaring Middle, we tend to the west for the Boston Roads red and white buoy that marks the entrance to the Freeman Channel. The international buoyage system is owned and maintained by the Port of Boston Authority, and is easy and excellent to follow, as it leads you, station by station from 'Alpha' the first in the actual channel, in impeccable alphabetical order, to Juliet, the last before Dolly Peg, Tabs Head and Welland. When used without cutting corners - for the channels are sometimes steeply-edged and narrow - it makes the approach a simple, safe and straightforward matter.

A favourite spot to anchor while awaiting a tide to permit you to pass over the bar and up to Boston is in the area of Clay Hole, and the nearby red Golf and green No. 11 buoys. While Clay Hole is as well a protected spot as you can hope to find in the Wash, I actually prefer not to go quite as far Clay Hole, but to use High Horn instead. However, no matter which place you choose, the chances are that you will be in the company of the local fishing boats queuing up just before opening time.

After that, Tab's Head and Dolly Peg show the way into the New Cut to the Haven and the River Witham. Tabs Head is left to port for Boston. It is possible to get closer in by watching your water through the channel almost up to the well-known trio of beacons. When I was there last, I determined to pass over the bar as soon as I possibly could, although I knew that would mean a necessarily slow trog up the New Cut and The Haven since the bottom is always close until well after half tide - and even if you succeed in getting up to the lock at Boston Grand Sluice you will have to wait for the first-level opening of the Grand Sluice. In order to do that, you need to be off to a good start and with no more than 3'3"/1.0m's draught, there will be no problem. Much more will require high quality skill to keep you out of keel-scraping trouble. In addition, the river bed is over-supplied with debris and detritus in a variety of forms from the occasional old car chassis to heavy tyres and supermarket trolleys. More still: there are concrete works on the steeply sloping banks; while eel nets and plastic bottles, harnessed together in mid-stream, also form some keel and prop-threatening formations. An inspection of the river at low water will convince you of the need for caution and accurate pilotage. Basically, tide times for entering the river are the same as the others in the Wash: no better than 3 hours before high water.

Be that as it may, I decided to stand watch by the Welland Beacon and move into the New Cut as soon as I could - that is, if I could get to the beacon in the first place. Eventually, I got within striking distance after a long series of stirring soft mud humps and touching slightly harder bottoms - and consequently consuming a lot of fuel by much use of Valcon's 56 horse power engines to go astern. In the event, I found that sitting just to the north of the Welland beacon was not a happy occupation. While I was on the bottom, looking at the Welland beacon, itself and hoping to go afloat, everything was fine, for it was an extremely pleasant evening. But when I did eventually come off, I found myself propelled powerfully to the beacon itself and not into the Bar Channel. It was no easy matter to avoid going aground yet at the same time trying to ensure that I moved in the right direction! All in all, it proved that such an exercise was definitely pointless; patient waiting is the name of the game; but nevertheless, the achievement of having tested it for myself gave me modest gratification.

The New Cut and the Haven

Once over the bar, and in the New Cut, joy and despair may await you in equal measures. For example, halfway between The Wash and the town of Boston, near the entrance to the Hobhole Drain, for those with a mind to see, there is a striking example, in the form of the Pilgrim Fathers' commemorative tablet. The best view, if you have an eye for that kind of thing, is from the river, not many managing to find it by an overland route; certainly not many of those contemporary Americans who make the pilgrimage to Boston (Lincolnshire) from Boston (Massachusetts, USA). The heart of Boston itself, is totally out of sight from the navigation that actually runs right through the centre of the town. What is, however, remarkably visible and obvious is the tower of the Church of St Botolph; and so high and mighty is it that it is almost impossible not to feel overawed by its dominating presence and you are seldom out of its purview for many a mile.

On the river, the channel is more or less central, with only the normal hazards of tide-time, port and river navigation to be overcome - and at Boston, these are not formidable. The banks are well marked with beacons, but normally they are needed only for interest or just to plot your progress and speed over the ground; and all is plain sailing until you reach the area of the docks, where life can become a bit hectic. A radio request to the Harbour Master (VHF channel 12) will bring information regarding shipping movements; information of some import since room to manoeuvre is never generous and in the immediate vicinity of the entrance it is at a premium: there is little space for amicable flirtations between commercial traffic and leisure craft. Nonetheless, it is comforting to know that co-operation has always been the order of the day at Boston, with none of the aggravation that sometimes mars relationships between big fishing boats and even bigger commercial shipping vessels, and leisure craft. The meeting of these different worlds has always been a pleasing aspect of Boston's river.

The docks are not available to yachts except in an emergency, and the nearest feasible moorings are just below the first bridge on the port hand where the bottom is soft mud. Under favourable circumstances, craft can stay afloat here at all states of the tide. However, laying alongside this short length of wall is a risky affair, only to be considered if you have a robust vessel with sturdy tackle and a stalwart crew who will be staying on board. To move any further upstream for yachts with masts means that they must be lowered in order to negotiate the river bridges and the Grand Sluice Lock.

There are also other possible moorings beyond the railway swing bridge to the docks. They are private jetties and berths, near-berths and so-called berths where, even if you could find the owner, it would take only one tide to convince you that they are not really suitable for leisure craft - fragile or otherwise. Nevertheless, they are in great demand and much valued by local fisherman and pleasure boaters since they afford access to The Wash without the constraints and disciplines that the Grand Sluice enforces. There have been what might be euphemistically termed 'vague ideas', 'sketch plans' and 'proposed projects' around for years to improve, refurbish or even to renew and reorganise the area and its facilities. But , as usual, riparian interests and the delays of local office stand in the way of boaters' progress. At the moment, boats are frequently tethered to unstable jetties and most of them take to the (soft mud) bottom every tide.

If you have lowered your gear to pass under all the bridges up the Boston River, you will be able to get through the Grand Sluice Lock without any trouble. The last stretch of the river before the lock is the one where special care must be taken especially if you are 'early' on the tide, trying to catch the first pen. The bottom is tricky: although there are fewer eel nets than there used to be, there are still enough to warrant a watchful eye. Rocks and a generally foul bottom are to be found reaching from the port bank out as far as mid-stream. Keeping the railway signal in line with the last lamp standard on shoresides will keep you clear of all the obstructions. The worst area is just after the footbridge, where it is foul on both sides and the stretch is generally shoal.

Finally, there is the immediate approach to the lock itself, Grand Sluice! It is an ugly-looking, threatening affair, with gates that can spew out its races at a tremendous rate of knots, and special care is required if sluicing is going on. The whole process can be vicious enough to turn and spin a small boat, so that the skipper really needs enough power to counteract the forces; and from time to time will need to manoeuvre speedily and then perhaps have to jill around; and the powerful eddies must be watched. If you let the lock keeper know of your ETA (preferably by phone since his VHF reception is poor) he can then ask the sluice controlling engineers to co-operate, and so ensure that cruising folk are put about as little as possible.

The lock office is equipped with a telephone and answering machine Tel. 01205 364864; and is also on VHF channel 16 and 74, on which dual watch is maintained. As a final resort the Boston Harbour Master will consider passing on a message from you via the telephone should necessity demand. The lock is in fact available at tide times during both night and day for anyone making a genuine seagoing passage or requiring a haven from the Wash, but since there is only one keeper, he appreciates not having to work nights as well as days. When the lock-master at Boston lays down the law, as he frequently does for he knows it well and is more than ready and willing to pass it on, he, who disregards it or fails to pay it proper respect, is indeed a sad and sorry man - although later he may well become a wiser one. The lock-keeper is one of the longest serving on the local waterways, and during that time he has accumulated a great deal of comprehension and apprehension of the ways of leisure craft and is thus well prepared for the vagaries of his job. His characteristic and particular style are singular to a degree - master's, of course.

If you have to wait outside the lock, moor only between the ladders, where if you draw less than 4'10"/1.5m you will be able to stay afloat at all times. If you draw more, you may touch bottom on springs and it is hard concrete. It is quite flat, but since it is hard, exposed engines or out-drives are at risk: the traffic signals are standard. While the navigation is theoretically open from October to April the river is often run low, so passage is frequently impossible.

There is little point in going to Boston, with all the trouble of taking down masts (if necessary), without going through the Grand Sluice Lock into the fresh water of the river. The first mooring facility is Boston Marina. In addition to the usual chandlery, there are Admiralty charts. There is mains water and electricity at the berths, with the marina's diesel pump nearby. You can telephone the marina at Boston (01205) 364420 to let them know you are visiting and they will do their best to have a place set aside and ready for you if at all possible. A phone call is a wise precaution since it is a very popular spot in the summer season. There are British Waterways Board moorings above the marina.

Boston has a boating season that stops and starts with absolute, definite dates; from the first day of November to the last day of April, mooring is prohibited between the Grand Sluice and any point on the river that may be immediately affected by any speedy sluicing operations that take place to combat flooding or to permit repairs to be carried out to the miles of bank. The sailing and cruising clubs uproot their scaffolding, buoys and finger pontoons; and the more permanent fixtures belonging to Boston Marina and the British Waterways Board become apparent as they are denuded of the craft that have clung to them throughout the summer. In season, it is hardly ever quiet, even in the middle of the night, for there is always someone 'messing about in a boat'; often accompanied by tea, coffee or alcohol in large or small doses.

However, no matter how strong the lure of the water, the waterside or whatever the season, Boston is a place that must be tasted shoresides if it is not to be considerably undervalued. Some cruising havens promise visitors the promised land but fail to deliver; on the other hand, Boston offers visions of glory by grace and favour of the tower of St. Botolph's Church. This famous church is better and more collo-quially known as Boston Stump; but that is to belie its size, stature and significance. The total area of the church, at more than 20,000 sq. ft. make it the largest parish church in England. The name 'Stump' has attached itself to the majestic mediaeval Lantern tower of this beautiful church - and no-one really knows how it came to be so called. Some say it is because the tower was never completed and that it was intended that a spire should be added. It has been suggested that the name refers to the steeple's appearance as seen from a distance across the marshes or flat Fenland country which sur-rounds Boston. It may be that the name goes back to the seventy years period during the 15th century when the steeple was in the process of construction.

On the left of the South Door is the Cotton Chapel. Originally a Guild Chapel, it was restored in 1857 in memory of John Cotton, the Puritan Vicar of Boston who went with many of the congregation to Boston, Massachusetts in 1633. The Choir Stalls are of late 14th century design and contain in the misericords a very fine series of cannings. The canopies above the stalls are of a later period and were erected between 1853 and 1860. Tracery removed from the window where the organ is now housed, was presented to Trinity Church in Boston, Massachusetts. The great tower is the highest in Britain, and at 272'/83m it virtually dominates the whole town. However, its topmost tiers are now prohibited to the public on account of the growing popularity of suicide attempts from its balconies.

Boston is indeed St. Botolph's town, being known by that name until the 16th century. On a pinnacle on the south side of the great church tower stands a figure, said to be St. Botolph. The Anglo-Saxon Chronicle says that he was a pious Benedictine monk with 'locks as white as wool, and a heart like the down of a thistle'. St. Botolph asked the King of the South Angles for a piece of waste ground as he did not wish to dispossess any one of his land. On this his monastery at Ikanho was founded, probably at Iken in Suffolk. It was destroyed by the Danes in 870, but more than seventy churches were dedicated in his name.

It is said that there are 365 steps to the very top of the tower - one for every day of the year. There are 12 pillars supporting the roof - equal to the months in a year. There are 7 doors for the days of the week, 52 windows for the weeks in a year. There are also 24 steps leading to the library above the south porch, whilst on either side of the chancel there are 60 steps by which the roof can be reached; these steps indicating the hours, the minutes and the seconds by which our days are numbered. If some energetic person should prove this information to be incorrect, remember that such sayings are not always meticulously accurate. In the main, St. Botolph's Church is a veritable Calendar in Stone.

You will also hear it said with some conviction, that the tower was built 'on wool'. This belief originated from the fact that during the 13th and 14th centuries Boston was the centre of the wool industry. In 1204 Boston was granted its first Charter by King John. Between 1279 and 1289 records show Boston as contributing a third more in customs duties than London and by 1300 it was considered to be England's leading port. The church which was begun in 1309 was financed mainly through the rich trade which Boston enjoyed at that time - hence the expression 'built on wool'.

The stump itself is mainly 15th century, and was heightened in stages, culminating in the delicate crowning lantern of the early 16th century. This was used as a lighthouse to guide ships and fen travellers, but was only completed at a time of severe decline in the port.

William Cobbett visited the medieval Fenland port and market town of Boston in April 1830 and wrote in 'Rural Rides': "The great pride and glory of the Bostonians is their church, which has a tower 300 feet high, which is both a landmark and a sea-mark. To describe the richness the magnificence, the symmetry, the exquisite beauty of this pile is wholly out of my power." The church has been flooded several times throughout the ages, as seen on the buttress to the right of the west door of the tower on the outside of the church. The most recent flood, on January 11th 1978, was the highest ever recorded: the boundary wall on the river bank collapsed, the church being flooded to a depth of 1'5"/45cms.

In 1607, one William Brewster together with William Bradford and other Separatists from Scrooby, Nottinghamshire, attempted to sail illegally from Scotia Creek near Boston, to Holland, where their 'heretical' beliefs would be tolerated. Their Dutch captain turned them in and they were imprisoned in the Town Hall. Eventually they got to Holland; and in 1620 some of them reached America. There these original Pilgrim Fathers became the Founding Fathers of New Plymouth.

Puritanically Puritan Boston became a hothouse led by the Earl of Lincoln. In 1629 the Massachusetts Bay Company was formed and the following year a fleet of 7 ships with 1,000 souls on board was skippered by John Winthrop to America. They pronounced upon their landing the single fateful word, 'Boston'. During the next decade, 10% of the town's population (250) emigrated. Among them were John Cotton, Richard Bellingham, later Governor of Massachusetts, and Edward Quincey of Fishtoft whose descendant, John Quincey Adams, became the 6th President of America.

The Boston lot dominated the colony for two generations and virtually ran the College of Further Education - which was to become Harvard in 1639. In 1851 a set of Corporation seals was sent to America and in 1879 stone tracery from St. Botolph's was sent to Trinity church. In return American money helped restore the Cotton Chapel in 1855, the Guildhall in 1915 and St. Botolph's in 1931; in 1938, Ambassador Joseph P. Kennedy opened the American Room in Fydell House.

John Cotton was a Non-Conformist, and this, together with his rebuttal of central church government, made him unacceptable, forcing him to resign as Vicar of Boston in 1632. Hiding in London, he changed his identity and escaped to Boston, Massachusetts. He was known as the 'unmitred pope of a pope-hating community', and laid down most of the colony's laws. In 1641, Parliament tried to persuade him to return as a religious and public affairs advisers but he refused, staying put to die in 1652. Quoth the City Fathers: "Both Bostons have reason to honour his memory and New England most of all, which oweth its name and being to him, more than any person in the world."

Jean Ingelow, another famous Bostonian, is best remembered for her famous poem 'The High Tide on the Coast of Lincolnshire' which appeared in 'Poems' 1863. It was inspired by one of the worst floods in Boston's history. It went into 4 editions in that year alone and by 1873 it had reached its 23rd edition. She was the daughter of William Ingelow, a Boston banker who lived in South Square, but she later moved to Ipswich and then to London. She gained considerable wealth and in America alone 200,000 copies of her work were sold.

Back in our own time again, Boston is still something of a hothouse, especially on the two well-known and important market days,

Wednesday and Saturday. The general market is situate more or less in that part of the town centre that is nearest the river and The Stump. It is traditional and contemporary all in one: from one relic of old-fashioned boiled sweets in the hands of an elderly Bostonian lady to a superfluity of cheap jean stalls leaned on by dark-skinned nomadic gentlemen. Nearby is an arcade with one of the best fishmongers in the area. The other market, near the 'other' town centre, namely near the Post Office, also manages to combine opposites: this time the esoteric and the eclectic. It would be a misnomer of great disservice to call it a car boot sale, unless one were to describe it as the great Car Boot Sale in The Sky – for it offers almost all things to all men and almost as many to all women. I have experienced many such markets from Brigg (Fair) to Benidorm and Boston, if not actually running an infamous Tea Party, easily manages to take the biscuit. For assertive bargain hunters, there are plenty of stall-holders who relish nothing better than banter and barter. One of the highlights is the auction (Dutch or otherwise) for all kinds of cuts and packages of meats from the mobile butcher – who, when the going gets tough, resorts to his personal public address system. In addition, there are alleys, tenfoots, lanes and back-streets, many of which house shops that embrace goods to intrigue and entertain if not actually to purchase; while for those who prefer the more mundane pre-packaging of the (improperly titled) Super Markets, opportunities proliferate. The untardy traders of Boston are in general a joy – and I never leave without a sense of regret.

So; considering leaving, we move on gently upstream past all the small-sailing, rough-rowing and solemn to-the-last-fishing all the short straight way up to the strangely named Anton's Gowt. Now, although Peewit/Peewee/Pyewipe birds and pubs abound, there is no cuckoo around – and a gowk is a cuckoo – it is also a fool (and there is little doubt that many folks have been fooled by thinking that this strange fellow at the entrance to the Witham Navigable Drains offers deep waters simply because they are still) but I have not as yet been able to bottom the mystery of the nomenclature – nor, for that matter, of the magical drains themselves. Now read on:

The Witham Navigable Drains

A drain, in this part of Lincolnshire, means a man-made waterway cut to drain the land. Since most of this area is below sea level, a drain is of vital importance. It can be as simple as clay tiles laid just below the surface of the land, it can be a narrow dyke, or a waterway the size of a river. Drains are usually straight in line, criss-crossing the whole area, each one leading to a larger deeper drain. The water, controlled by sluices, locks and pumps, eventually flows into the sea, leaving good arable land. The cutting and maintenance of these drains is as important today as in the 16th century when the first effectual drainage of the fens began.

The history of the River Witham Fourth District Drains is fascinating and deserves wider promulgation.

60 BC Romans occupied the area but there is no proof of drainage works as such. Wainfleet was an important port to serve Lincoln and the River Witham was made navigable from Lincoln to Dogdyke. Car Dyke was cut on the western edge of the Fens for navigation. Boston did not exist.

420 - 866AD The Saxons inhabited the area, their settlement names terminating in ton', 'ey' and 'fleet' In 654 St. Botolf founded a monastery.

866 - 1050AD This was the period of invasion by the Danes who sacked many of the Fenland monasteries, including St. Botolf's, and occupied settlements on the higher ground in places with names now ending in 'by' King Alfred the Great defeated the Danes in 878AD but allowed them to administer lands adjacent to and in the Fens (Danelagh) but the Saxons also remained and the monks returned. King Canute allotted Common Rights in the Fens and parcelled the land to surrounding parishes.

1066AD Norman Conquest. Numerous lands were granted to the Normans. In 1086 the Domesday Book was compiled and recorded churches existing at Butterwick, Fishtoft, Leverton, Skirbeck Stickney, Steeping, Stickford, Sibsey, Thorpe and Toynton St. Peter.

11th/12th cent. During this period the monks made various attempts to drain the land and protect it from sea and river flooding. It is from this period that the earliest mention of the sea bank is made, referred to now as the 'Roman Bank' The duty of repairing banks and sluices devolved upon frontagers, but the works were neglected and many petitions were put to the King by people who suffered flooding.

1142 A sluice was built below Boston to increase scour in the River Witham for the benefit of navigation.

13th cent. Commissions of Sewers were set up. These were the earliest drainage authorities with powers to investigate drainage problems; to direct by whom works were to be carried out; and to assess the

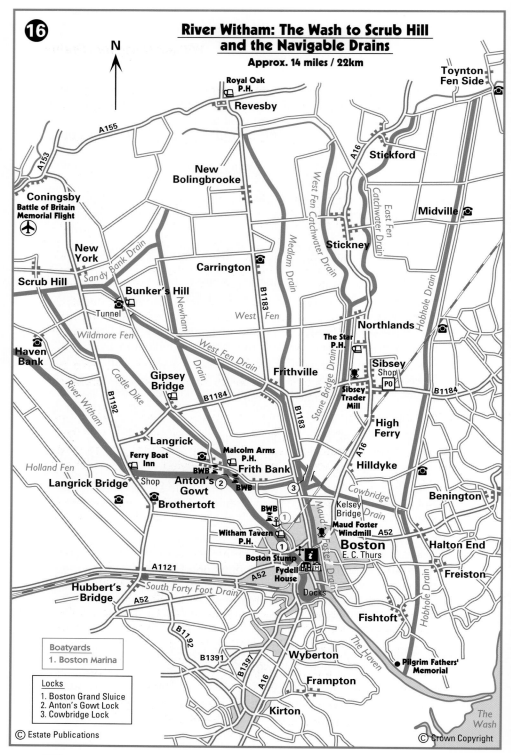

River Witham: The Wash to Scrub Hill and the Navigable Drains

Approx. 14 miles / 22km

16

N

Royal Oak P.H.
Revesby

A155

A153

Coningsby
Battle of Britain
Memorial Flight

New
Bolingbrooke

Toynton
Fen Side

A16

Stickford

Midville

New
York

Carrington

Scrub Hill

Stickney

West Fen Catchwater Drain

East Fen Catchwater Drain

Medam Drain

Sandy Bank Drain

Bunker's Hill

Tunnel

Newham

West Fen

Northlands

The Star
P.H.

Sibsey
Shop
PO

Hobhole Drain

Wildmore Fen

Haven
Bank

Castle Dike

Gipsey
Bridge

West Fen Drain

Drain

B1184

Frithville

Sibsey
Trader
Mill

B1184

River Witham

B1192

B1183

Stone Bridge Drain

B1183

High
Ferry

Holland Fen

Langrick

Ferry Boat
Inn

Shop

Malcolm Arms
P.H.

Frith Bank

A16

Hilldyke

Langrick Bridge

BWB

Anton's
Gowt

BWB

Cowbridge Drain

Benington

Brothertoft

BWB

Kelsey
Bridge

Maud Foster
Windmill

A52

Halton End

Witham Tavern
P.H.

Boston Stump

Fydell
House

Maud Foster Drain

Boston
E. C. Thurs

Freiston

A1121

A52

South Forty Foot Drain

Hubbert's
Bridge

A52

Docks

Hobhole Drain

Fishtoft

B1192

B1391

Wyberton

The Haven

Pilgrim Fathers'
Memorial

B1397

A16

Frampton

Kirton

The
Wash

Boatyards
1. Boston Marina

Locks
1. Boston Grand Sluice
2. Anton's Gowt Lock
3. Cowbridge Lock

method of payment. (These Commissions were renewed by succeeding sovereigns until Henry VIII made them permanent in 1531).

1287 Boston and district was overwhelmed by a sea flood 'caused by much wind'

1316 Inquisition held at Boston into condition of the Great Sluice.

1394 Inquisition at Bolingbroke presented a verdict to the Kings Bench at Lincoln showing that marshes of the East Fenne and West Fenne, and also divers lands, meadow and pastures lying in the towns of Leek Wrangle, Friskeney, and Waynflete, betwixt the waters of Wytham and Waynflete, were drowned by a great inundation of water so that all inhabitants of those towns did wholly lose the benefit of their lands through defects of a certain floodgate at Waynflete which was too narrow and that it would be necessary to have another erected with the towns of Leek Wrangle, Friskeney, and Waynflete, and all others having rights of common, making a contribution to the cost.

1430 Court at Sibsey Hall found that the Abbot of Kirkstead had neglected to repair the Witham banks near Langwarthe Grange so that the river flowed into the West Fen.

1483 King's Court at Bolingbroke fined the inhabitants of Boston and Skirbeck for neglecting to repair the New Gote Sewer in Sibsey.

1500 Sluice built across the river in Boston by the Dutch engineer, May Hake, to stop the tide. An acre rate was levied on local parishes to pay for it.

1532 From the Duchy of Lancaster records it appears that an attempt was made to drain the East and West Fens by enlarging certain drains.

1568 One of these drains was the Maud Foster, cut from the Boston Haven to Cow Brygge. The Boston Corporation Records of November 1st 1568 read as follows: 'A new cut to Cowbrigge shall be coon with such spede as may be couvenientlie and for the charge thereof it is agrede that He Mayor shalle disbourse of the townes money the sum of twentie marks till further order be taken.' Queen Elizabeth I ordered a report on the condition of the East and West Fens but no action appears to have been taken. (However, we do know a bit more about Maude for the Corporation records state:
1568 'Maude Foster shall have two cellars and one cottage, and three acres of pasture, being the towns, during her life, for the

yearly rent of 49s 8d to be paid on the usual days. She to bear all reparations and charges'.

1570 'Maude Foster shall give an obligation with sufficient surety to the Mayor and Burgesses, to pay £10 to the Corporation immediately after her decease'.

1580 'Maude Foster discharged of sundry tenements and garth, and three acres of pasture in the Holms and a house and celler next the Grete hedd if she will not repair the same'. While the Parish Registers show that she was buried on the 10th November 1581.)

1603 King James I declared that he would undertake to drain these Fens but the House of Commons rejected his proposals and he confined his activities to the Great Level in Cambridgeshire.

1631 Court of Sewers at Boston found that the lands of the West and East Fens were overflowed with water and that they were capable of recovery. A tax of ten shillings an acre was levied for repairs to the natural outfalls and other works. Sir Anthony Thomas with others then undertook to drain these Fens and began by erecting a new Maud Foster outfall sluice and widening the drain. The works of Sir Anthony Thomas are indicated on a map in Dugdale, dated 1661.

1642 The Commoners, incensed by loss of lands to the Adventurers broke down the sluices and the matter was taken to the House of Commons. The Commoners commenced proceedings under common law against the Adventurers in which they were successful and the Court of Sewers resumed charge of the district.

1734 Court of Sewers held that various works should be carried out including a new Maud Foster sluice and drain improvement.

1754 Head of Medlam Drain improved and a cut made to Cherry Comer and sluice removed to allow West Fen water to pour down Mill Drain to Maud Foster sluice. Attempts were made to drain other parts of West Fen to Cherry Corner but this was opposed by Boston Corporation who required water to pour through the town for navigation, and this was upheld by a Court. This controversy raged for some time and on one occasion led to rioting near Sibsey.

1762 An Act of Parliament was passed which, among other things, defined the boundaries of the Fourth District of the Witham Commissioners. This excluded the East Fen and the Court of Sewers area. This same Act provided for the appointment or election of both General and District Commissioners to deal with works and to raise toes to finance them.

1766 Grand Sluice, Boston, opened.

1784 Mill Drain deepened and partial drainage of East Fen diverted in this direction, only to be blocked off by the Fenmen whose livelihood of fishing, fowling and reed cutting was threatened. During the late eighteenth century several reports were prepared on the condition and drainage of the East and West Fens and finally, upon the instigation of Sir Joseph Banks, Mr. John Rennie recommended a scheme which, after some modification and much discussion, was put into being by Acts of Parliament in 1801 and 1803, under the direction of the Commissioners.

1801 The main Act was passed which defined the works and also extended the Fourth District to include East Fen.

1806 Hobhole Sluice opened.

1807 New Maud Foster Sluice opened.

1810 Boston flooded by storm tide.

1814 East and West Fens reported to be in good condition.

1817 Sea banks raised two feet above 1810 tide level.

1818 5,000 acre District was taken into the Fourth District and Thorpe Culvert was built.

1861 Land Drainage Act amended the powers of Courts of Sewers.

1862 Skirbeck Court of Sewers issued a Verdict detailing all maintained watercourses in the parishes of Boston East, Skirbeck Fishtoft, Freiston, Butterwick Benington, Leverton, Leake, Wrangle, Friskney and Sibsey.

Towards the middle of the nineteenth century it became evident that conditions in the East Fen were deteriorating due to shrinkage and the poor condition of the Witham outfall below Hobhole sluice. With the advent of the steam engine power became available for pump operation.

1867 Witham Drainage (Fourth District) Act passed which provided for steam pumping engines to be installed at Lade Bank and for channels etc. to be constricted to allow West Fen water to flow to Hobhole Sluice instead of Maud Foster Sluice in adverse conditions. Pumping station commissioned in September. Witham Outfall Improvement Act passed to authorise channel improvements.

1880 Boston Dock opened.

It is not only Boston folk who get hung up about the Witham Navigable Drains. Folk come from far and wide to experience the delights of the Nav-Drav as opposed to those of the Des-Res – and it is indeed salutary to ponder that coming, as they do from the far and the wide, that is exactly what they are not going to find, for the Drains are extremely near and narrow. And no matter how near and dear they may be to any narrow-boat skipper's heart, it has to be remembered at all times that while Drains they certainly are – Navigable they only sometimes are: and definitely only from May to October.

These Witham Navigable Drains occupy the area that lies north of the Witham and south of that line that joins Spilsby to Dogdyke and comprise about 90 miles/145km of man-made waterways of which about 59 miles/ 95km are navigable. While they have become more interesting to leisure cruisers of late, they are still first and foremost functional – and indeed they do work well. It was only after much draining had taken place that it was realised they could usefully carry traffic – and it was not long before agricultural produce, wood and coal were being moved around the area. Today, the most regular, if not the most overworked, activity is that of the protection of the Rights of Navigators: boat owners get together betimes and cruise over every acre that is covered with sufficient water – just to preserve their privileged claims and to remind the authorities (whomsoever they may be) of that right. Owners of craft to whom this right of way is important need to be possessed of boats that are absolutely no more than 60'0"/18.3m LOA (and since this means very few turning places, perhaps 30'0"/10.0m LOA is wiser) with a beam of no more than 11'0"/3.4km (better is 10'0"/3.0m), an air draught of 8'0"/2.4m (better is 6'6"/2.0m) and a water draught of 3'6"/1.1m – at the outside. These figures may not seem very optimistic to those who are great fans of the fens (and experimenters to boot) but caution dictates them since the levels can rise and fall very quickly (and may even be dropped dramatically from time to time without warning). Skippers have been known to be stranded for more than just a short weekend.! It is wisest to take local advice: best obtained from the Drains Officers (Tel. 01205 310099/353758) who are always happy to counsel and oblige. For those whose craft can and will, the Drains offer an intriguing experience; but, don't forget, that once you are in you are in – for Anton's Gowt is the first and the last: the only exit and the only entrance. This lock is boater operated and has max. dimensions of 60'0"/18.3m long by 16'9"/5.1m wide. It is possible to get to the centre of Boston via Cowbridge Lock (71'0"/21.5m x 11'6"/3.5m) which needs a BW key and the Maud Foster Drain but there is no access through onto the Witham.

Not to be missed are the quaint names that abound in the area: New York, Bunkers Hill, Maud Foster, Hobhole, Cowbridge, Bolingbroke,

Lush's, Bellwater and Howbridge.

The BWB moorings outside Anton's are popular for those craft whose size prohibits entry, for the pub is very popular. Apart from weekends, however, the place is quietness itself.

Moving upstream from the Gowt, the river, seldom becoming picturesque in this stretch, feels isolated, remote – if not indeed pretty bleak in all respects. Its best feature is, perhaps, that is no more than a modest hour's run before the nest staging post at Langrick Bridge, about which, it must be said that there is little again that is not desolate, dreary or joyless. For craft with more than 3'3"/1.0m, it is almost impossible to moor to the bank or the bridges – the older of which was built in 1907, putting out of business the ancient ferry. There are general stores, a garage and a public house with food, but with no easy acces and even once you are shoresides there is no cause for complacency or celebration, for the traffic is thunderously threatening and the company hardly less so. Take heart! The river has better things to offer as we move towards Lincoln, the first of which is the engaging stretch of waterway between Kyme Eau (pronounced 'ugh' as in an aitchless Hugh and locally known as Sleaford Cut) and the old (now retired, retiring and silting) Horncastle Canal.

The moorings in Kyme Eau are exclusively private – and, as such, are well marked. The word 'riparian' does not immediately spring to the lips as a way of describing what is to be found here, but 'territorial' certainly does. And no more so than on the balustraded stone bridge at Chapel Hill, where it is possible to stand with one foot in one political, parochial patch and one foot in another, for its used to mark the divide between Kesteven and Holland. It is a pity that there are few opportunities to moor easily and happily here since I have always found it a most appealing spot.

The old river Slea was used as far back as the 13th century and, like all the Fens waterways, has been critical in controlling water levels throughout its area. This waterway, opened on May 6th 1794, and known as the Sleaford Navigation, made completely navigable the twelve mile passage between the town of Sleaford and the River Witham.The canal prospered greatly during the early middle of the 19th century, but the Iceman Cameth, in the form of the railways, froze its assets and chilled it to death. From 1878 (when the canal was abandoned by Act of Parliament) until 1986, when Bottom Lock was re-opened, it slowly descended into disrepair – being useful, it was deemed, for drainage only. The first stretch of the canal is now once again navigable: this rejuvenation is due to the stalwarts of the Sleaford Navigation Society, who were also responsible for the agitation

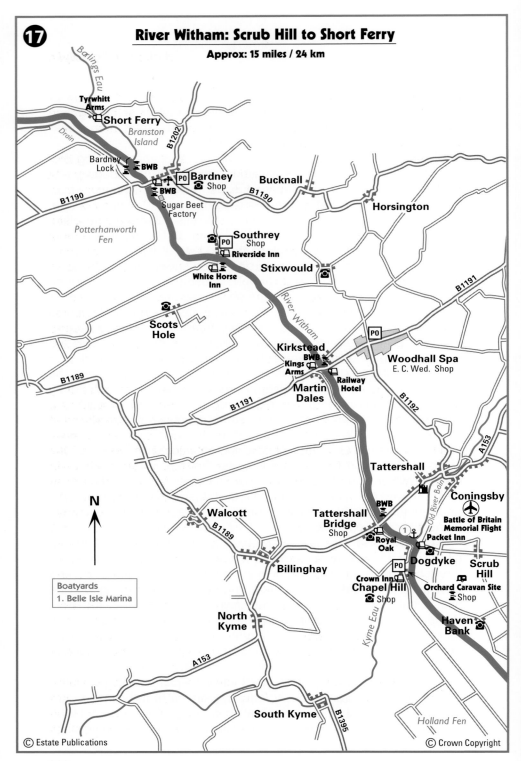

River Witham: Scrub Hill to Short Ferry

Approx: 15 miles / 24 km

17

Bailings Eau

Tyrwhitt Arms

Short Ferry

Branston Island

Drain

B1202

Bardney Lock

BWB

BWB

PO

Bardney
Shop

Bucknall

B1190

Horsington

Sugar Beet Factory

Potterhanworth Fen

B1190

Southrey
Shop

PO

Riverside Inn

Stixwould

White Horse Inn

River Witham

B1191

Scots Hole

B1189

PO

Woodhall Spa
E. C. Wed. Shop

Kirkstead
BWB

Kings Arms

Martin Dales

Railway Hotel

B1191

B1192

Tattershall

A153

B1189

Walcott

Tattershall Bridge
Shop

BWB

Coningsby

Battle of Britain Memorial Flight

Old River Bain

(1)

Packet Inn

Royal Oak

Dogdyke

Scrub Hill

Orchard Caravan Site
Shop

Billinghay

PO

Crown Inn

Chapel Hill
Shop

North Kyme

Kyme Eau

Haven Bank

N

Boatyards
1. Belle Isle Marina

A153

South Kyme

B1395

Holland Fen

© Estate Publications

© Crown Copyright

that brought about the Cobblers Lock work and the 1996 grant of funds for further improvement. It is their fervent hope that the Sleaford Navigation will shortly be returned to the majority of its former glory – even to the waters above Cogglesford.

Navigation is to be undertaken with caution, as the waters not only rise and fall, but also attract more than a goodly share of weed. In particular, it should be remembered that 6' 6"/2.0m air draught is no better than 6' 6"/2.0m at the South Kyme bridge. The locks are all a delight to observe: Haverholme (with its adjacent Priory); Paper Mill (named after the once Boston-busy Evedon Paper Mill); Corn Mill (which once made flour); Bone Mill (for which no name-guessing prize is given); and Cogglesford Mill (known for its old stone cobbled ford) and currently the head of navigation.

Chapel Hill has more facilities than at first seem apparent: a grocer post master whose stocks are plentiful; and a pub with a landlord who goes out of his way to serve – and to be seen to do so. Nearby Orchard Caravans warmly welcome visitors and offer toilet, showers, laundry facilities and a heated swimming pool from June to September. It is well worth a two-day break.

By Dogdyke itself there is a pub, the Packet, and the splendidly named Belle Isle Marina (just up the cut of the Old River Bain). However, appellation is one thing; reality is another – and reality must be all to the point here where the bed of the river is never far away and the banks are all in need of care and attention. Everything is 'Old' in this propinquity (NB: nearness in space, kinship, culture or kind – in truth very true round here): not only in name, but, superficially at least, but also in fact. For example, the 'Old' River Bain; the 'Old' Ferry that no longer exists; the 'Old' Horncastle Canal, now blanked off from the main river where cattle meet for a wet; 'Old' Tattershall Castle; and, finally, the 'Old' Pumping Station. This last is of special interest. The first pump at Dogdyke was built just before the 19th century was born. It was of the genuine windmill genre and lived and worked for sixty years, after which its load was taken up by a coal-fired steam engine. In turn, its days were numbered and in the early part of the last war it was superseded by the present diesel engine. It has, though, been happily retired and properly pensioned by the Trust formed in 1973 that keeps it open for visitors and from time to time, it is fired into life.

It is only about a mile to the 'old' and 'new' Tattershall Bridges where the A153 crosses the Witham. There are good BWB moorings here affording access to the shoreside facilities of basic grocery and hostelry. Apart from immediate spirituous charms, it is Tattershall

Castle that must take pride of place. The present village of Tattershall, lying on the River Bain in east Lincolnshire, has no market, although the spacious market place is a reminder of a more prosperous past. The market is indeed recorded from the beginning of the 13th century, and shortly afterwards, in the early 1230s, the first castle built of stone was erected. In 1430-50 Ralph, Lord Cromwell extended the area of the castle and added many new buildings of brick, of which the most notable was the Great Tower. Domestic (if it can be called that) occupation con-tinued until the late 17th century, but after its final abandonment the ruins were largely cleared away and the moats filled in. In 1911 the site was bought by Lord Curzon, who, after extensive treatment of the buildings and restoration of the earth-works, bequeathed them to the National Trust in 1925.

As a young man, Ralph, Lord Cromwell went for a soldier to France and was at Agincourt - and country and battle both impressed him greatly. Back in his home territory, he ascended the power scale rapidly: Constable of Nottingham Castle; Warden of Sherwood Forest; and England's Treasurer for the ten years from 1433-1443. This last office so appealed to him that he had purse icons fashioned in his chimney pieces. There are even some (difficult to read) bills of trade and carpenter services still available for inspection.

The main interest has to be the magnificent brick tower, referred to in 1446 as the 'great tower called 'le Dongeon'. It is one of the most striking monuments of the later Middle Ages in this country. The feudal/tyrannical regime of the Middle Ages inspired not so much churches for the body spiritual but houses for the body corporeal: tall towers for residential occupancy - but with small windows and entrances at first-floor level. Although the Tattershall tower is generally in keeping with the tradition, possessing three ground-floor door-ways and large ground-floor windows and was definitely meant to show itself really like one, it could not really have been used as one. It may have given rise to second thoughts in the hearts and minds of brigands - but would not have completely deterred them. While keeps had been out of fashion in England since the 13th century, in France they were a normal feature of the late 14th and 15th century castles. It is fair, there-fore, to assume that Cromwell brought back from his foreign travels the idea of building one. Few buildings so tellingly reveal on the one hand so much of the artificiality of the secular life of the period in which they were erected, and on the other the aspirations of the man for whom it was built.

No more than half a mile from the bridge on the way to Kirkstead is a most attractive and remote spot where once led off the Horncastle

Canal. There is an obvious large 'dent' in the bank where the water-way is now dammed, and this is an excellent place to nudge or nestle your way to the side and settle down in peace and quiet. Built at the turn of the 19th century, the (short) 10 mile/16km canal to the eponymous community had only a (short) 75 year life-span. Bits of the lost lock are to be examined by the river, and some short stretches are still damp. Its chief claim to glory was to provide the wet wherewithal for the castle's moat.

Less than an hour's cruising upstream brings Kirkstead Bridge into view. An excellent stopping place, it is now favoured with a another good BWB mooring. Kirkstead is on the east bank with the much smaller Martin Dales on the other; although there is life and talent galore on both sides – so don't miss out on either of the pubs. Fishermen abound.

Woodhall Spa, is hardly a mile away, and a very pleasant mile it is - with good old-fashioned hedges with good old-fashioned seasonal natural goodies. Mushrooms and blackberries in particular can not only abound but also do as lush and luscious crops. Half-way to the Spa, across a cow-pat covered, rabbit and hedgehog infested field, is to be found all that remains of the seat of the once powerful abbots of Kirkstead Abbey. Beware of ghosts and falling stones.

I have always found Woodhall to be a dream of a place – in spite of having had to suffer too many Sunday afternoon teas in the woods impaled on the thorns of my parents' hateful relationship. The Spa has three fascinating features: almost hidden away in the woods is the Kinema; the Petwood Hotel, a one-time seriously lush hang out for the seriously rich – and now a monolith dedicated merely to the expensive mediocre. The local heroes of the Royal Air Force (the commissioned officers of the Damn Busters) made it their headquarters during the last war. The third part of the trio still abound: squirrels – much to the annoyance of many of the locals, for they, the squirrels that is, are grey, with the indigens being red in the face from trying to get rid of the 'pestilential critters'!

Half an hour from the river bridge brings us to Southrey: a small community divided by the river – although never the twain-twins shall meet. On the north side, the Riverside Inn flaunts this notice skywards: 'If you can read this, you are too close'. Sadly, there is no proper landing stage and getting ashore is worth neither the risk nor the effort. On the south side are the moorings for the White Horse pub – where there is an almost ever open-door atmosphere, and very good facilities. the mooring fee can be reclaimed at the bar – in exchange for victualling! A decent bargain, this; since it is not long ago that the privately laid mooring was nearly all taken away when a travelling troupe of thespian chappies tried to tow it away with their narrow boat. After another three miles up the river is the sugarbeet factory, with the first BWB moorings for the village – much closer than the ones at the lock. This is followed by a big river bend and bigger chimneys. Three waterways divide here: dead ahead proceeds the drainage dyke that reaches up to Lincoln; to the north is the navigation, which then bends to port, leaving the course of the old river that goes to Short Ferry where there was once a marina. The 'old' river rejoins the navigation upstream of Bardney lock which is immediately next – complete with its clean piling against which it is a pleasure to tie up: the water is deep; there are plenty of rope holds, hand holds and foot ladders. The final entry to the lock is guarded by a quaint footbridge.

Bardney Lock was at one time manned, but those days are gone. It is, as BWB so charmingly puts it 'boatman operated'. However, the good news is that the whole 'operation' has been improved - although the actual hand-working of the gates still requires goodly effort. For once, there are plenty of places to moor: the quayside with the water point, loo and showers is seldom busy enough to prevent an overnight stay; while the first few spaces by the new pontoon moorings above the lock are usually available to visitors. If all else fails, there is a very quiet patch back at the first drain: the open area just in front of the railway arches. The environs are host to many friendly folk and even more feral cats – but both take a lot of chasing; even more seducing - and are almost all impossible to catch. The village itself has a good array of 'proper' village shops and pubs – making the substantial walk a worthy effort with an excellent reward.

Moving on towards Lincoln, the canal carries very little water; and if you are near the 6'0"/1.8m mark you will start encountering the bottom. True, the bottom is all soft mud and silt with no hidden rocks; but there are still unpleasant items such as barbed wire, fan belts and part of mattresses waiting to be plucked by deep-searching props. However, once past the chained-off weir and pumping station on the right (the old river and no doubt the cause of the lesser depth) the danger of finding bottom is over if you keep to a central course.

Five miles before Lincoln comes (surprise!) Five Mile Bridge. This is an attractive staging post if you want to go to Fiskerton (known as Fishers' Town when boats worked the 'port' years ago) or pretty Cherry Willingham. Both are within walking distance, and are interesting because of their past connections with the old Viking Way. Nearby, across the water, is Washingborough; an entirely different kettle of fish(k). It is a popular spot, but there is a shortage of water at

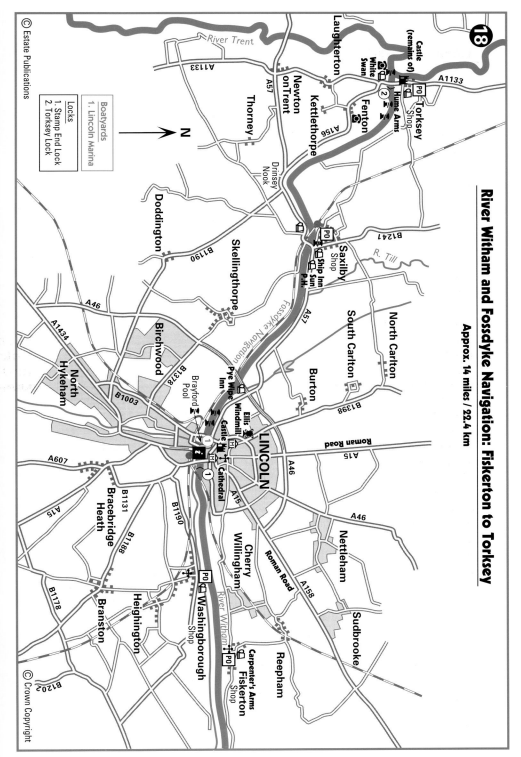

Boatyards
1. Lincoln Marina

Locks
1. Stamp End Lock
2. Torksey Lock

N

© Estate Publications

© Crown Copyright

215

the banksides and cautious bows-on mooring is required. Nevertheless, Washingborough is not a place to be idly dismissed if you have the few hours it will take to assess the charm and facilities.

The first signs of Lincoln are the piercing cathedral spire and Saint Hugh's soul on high, and the old and ugly disintegrating factories below. The whole area possesses a collection of floating rubbish and underwater detritus; but, on the other hand, it no longer proffers the factory electric lift bridge that used to cause so much aggravation and delay. It is no distance at all to the lock known as Stamp End, which marks the beginning of Lincoln City proper. The lock is an electric, boater operated, guillotine; and delivers the usual assaults from that kind of action. Stout ropes are recommended and umbrellas and oilies are appropriate.

Next comes a series of pipe, road and foot bridges, including the well known Glory Hole or High Bridge. The facades on this mile or so of urban waterway are as attractive as they are old - although some have been treated to much tasteful refurbishment. They disguise the easy access that is afforded to the old established markets and the newly arrived arcades. The Glory Hole is generally accepted as the restricting factor between The River Trent and The Wash, being low, narrow and severely arched; and there is no doubt that it is impossible to negotiate it at anything more than a crawl. However, the modern road bridge, which is the last before the great acreage of Brayford Pool is actually the lowest on the stretch. It is possible to get under the bridge if the craft has some of the maximum dimensions, but if it is at the extremes of all, considerable caution and a snail's pace are required if the vessel is not to get jammed. My personal assessment of the restricting dimensions (made on a number of occasions and with neck-aching/finger-nail scraping efforts are: draught 4'6"/1.4m; beam 14'0"/4.3m; air draught no more than 9'0"/2.7m when the span of the wheelhouse exceeds 9'0"/2.7m.

The Pool attracts hundreds of boat folk from far and near, many of whom are permanent. Visitors moorings are to be found by the Harbour Master's office. Here, you will find a warm and helpful welcome. Across the way, the island looks tempting, but, while the bottom is clean and free from everything, it is also very close to the surface. The much-vaunted (but charisma-less) 'new' university is on the island and rail-track side – as are the 'very new' (incomplete at the time of going to press) facilities of Lincoln Marina.

The city has many shops and eating places; especially up the 'Steep Hill' (many pauses for breath needed) that ascends to the cathedral. There is another place of spirit here too: The Whisky Shop, in

Bailgate. It is run by a Scot who lived as a boy next the Scottish boat-yard where Valcon was built, and later was Station Officer at Niton Radio. The long haul from the Pool, is justified if only for their array of single malts; but there are delights galore in the whole locale. The main attraction for many folk is the Cathedral of St Hugh.

Lincoln to Torksey

Leaving Brayford Pool, with the Perkins boat-obsessed engineers to the right and Lincoln Marina to the left, there used to be another old bridge to be negotiated. Times have changed: together with all the new academic and commercial building that has occurred around the pool, there will shortly be a brand new bridge to celebrate the upsurge in road traffic.

After the bridge comes the BWB office, followed by a long line of moorings. Most of these are 'occupied' by fee-paying tenants who are among the most territorially minded land-bound boating folk I have ever met. Along this Main Drag (and what a drag it is) the craft come in a variety of forms - and also a variety of states. On the opposite bank are the comparatively safe havens of the Lincoln Race and Golf courses.

However, a positive attraction lies not far ahead: the Pye Wipe Inn (of the famed omnipresent eponymous bird). It is an isolated hostelry, but very popular with boaters, for, although its exterior does nothing to tempt you in, once inside, both interior and company make the mooring up worthwhile.

From the Pye Wipe to Saxilby is about 4 miles/6.4km and most of the route is fairly low-key in most ways. Saxilby is a pleasant village; its 'High' street running with the canal. Within walking distance are fish and chip shops, hairdressers, DIY merchants, grocers and two public houses: the Ship and the Sun. Just beyond the village, on the other side from the shops, is a hotel-manque-type establishment with easy access from the canal. Between the village and Drinsey Nook, the banks are likely to be strewn by fishermen and their tackle - in or out of season.

After Drinsey Nook, not much happens for a long time. In general it is akin to 'Waiting For Godot': 'nobody comes, nobody goes ... it's awful' - except in this case it is not 'awful', merely uneventfully straight and flat until you reach the end of the navigation at Torksey Lock. The generally slow progress creates time to observe the many arrays of wild life - mostly of the low-flying breed - but also lots of rats. Long before the lock, there are moorings on each bank. Twenty years ago when I first went there, there were masses of them, but now there are masses and masses as it were. On the bank, the hostelry, 'Wheelhouse' comes first. Torksey has many attractions, and the most outstanding must be the castle, sadly now in a poor state but still with a proud facade that is best seen from the river.

The lock itself is a classic black and white affair, with keepers who are always ready to help when it comes to working the Trent's sometimes baffling timetables. Just beyond the lock are two floating pontoons which offer over-night and over-tide moorings so that it is never actually difficult to get to Cromwell Lock upstream or the Stockwith or Keadby locks downstream - even when your speed is, like Valcon's: a standard 6 knots.

I have a special liking for the Witham and Fossdyke. Its 40 miles/64km offer peace and quiet most of the time, and three really good spots to stay: Torksey, Lincoln and Boston. Then there are water-borne treats and challenges at each end: the provocations and relaxations of the River Trent; and the prodigious phenomenon of The Wash. It can also claim to be one of the oldest artificial Navigations in Britain, dating back to Emperor Hadrian, who around 120AD apparently had enough sense and clout to dig the Fossdyke as well as to build his wall.

The Witham and Fossdyke must rate as one of the most under-rated waterways of the UK: attractive but under-appreciated ... worthy of real admiration yet mostly overlooked and underpraised.

Facilities

Boston Marina	01205 364420
Belle Isle Marina, Dogdyke	01526 342124
R.Keightley & Son	01205 363616
Brayford Pool, Lincoln	01522 521452
Lincoln Marina, Brayford Pool	01522 526896
Witham Fourth District Internal Drainage Board	01205 310099
7 Norfolk Street, Boston	
Foreman	01205 353758
Sleaford Navigation Society	01529 240501

Places of interest

Fydell House, Boston
Tel. 01205 351520
18th century town house: open all year mon - fri 0930 - 1230 and
1330 - 1630 during university term time

Boston Guildhall Museum
Tel.01205 365954
15th century building with original cells where the Pilgrim fathers were
imprisoned: tel for opening times

Dogdyke Steam Pumping Station
Tel. 01526 342352
only known land drainage engine worked by steam: open Apr - Oct,
1st sun in every month 1330 - 1700

Tattershall Castle (N.T.)
Tel. 01526 342543
fortified and moated mediaeval red brick tower: open 3rd Apr - 31st
Oct daily except thurs and fri 1030 - 1730 and 6th Nov - 19th Dec sat
& sun 1200 - 1600

Lincoln Castle
Tel. 01522 511068
mediaeval castle with Magna Carta exhibition: tel. for opening times

Lincoln Cathedral
Tel. 01522 544544
mediaeval Gothic cathedral : open daily from 0715

Sibsey Trader Windmill
Tel. 01205 750036
restored 19th century 6-sailed windmill: tel. for opening times

USEFUL ADDRESSES

Broads Authority
18 Colegate
Norwich   NR3 1BQ   01603 610734

Blakes Holidays Ltd,
Wroxham
Norwich   NR12 8DH   01603 739300

British Waterways
(Witham & Fossdyke)
North East Region
1 Dock Street
Leeds   LS1 1HH   01532 436741

Cam Conservancy
(River Cam)
The Guildhall
Cambridge   01223 457000

East of England Tourist Board
Toppesfield Hall
Suffolk   IP7 5DN   01473 822922

Environment Agency
Anglian Region Office
Kingfisher House, Goldhay Way
Orton Goldhay
Peterborough PE2 5ZR
01733 371811

Environment Agency
(Rivers Nene, Welland and Glen)
Northern Area
Waterside House, Waterside North
Lincoln   LN2 5HA   01522 513100

Environment Agency
(River Great Ouse)
Central Area
Bromholme Lane
Brampton, Huntingdon
Cambs   PE18 8NE   01480 414581

Great Yarmouth Port Authority
20 South Quay
Great Yarmouth   01493 335500

Hoseasons Holidays Ltd.
Sunway House
Lowestoft
Suffolk   NR32 2LW   01502 502602

National TrustEast
Anglian Regional Office
Blickling
Norwich   NR11 6NF   01263 733471

Norfolk Wherry Trust
Hon. Sec
14 Mount Pleasant
Norwich   NR2 2DG   01603 505815

Norfolk Wildlife Trust
72 Cathedral Close
Norwich   NR1 4DF   01603 625540

Norfolk Windmills Trust 01603 222222

RSPB
Stalham House
Norwich   NR1 1UD   01603 661662

Suffolk Windmills Trust 01473 890089

INDEX

Bold type indicates map

Abington Lock **163**, 165
Acle 21, **27**, 28, 39, 78
Acle Bridge **27**, 28, 29
Acle Road Bridge 17, **18**, 20, 22, **24**, 25, **59**
Aldeby Staithe **67**, 68, 97
Aldreth Bridge 125, **128**
Aldwincle **159**, 161
Alwalton Lock **156**, 158, **159**
Angle Bridge **170**, 174
Anglesey Abbey **147**, 151
Ant, River 9, 30, 50-4, 56-7
Anton's Gowt 202, **204**, 208
Ashline Lock **170**, 172
Ashton Lock **159**, 160
Ayscoughfee Hall 187, 192
Baits Bite Lock **147**, 149
Bardney Lock **210**, 214
Bargate Water 87
Barnack Stone 127, 174, 190
Barnwell **159**, 161
Barton Broad **49**, 51-2
Barton Turf **49**, 51-3
Beccles 60, 63, 64, 66, **67**, 79, 97
Beccles Bridge 66, **67**, 68
Beccles Museum 66, **67**, 69
Beccles Yacht Station **67**, 69
Bedford 127, 135, **136**, 137-8
Bedford Level 102-103
Bedford Lock **136**, 138
Belaugh **32**, 37, 39
Belle Isle Marina **210**, 211, 219
Benwick **170**, 174
Berney Arms 21, 58, 60, **62**, **77**, 78, 96
Berney Arms Mill 12, **62**, **77**, 78, 95
Bevill's Leam **170**, 173-4
Bill Fen Marina **170**, 176, 181
Billing Lock **163**, 165
Billing Aquadrome **163**, 165, 167
Boal Quay 109, 113
Boatworld **65**, **72**, 76
Boston 110, 184-6, 193-205, 218, 219
Boston Grand Sluice 110, 193, 195, 197-8, **204**-7
Boston Guildhall Museum 219, **204**
Boston Marina 198-9, **204**, 219
Boston Stump 102, 199-200, **204**
Bottisham Lock 101, 125, **147**, 149
Bramerton Common **85**, 93
Bramerton Woods End **85**, 87, 98
Brampton Lock **131**, 133
Brandon 118, **119**, 138
Brandon Bridge **119**, 120
Brandon Creek **116**, 118, **119**, 138
Brayford Pool **215**, 216, 217, 219
Breydon Bridge 17, **18**, 19, 21, 58, **59**
Breydon Water 15, 17-21, **24**, 58-60, **62**, **77**, 78
Bridewell Museum 91, 95
Broads Authority 10-14, 21-2, 39, 51, 53, 75
Brownshill Lock 127, **128**

Brundall 83, **85**, 86-7, 94, 98
Buckden **131**, 133
Buckden Marina **131**, 133, 143
Buckenham Ferry **82**, 84, **85**
Bure Valley Railway **32**, 40
Bure, River 9, 15-21, **24**, 25-41, 57
Burgh Castle 21, 58, 60-2, 68, **77**
Burgh Castle Marina 61, **62**, 69, **77**
Burgh St Peter 64, **65**, **67**, **72**
Burghley House **183**, 190, 192
Burnthouse Bridge **170**, 172
Burwell **147**, 148
Burwell Lode **147**, 148
Cam, River 101, 125, **128**, **147**-51, 180, 220
Cambridge 101, 115, 125, **147**, 149-150, 190
Candle Dyke 43, 44, **45**, 46, 55
Candlemaker Model Centre **24**, 40
Cantley **82**, 83
Cardington Lock 135, **136**, 138
Carlton Rail Bridge **65**, **72**, 76
Carrow Lifting Bridge **85**, 88, **93**
Castle Mill Lock 135, **136**
Central Museum and Art Gallery 165
Chapel Hill 209, **210**, 211
Chedgrave **82**, 83, 93-4
Chet, River 81-3, 98
Clifford Hill Lock **163**, 165
Cockshoot Broad 11, 31, **32**
Cogenhoe **163**, 165
Coltishall 25, 29, **32**, 33, 37-9, 57
Cotton End Lock **163**, 165
Cowbridge Lock **204**, 208
Crowland **183**, 187, 192
Croyland Abbey **183**, 187, 192
Deep Dyke **45**, 47, 55
Deeping St James 182, **183**, 187-8
Delph Bridge **171**, 178-9
Denford Lock **159**, 162
Denver 111, **112**, 115-8, 138, 143, 145
169, **171**, 174, 179, 180
Denver Cruising Club 110, 118
Denver Sluice 105, 110-17, 127, 148
169, **171**, 179, 181
Dilham **49**, 50, 52
Dilham Dyke **49**, 50, 52
Ditchford Lock **163**, 164
Doddington Lock **163**, 165
Dog-in-a-Doublet 154-7
Dogdyke 208, **210**, 211, 219
Dogdyke Steam Pumping Station 219
Downham Market **112**, 115, **171**
Downham Market Bridge **112**, 113, 114, **171**
Drainage Engine Museum 121, **122**, 144
Earith 127, **128**, 143, 145
169, **170**, 179-80
Earls Barton **163**, 165
Eaton Ford **131**, 134, **136**
Eaton Socon **131**, 134, **136**, 143, 145

221

Elgoods Brewery **153**, 167
Elizabethan House Museum **18**, 22, **59**
Ely 115-117, 120, 123-25, **128**
138, 143-5, 169, **171**, 176, 190
Ely Boat Chandlers 124, 126, 145
Ely Cathedral 102, **116**, 121, 124, **128**, 174
Ely Marina 113, **116**, **128**, 143
Ely Museum **116**, **128**, 144
Environment Agency 101, 111, 138-9
181, 176, 220
Exhibition Bridge **170**, 176
Fairhaven Garden Trust **27**, 40
Filby Broad 28, 55
Fish & Duck 125, **128**, 145-8, 151
Fish & Duck Marina **128**, 143, **147**, 151
Fishing 55-7, 97-8, 146, 168, 191
Fiskerton 214-5
Five Miles From Anywhere **147**, 148, 151
Forty Foot Drain 169, **170**, 176
Fosdyke 110, 155, 184-6, **183**, 191
Fosdyke Bridge 182, **183**, 184-6
Fotheringhay Castle **159**, 160-1
Foundry Bridge **85**, 89
Fox's Marina **170-1**, 177-8, 181
Free Bridge 113-14
Freedom Bridge **153**, 154
Fritton **62**, 63, **77**
Fritton Lake Country Park **62**, 63, 69, **77**
Fulney Lock **183**, 184, 186, 192
Fydell House **204**, 219
Gariannonum 58, 61, **62**, **77**
Gay's Staithe **49**, 51, 53
Geldeston 63, 66, **67**, 68
Glen, River 101, 182, **183**, 191-2
GOBA 109, 118, 121, 125, 129, 140-2
Godmanchester **131**, 132, 143
Godmanchester Lock **131**, 133, 139
Gordon Boswell Romany Museum 192
Grand Union Canal 165, 169
Great Addington 162, **163**
Great Barford 135, **136**, 141, 143, 145
Great Ormesby Broad 55
Great Ouse, River 9, 101, 105-46, **171**, 180
Great Paxton **131**, 134
Great Yarmouth 11, 15-25, 38, 52, 58, **59**, 61
Great Yarmouth Marina **24**, 25, 39
Great Yarmouth Maritime Museum 23
Great Yarmouth Port Authority 22, 220
Great Yarmouth Yacht Station **18**, 19-22, **24**-5
28-9, 39, **59**
Guyhirn **153**, 155, **156**, **170-1**
Haddiscoe Bridge **62**, 68, **77**
Haddiscoe Cut **62**, **77**, 79-80, **82**
Halvergate **62**, **77**, 78
Hardley Dyke **82**, 83-4
Hardley Flood Nature Reserve **82**, 95
Hartford **131**, 132, 145
Hartford Marina **131**, 132, 143
Haven Bridge 15-9, 22, **59**, 60
Hemingford Abbots 130, **131**
Hemingford Grey 130, **131**, 145
Hemingford Lock **131**
Hemingford Meadow 130, 141

Hermitage Lock 125, **128**, **170**, 180
Hermitage Marina 127-8, 143, **170**, 180
Herringfleet Mill 63, **65**, **72**
Hickling Broad 44, **45**, 47, 52, 55
Hilgay **116**, 118, **119**, 145
Hire Boats 12, 17, 21, 35, 44, 71
Hobhole Drain 196, **204**, 208
Holme Fen **170**, 173-4
Horning 29, **32**, 33, 39, 57
Horning Ferry **32**, 33
Horning Sailing Club **32**, 33
Horsey **45**, 46
Horsey Mere 42, 44-6, 52, 55
Horsey Mill 12, **45**, 46, 48
Horsey Staithe **45**, 46
Houghton **131**, 132, 139
Houghton Mill **131**, 132, 144
Hoveton Great Broad **32**, 34, 40
Hoveton Hall **32**, 34, 40
Hoveton Little Broad **32**, 33
Hoveton St John **32**, 34, 39
How Hill **49**, 50, 53
Hundred Foot Drain 114, 146, 169, 179, 180
Hunsett Mill **49**, 52
Huntingdon **131**, 132-3, 143-4
Huntingdon Boat Haven **131**, 143
Infields Bridge 174
Irchester **163**, 164
Irstead **49**, 50, 51
Irthlingborough 162, **163**
Isleham 121, **122**
Isleham Marina 121, **122**, 142-3
Islip Lock **159**, 162
Judes Ferry 121, **122**
Kings Dyke **156**, 169-72
King's Lynn 105-15, 144, 179
King's Lynn Port Authority 109-10, **112**
Kirkstead Bridge **210**, 213
Kyme Eau 209, **210**
Lake Lothing 9, 58, **65**, **72**, 73
Langley Dyke **82**, 84
Langrick Bridge **204**, 209
Lark, River **116**, 121-3, 138, 146
Lazy Otter Inn 125, **128**, 141, 145, **171**
Lilford Lock **159**, 161
Lime Kiln Dyke **49**, 51
Lincoln 188, 190, 209, 214-216, 218, 219
Lincoln Castle **215**, 219
Lincoln Cathedral 102, **215**, 217, 219
Lincoln Marina **215**, 216, 217, 219
Little Ouse, River **116**, 118-20, 138, 146
Little Thetford **128**, 139
Littleport **116**, 120, 138, **171**, 180
Littleport Boat Haven **116**, 120, 143
Loddon 81, **82**, 83, 93, 94, 98
Lode **147**, 151
Lodes End Lock **170**, 174, 175, 181
Lower Ringstead Lock **159**, 162, **163**
Lowestoft 9, 15, 58, 60-5, **72**, 73-6
Lowestoft Maritime Museum **65**, **72**, 76
Lowestoft Museum **65**, **72**, 76
Ludham 29, 42, **43**, **49**
Ludham Bridge **49**, 50, 53

Malthouse Broad 30-2, 56
March 169, **170-1**, 176, 178, 181
March Museum **170-1**, 176, 181
Market Deeping **183**, 188, 191
Marmont Priory Lock **171**, 178
Martham **43**, 44, **45**
Martham Broad 42, 46, 56
Maud Foster Drain **204**, 205-8
Meadow Dyke **45**, 46
Mepal **171**, 179
Middle Level Drain **112**, 114, **171**
Middle Levels 101, 103, 115, 157, 169-81
Midsummer Meadows **163**, 167
Morton's Leam 103, 125, **156**, **170**, 174
Muck Fleet 26, **27**, 28
Museum of the Broads 54
Mutford Lock 9, 15, 58, **65**, 71, **72**, 75
Mutford Lifting Bridge 15, **65**, **72**, 75, 76
Nassington **159**, 160
Neatishead 29, **49**, 51
Nene, River 101, 125, 152-69, 174, 188
Nene Valley Railway **156**, 158, **159**, 168
New Bedford River 114, **116**, 117, 146
169, **171**, 176, 179-80
Nordelph **171**, 178
Norfolk Broads Yacht Club **32**, 34
Norfolk Rare Breeds Centre 28, 40
Norfolk Wherry Trust 14, 220
Norfolk Wildlife Trust 10, 31, 40, 46
47, 51, 54, 220
Norfolk Windmills Trust 12, 40, 220
North Walsham and Dilham Canal **49**, 50, 52
Northampton 155, **163**, 165-9
Norwich 11, 61, 63, 78, 79, 81, **85**, 88-96
Norwich Castle Museum 95
Norwich Cathedral **85**, 90, 107
Norwich Yacht Station **85**, 89, 94
Octavia Hill Birthplace Museum 155, 168
Offord Cluny **131**, 133, 145
Offord D'Arcy **131**, 133-4
Offord Lock **131**, 133, 141
Old Bedford River 114, **116**, 117, 127
146, **171**, 176, 178-9
Old Bedford Sluice **171**, 178
Old Nene 125, 169, **170-1**, 174-9
Old West River 125, 146, **171**, 180
Oliver Cromwell's House, **116**, **128**, 144
Orchard Caravans **210**, 211
Orton Lock **156**, 158, 168
Oulton Broad 11, 60, 64, 71-6
Oulton Broad Yacht Station **65**, 71, **72**, 76
Oulton Dyke 64, **65**, 68, 71, **72**
Oundle **159**-61, 168
Oundle Marina **159**, 160, 167
Outwell **112**, 169, **171**, 178
Oxlode Railway Bridge **171**, 179
Peakirk **183**, 188, 192
Peckover House **153**, 154, 167
Peterborough 102, 154-8, 168-9, **170**
174, 176, 186, 188, 190
Peterborough Embankment **156**, 158, 167
Pettitt's Animal Adventure Park **82**, 95
Pike & Eel Marina **128**, 129, 141, 143, **147**

Pinchbeck Engine Musem **183**, 191-2
Popes Corner 125, **128**, 145, **147**
148, 151, **171**, 180
Popham's Eau **171**, 178
Port of Fosdyke Ltd 182, 185, 192
Postwick **85**, 87, 93
Postwick Viaduct 78, **85**, 87, 93
Potter Heigham 37, 42, **43**, 44, 47, 57
Potter Heigham Old Bridge **43**, 44, 47
Prickwillow **116**, 121, **122**, 138
Prickwillow Drainage Engine Museum **116**,121
122, 144
Priory Marina 135, **136**, 141, 143
Purvis Marina **131**, 132, 143
Queen Adelaide **116**, **122**, 138
Quiet Waters Boat Haven 127, **128**, 143
Railworld 168
Ramsey **171**, 174-6
Ramsey Abbey 129, 130, **171**, 173, 175
Ramsey Rural Museum **171**, 175, 181
Ranworth 31, **32**
Ranworth Broad 31, **32**, 56
Ranworth Staithe 39, 41
Ranworth Wildlife Centre 31, **32**, 40
Reach Lode **147**, 148
Red Hart **171**, 177-8
Reedham 21, **62**, 63, **77**, 78-**82**, 93-6
Reedham Swing Bridge **62**, **77**, **82**, 93
Ringstead **159**, 162, **163**, 168
Rockland Broad 84, **85**, 86, 97
Rollesby Broad 28, 55
Roxton Lock 135, **136**
Royal Norfolk and Suffolk Y.C. **65**, **72**, 73
Sacrewell Farm and Country Centre **159**, 168
Salhouse Broad **32**, 34, 56
Salhouse Little Broad **32**, 34
Salters Lode Lock **112**, 114-15, **116**, 127
169, **170**, 178-9, 181
Saxilby **215**, 217
Scrub Hill **205**, **210**
Short Ferry **210**, 214
Sibsey Trader Windmill **204**, 219
Sleaford Navigation 209, 211
Sleaford Navigation Society 209, 211
Somerleyton **62**, 63, 64, **65**, 68, **72**, **77**
Somerleyton Bridge **65**, 68, 71, **72**
Somerleyton Hall 63-5, 69, **72**
South Kyme **210**, 211
South Walsham **27**, 31, 39
South Walsham Broad **27**, 30, 56
Southrey **210**, 213
Spalding 137, 176, 182, **183**, 185-7, 191-2
Spalding Bridge 184
Spalding Tropical Forest 192
St Benet's Abbey **27**, 29-30, 42
St George's Guildhall 144
St Germans Bridge 113-114
St Ives 125, 129-31, 142, 145, 176
St Neots **131**, 134, 143
St Neots Lock **131**, 134
St Olaves 21, 60-3, 68, **72**, 79
St Olaves Bridge **62**, 63, 68, **77**
St Olaves Priory **62**, 63, 69, **77**

St Olaves Windpump 62, 69, **77**
Stags Holt Farm **170-1**, 176, 181
Stalham 49, 51-2, 57
Stalham Dyke **49**, 52
Stamford **183**, 187, 190-192
Stamp End Lock **215**, 216
Stanground Creek **170-1**, 172
Stanground Sluice **156**, 157, 167, 169-172, 181
Stibbington 158, **159**, 168
Stoke Ferry 118, **119**
Stokesby 24, 26, **27**
Stonea Camp **171**, 176
Stowbridge **112**, 113-4, 180
Stracey Arms 21, **24**, 26, 57, 78
Stracey Arms Mill 12, **24**, 26, 40, 78
Stretham 125, **128**, 139, 144, 145, **171**, 180
Stretham Ferry Bridge 125, **128**
Strumpshaw **85**
Strumpshaw Fen **85**, 86, 95
Strumpshaw Steam Museum **85**, 86, 95
Surfleet Seas End **183**, 191
Surfleet Sluice **183**, 192
Surlingham 83, **85**, 87, 98
Surlingham Broad **85**, 87
Sutton **49**, 51
Sutton Bridge 152, **153**, 154, 155
Sutton Gault **170-1**, 180
Sutton Mill 51, 54
Sutton Windmill Pottery **49**, 54
Tales of the Old Gaol House 144
Tattershall **210**, 211-2
Tattershall Bridge **210**, 211
Tattershall Castle **210**, 211-2, 219
Ten Mile Bank **116**, **119**, 138, 145, **171**
Thorpe St Andrew **85**, 88, 93-4
Thorpe St Andrew Railway Bridges **85**, 88, 93, 98
Thrapston **159**, 162
Thrapston Lagoon **159**, 162
Thrapston Marina **159**, 162, 167
Three Holes Bridge **171**, 178
Thrigby Hall Wildlife Gardens **24**, 40
Thurne Dyke Windpump **27**, 12, **43**, 47
Thurne Mouth **27**, 29, 42, **43**
Thurne, River 9, **27**, 29, 30, 33, 42-8, 57
Tip Tree Marina **147**, 151
Titchmarsh Lock **159**, 161
Toad Hole Cottage Museum **49**, 50, 53
Tolhouse Museum **18**, 22, **59**
Tongue End **183**, 191
Torksey 194, **215**, 218
Torksey Lock **215**, 217
Trent, River **215**, 216, 218
Trinity Broads 26, **27**, 28
Trowse **85**, 88-9, 98
Trowse Swing Bridge **85**, 88, 93
True's Yard Museum 144
Twenty Foot River **156**, **170**, 174
Twenty Pence Bridge 125, **128**
Twenty Pence Marina 125, **128**, 143, **171**, 180
Upton **27**, 29, 39
Upton Broad **27**, 29
Upton Dyke **27**, 29
Upton Fen **27**

Upware **128**, **147**, 148, 151
Upware Marina **147**, 148, 151
Upwell **171**, 178
Vauxhall Bridge 17-9, 22, **59**
Vermuyden's Drain 169, **170**, 176
Water Newton Lock 158, **159**
Waveney, River 9, 21, 60-71, **72**, **77**, 97
Waveney River Centre 64, **65**, 69, 71, **72**
Waxham Bridge **45**, 46
Waxham New Cut **45**, 46
Wayford Bridge **49**, 52-3
Welches Dam Lock **171**, 176, 181
Well Creek **116**, 169, **171**, 174, 178
Welland, River 101, 182-92
Wellingborough **163**, 164
Wellingborough Embankment **163**, 167
Welney **171**, 178-79
Wensum, River **85**, 88-90, 98
West Row 121, **122**
West Somerton 42, **45**, 47
Weston Favell Lock **163**, 165
Westview Marina 127, **128**, 143, **170**
Wheatfen Broad **85**, 95
Whiston Lock **163**, 165
White Mills Lock **163**, 165
Whitlingham 93
Whittlesey **156**, 157, **170**, 172, 174
Whittlesey Dyke 169, **170**, 172, 174
Whittlesey Mere **170**, 173
Whittlesey Museum 172, 181
Wicken Fen National Nature Reserve 141, **147**
149, 151
Wicken Lode **147**, 148
Wiggenhall St Germans **112**, 114
Wiggenhall St Mary **112**, 114
Wilburton 125, **128**, 143
Wildfowl and Wetlands Trust **171**, 179, 181, 188
William Clowes Print Museum 66, 70
Windpumps 11, 12
Wisbech 105, 137, 152-4, 164, 167-8, 174, 176
Wisbech and Fenland Museum 168
Wisbech Canal 178
Wissey, River **116**, 118, **119**, 141, 146
Witham, River 193-218
Witham and Fossdyke 193-218
Witham Fourth District Internal Drainage Board
203, 219
Witham Navigable Drains 148, 202-208
Womack Water 42, **43**, 47, 56
Worlingham **67**, 68, 97
Worlingham Staithe **67**, 68, 97
Wroxham **32**, 33-7, 39, 41
Wroxham Barns Craft Centre **32**, 41
Wroxham Broad **32**, 34, 56
Wroxham Rail Bridge **32**, 38
Wroxham Road Bridge **32**, 35-8
Yare, River 9, 21, **62**, **77**, 78-81, **82**, 83-96
Yarwell Mill **159**, 160, 167
York 103